JUSTIN MARSHALL

Angus Gillies

Hodder Moa

National Library of New Zealand Cataloguing-in-Publication Data

Gillies, Angus.
Justin Marshall / Angus Gillies. 1ˢᵗ ed.
ISBN 1-86971-023-1
1. Marshall, Justin, 1973- 2. Rugby Union football players—New
Zealand—Biography. I. Title.

796.333092—dc 22

A Hodder Moa Book
Published in 2005 by Hachette Livre NZ Ltd
4 Whetu Place, Mairangi Bay
Auckland, New Zealand

Designed and produced by Hachette Livre NZ Ltd
Typeset by *Book*NZ
Printed by Everbest Printing Co. Ltd, China

Front and back cover images: Fotopress
Bad to the Bone words and music by George Thorogood © Del Sound Music/Universal Music Publishing P/L
Reprinted with permission. All rights reserved.

Justin would like to dedicate this book to his wife Nicolle and their children, Lachlan and Fletcher, to his parents Warren and Lois and his brothers Paul and Darren.

Angus would like to dedicate his work on this book to his wife Tui and his son Rogie.

Writer's Note

Justin and I would just like to explain how we've put this book together. It is predominantly written in the first person. Stories or opinions are generally recounted as told to the writer, in their own words, by Justin or by other people interviewed for the book.

Occasionally the writer will intrude on these first person accounts. You'll know this is happening when the print changes to a different font. The writer does this to offer background, to set up stories, to provide links between anecdotes, to explain, illustrate or hammer home a point made by Justin or because he gets carried away and can't help himself. Hopefully, this hasn't happened too often.

Interestingly, Justin chose these lines from a song to describe himself:

On the day I was born
the nurses all gathered around.
They gazed in wide wonder
at the joy they had found.
The head nurse spoke up.
She said, 'Leave this one alone.'
She could tell right away
that I was bad to the bone.
— George Thorogood, blues singer

'I think Justin's a guy whose personality has changed dramatically over the years. And rugby's had a lot to do with that. In Justin Marshall's case, rugby has been a life-changing experience. Rugby's actually made him a better person.'
— Daryl Gibson, Marshall's cousin and former Canterbury, Crusaders and All Black team-mate.

Contents

Acknowledgements

Justin would like to thank his mum Lois for filling up 12 huge scrapbooks with every article written about him since he was five years old and his dad Warren for videotaping all his tests plus Canterbury and Crusaders games. These were invaluable research tools and a source of much information that couldn't have been found elsewhere.

Justin would also like to thank Nicolle for her patience, sound opinions and great ideas (she suggested an interview with referee Steve Walsh!) and Angus for being so passionate and enthusiastic about the project.

Angus would like to thank his wife Tui, son Rogie, and employers 3 News for giving him the encouragement, time and space to work on the book and, of course, Justin, for having such an interesting life and being so honest about it.

Justin and Angus thank editorial director Warren Adler at Hachette Livre for having the confidence to let us do it our way, the rugby writers we've quoted, Ellen Anderson at the *Southland Times* and all the other people who agreed to be interviewed for the book: Hemi Mathias, John Hart, Steve Walsh, Paddy O'Brien, Laurie Mains, John Mitchell, Wayne Smith, Steve Hansen, Mike Banks, Aussie McLean, Daryl Gibson, Tabai Matson, Scott Robertson, George Gregan, Byron Kelleher, Paul Henderson, Reuben Thorne, Andrew Mehrtens, Taine Randell, Kevin Phillips, Mike Anthony, Errol Collins, Robbie Deans and Peter Sloane. Special thanks to Leanne McGoldrick, for helping bring the project together, and to Photosport, Fotopress and the NZ Rugby Museum for the use of the photographs which appear in the book.

Finally, Justin would like to thank the other players, administrators and fans who have helped make his career such a success.

Foreword

To be asked to write the foreword for Justin Marshall's book is a real honour and a privilege, and it says a lot about our relationship as both footballers and people.

While we're both fiercely competitive on the field, we also have enormous respect for each other as professional rugby players. I've always known that when I play against a team that has Justin in it, we'll be in for a tough match.

The reason for this is simple: he plays in a manner that draws the best out of the players around him. He demands a total effort from himself, which is clear when you watch him play, and he expects this from all of his team-mates. It is no coincidence that all the teams with whom he's been involved have been amazingly successful.

I've spoken a lot about him as a rugby player but probably the most pleasing aspect about Justin is his character. We've been playing against each other since 1993 but it's probably in the last five to six years that we have really got to know each other properly away from rugby.

Over this period we've shared similar experiences such as marriage, children and building our homes. And we've made a conscious effort to catch up with each other, with our wives and families whenever possible, be it in Christchurch, Sydney, Canberra, Melbourne, Wellington, Auckland or wherever; if we could catch up and have a few coffees or beers then we would. And it's during these times that I feel we've got to understand and share a lot of funny things that have occurred in our lives. We both enjoy a good laugh and this is normally obtained by one of us taking a shot at the other or at some totally innocent victim. Either way we're normally on the same wavelength with the major difference being the slang we use in our story telling. I would hate to think of the amount of cross-pollination of slang that has occurred over the last few years, but I'm sure it's a lot.

I will conclude in saying that to have shared my playing career with such a great player is a real highlight. However, the most important and rewarding aspect is our friendship. Unlike a playing career it will not end and soon be forgotten. It will grow and prosper in years to come, which means a lot to me.

George Gregan
Wallaby captain
Durban, March 2005

Prologue

The day I made my test debut was the proudest day of my career. It was also the most brutal. And if not for the quick thinking of a team-mate, it could have been my last, because I almost choked.

It was late 1995 and the All Blacks had come back from a first-test loss to beat France 37–12 in Paris.

Afterwards in the dressing room, Zinzan Brooke presented me with my first-test tie. You're given plenty of ties during your All Black career. But you only ever get one first-test tie. If you lose it, you don't get another. So you've got to look after it.

I remember that day better and more clearly than any other in my entire rugby career.

I remember getting on to the bus feeling happy about how I'd played and about being part of a great All Black win. It was the last game of the tour and everyone was in a good mood. It was Laurie Mains' last game as coach and we'd sent him off on the right note.

I was sitting in the bus thinking, 'This is the life for me,' when my team-mates Tabai Matson and Taine Randell came up.

Tabs said, 'I think we're gonna have to take the back of the bus.' And my moment was gone. All those great feelings and positive vibes just vanished.

On All Black tours, the back seat is reserved for senior players. There is a tradition of younger guys trying to take it by force. But no one's ever succeeded.

We sat down together and made our plan. Sean Fitzpatrick was right at the front because he was the captain. So we didn't have to worry about getting past him. But there were plenty of other hard men like Richard Loe, Craig Dowd, Norm Hewitt, Bull Allen and the Brooke brothers waiting for us.

We decided Tabs would lead the way, I'd come in second and Taine would come in behind. We figured surprise was the only tactic with a hope in hell of success. So we waited for the right moment.

The bus was rolling along and everyone was chatting away, having a beer or two, just relaxing. On the word, we jumped up and went charging down the middle of the bus. Everyone else sat bolt upright and set about stopping us as best they could. We didn't make it too far before Tabs was stopped in his tracks. It was pretty hard to see what was happening because Tabs is quite tall. Soon he was down on the floor like a big walrus blocking the way forward. I tried to clamber over him. That's when they got into me. I copped one in the back of the head. I managed to hold my feet for a while but I was just throwing windmills, one arm after the other. They were keeping people off me but they weren't really connecting with anything.

I managed to get myself ahead of Tabs but also ended up on the floor of the bus. Everyone came over and gave me a bit of a crack around the mid-section, a bit of a rucking and the odd punch. I remember trying to fight to get back to my feet because it was a really awful feeling being on the floor, not being able to comprehend what was going on above me, just feeling all this rucking and punches raining down on me.

I half made it to my feet and saw Norm Hewitt just up above me. So I threw an upper cut and clocked him square on the chin. He came back at me and grabbed me with one hand while he went to throw a punch at me with the other. But when he grabbed me, he got hold of my tie and tried to lift me up off the ground with it. He grabbed me just under the knot of my tie and hoisted me up so only my toes were touching the ground. I had all this weight of everyone else trying to get me down while he was still trying to pull me up at the same time. And the tie just kept getting tighter and tighter around my Adam's apple. And I couldn't breathe because the tie had cut off my windpipe and I couldn't speak either. I was starting to go, 'Uuurgghh,' so that hopefully someone would see I was in trouble.

I could feel myself turning really red and started waving my arms back and forth in front of my chest with my palms facing out and my fingers spread apart, trying to get everyone to stop. But it took a bit for people to realise what was happening because everything else was still going on. Taine was still going crazy, trying to bash his way through. Tabs was still trying to get to his feet. And I had this problem with my tie.

Normy had let it go by this stage. But he didn't know that it had choked up around my throat. So he was just getting on with whatever he was doing. But I still couldn't breathe or talk and I was getting desperate.

Somehow I managed to make my way back towards the front of the bus. I was starting to get quite panicky. I could feel that my face was going really, really red and I knew that my condition was starting to get reasonably serious. I was making this strangled, gurgling sound and then I could hear someone saying, 'He's choking! He's choking on his tie!'

I was still conscious, but I was very aware that I was starting to struggle. It was uncomfortable and I was starting to feel a little light-headed, like I was going to pass out. And I was thinking, 'This has got to come off real quick.'

Guys were grabbing at me trying to pull the tie off. But the knot was so tight it wasn't budging. People were trying to put their hands down my neck and pull the tie away from me. But that just caused more pressure on my throat.

In the end Todd Blackadder smashed a bottle. He wanted to cut the tie off me with that. So everyone got me to calm right down and stay still. You don't want to flail about too much when someone's cutting a tie off your neck with a broken bottle. And that's just what Todd did. With the nerve of a surgeon, he removed the tie.

The relief when it came off was incredible. And my face didn't look too bad, all things considered. My eyes were watering and I had a little bit of claret coming out of my nose from the punches I'd taken. But Tabs and Taine looked much worse.

The thing people have to realise is that it's just a tradition. It's like an initiation. We just wanted to try it and keep the tradition alive.

I know that to some people it probably sounds stupid and thuggish. But it's just something that's always been done and we gained a lot of respect with that. All that night and the next day everyone was talking about it, saying, 'Good effort last night. That's one of the best ones we've seen for a while. Good on ya. You should've had a few more helpin' ya.'

When you think about it, it's probably not a sensible thing to do. But a lot of things we do aren't sensible. And if you get the right outcome out of it — for us it was gaining respect — what does it matter?

There was one stroke of luck in the whole episode. It wasn't my first-test tie that was cut off my neck. I hadn't been stupid enough to put that on. I've still got that tucked away in a special place at home.

Part One: Pre-test build-up

Welcome to Mataura

The day I was born Mataura won the Eastern district club final for the first time in years. Dad played in the game and Mum, a week overdue, cheered like mad on the sideline.

After the game they went to the clubrooms to celebrate, then on to the captain's place for a few more.

Mum wasn't drinking, of course. So she was able to drive Dad home. When they got there Dad fell into a deep sleep. Mum went into labour.

There was nothing she could do but drive herself to Gore Hospital. With the contractions coming quicker all the time, she rang ahead to warn them she was on her way. I can't even imagine how she got Dad down the stairs. What is it about drunk people that suddenly makes them seem as though they're bolted to the floor?

Eventually she lugged him into the passenger seat like a sack of potatoes and set off in the blue-and-white Hillman Minx. Fifteen minutes later she was there.

Walking into reception, bag in hand, she said, 'I'm in labour. Can I have a wheelchair, please?'

A nurse brought one out and went to help Mum into it.

'Not for me,' she said, 'for him.' She pointed a thumb at Dad, who was still struggling.

For most of the night Mum was on a bed in the delivery room giving birth to me, while Dad was on a bed in a little side room fast asleep.

Before the Lions tour of New Zealand in 2005, Justin Marshall had played 77 tests for the All Blacks. Only Sean Fitzpatrick and Ian Jones had played more.

He became the All Blacks' fifty-fourth test captain in 1997, when as a 24 year old he led the side in four tests in Britain.

He is the highest capped back in New Zealand rugby history, seven tests ahead of the next highest, his old mate Andrew Mehrtens.

He is the highest capped New Zealand halfback, more than doubling his nearest rivals, Byron Kelleher with 32 and Graeme Bachop with 31.

His 24 test tries are a record for New Zealand halfbacks, more than doubling the 10 scored by 'Super' Sid Going.

He has the most criticised pass in New Zealand rugby.

And at different times it's seemed half the All Blacks' fans didn't think he should be in the team.

Andrew Mehrtens (All Black great): The one word I'd use to describe him is extraordinary. He's had an extraordinary career.

Andrew Mehrtens is one half of the famous Marshall-Mehrtens combination that has played for the All Blacks, the Crusaders and the Canterbury NPC team. They have been the half pairing in 43 All Black tests. If anybody is qualified to sum up Justin Marshall and his career in one word, it's Mehrts. Our aim in this book, and the challenge we've accepted, is to prove him right.

People often ask young players who they want to be like when they grow up. Well, I spent most of my Saturday afternoons as a kid down at The Rec in Mataura watching Dad play. And I can honestly say that the player I looked up to and wanted to emulate was my father. I wanted to be like Dad one day and play for the Mataura Seniors. Dad was a halfback so I wanted to be halfback too. I was quite small for my age, so that suited the coaches.

Funnily enough, growing up down home, I can never recall actually watching the All Blacks or a lot of provincial rugby. I don't have recollections of sitting up crouched around the TV and watching games in the middle of the night or listening to the radio or following sport that enthusiastically.

So Dad was it as far as heroes went. I didn't know much about any of that other stuff outside of Mataura.

There was a big hedge surrounding the ground and all the kids used to gather there on match days. All the parents used to dress the kids in gumboots and blue, green or brown overalls just like what mechanics wear nowadays. That way we could all climb up and down the hedge and roll around having our own game of rugby and get as dirty as we wanted.

Our parents would be keen to go to the clubrooms afterwards. So they'd strip off our overalls and we'd have a nice tidy outfit on underneath. A quick comb through the hair and we'd look as good as new. All the kids from Mataura went through the same routine every weekend.

I have vivid memories of going to watch Dad play rugby from the age of four until I was about eight, whereas I struggle to recall a lot of that other stuff from childhood.

Mataura is a small town of some 3000 people 50 kilometres north-east of Invercargill at the bottom of New Zealand's South Island. It once boasted a mayor who raced big-rig trucks for fun.

As far as industry goes, there's farming, the freezing works, coal mining, sawmilling and the country's oldest paper mill.

A resilient town, which has survived flash floods, Mataura was immortalised in song by former resident Jon Gadsby. 'I'm proud to be a scourer from Mataura,' he sang, 'where you can even wear a bush shirt in the lounge bar, singing God Defend New Zealand, and DB.'

I used to look out the window in standard three and four at the Mataura School and look at the fields, thinking, 'Wouldn't it be great if I could play rugby or cricket or any sport for a living?'

My first run-in with the police

Justin's dad Warren Marshall: Did he tell you about the time that they were caught chucking acorns at cars? They just looked so funny with their three little heads in the back window of the police car.

Warren Marshall is one of those Southern men who have turned economy of words into an art form. Why use a complete sentence when a phrase can work wonders? Why use a greeting when a friendly nod is all that's required? But I knew he was pointing me towards a good yarn. So I asked Justin, who takes more after his mum in the verbal department, to flesh it out for me.

Justin: Okay, I'll tell you about the first ride I ever had in a police car. It was down in Mataura with my good mate Mental, Mark Morton, who ended up being my best man.

Mental and I lived up the same hill. On one side of the hill there's a big grove of trees which is about 10 metres higher than the road itself. Mental and I were playing there with our little brothers, my brother Mouse (Paul) and his brother Moose. So we had Mental, Justin, Mouse and Moose down in the trees.

They were all oak trees. So we decided it would be a great lark to hide in the trees and every time a car went past we'd see if we could hit it with some acorns.

We would all throw at the same time. So usually two, but if we were lucky four, acorns would hit the car.

We'd see the car brake and we'd duck down into the trees, and then it would carry on. You can imagine the driver was thinking, 'What the hell was that? Ah, it was probably nothing, maybe just some stones on the road.'

Of course, we were having lots of fun. And we were doing it quite regularly. Until Mental thought it would be a great lark to throw an acorn at the local police car as it went past.

Now the rest of us all said, 'No, no, don't do it, don't do it, man.'

But sure enough, he did.

The police car braked a bit then carried on down to the bottom of the hill. Then of course it came back up and parked next to where we were hiding.

The police officer obviously knew there were some larrikins in there and they were up to something. So he gave it the old: 'I know you kids are in there. Out you come or there's going to be big trouble.'

We're all whispering away, thinking, 'What are we going to do? What are we going to do?'

Mental's going, 'Let's do a runner, we've got to get out of here. I'm not going out. There's no way I am.'

But I was going the other way. I wasn't a bad kid. And even when it was fun, I knew when I was doing things wrong. And I've got this really guilty conscience in me, this really bad guilt streak, which I suppose has been more of a saving grace than a curse over the years, but only just. Anyway, I was saying, 'No, this is bad. This is bad, guys. This is the police.'

And the police officer was still moving around saying: 'I know you're in there. I know you're in there. Don't make me come in there.' That old classic: 'Don't make me come in there and find you.'

Mental was starting to move his way down through the forest and trying to hide himself. The two little brothers didn't know what to do. And in the end I came out with my hands up.

I was pretty young. I can't remember how young. I'd have to ask Mum. But probably about eight or nine.

Anyway, I came out with my hands up. 'Okay, I'm coming out,' I said. 'It's me, Justin. I'm coming out now. Mouse and Moose and Mental are here with me.'

Sure enough, Mouse and Moose followed in behind, but no Mental.

The policeman said, 'Are there any more in there?'

And I said — and Mental will curse me to this day for it, 'Yeah, yeah, there's one more. Come on, Mental. Come out. Come out, mate. Come on.'

But he didn't come out.

And the policeman said, 'I know you're in there, Mr Morton. Don't make me go and see your mother and tell her what you've been up to.' In the end he managed to coax him out of there.

Mental came out and gave me a big glare because obviously I'd been the one who'd come out first. And all we'd been doing was throwing acorns for God's sake. And I'd come out with my hands up and confessed to the police that we were in the wrong and that we were doing this and doing that wrong. I could see Mental's brain ticking over.

The officer put us in the police car, all four of us in the back because we were quite small and quite young. That was my first ride in a police car.

He took us to Mark and Glen Morton's place first. He went up and knocked on the door. I don't think their mother was home, actually, or their father. So they got off quite lightly.

Then he took us home and Mum and Dad were there. It never looks good: a policeman bringing your kids home. He gave us a big speech in front of Mum and she was pretty upset.

So that was obviously my first little run-in with the police. It wasn't my last. And I became quite familiar with the process for a while there.

Home-made rugby posts

Warren Marshall: I remember when they were kids the three boys — Justin, Paul and Darren — and their mate Mental went and cut down some small trees. They made their own set of goalposts, dug a couple of holes and set them up across from the house. They used them for kicking goals, half-field games and that sort of thing. Eventually the tops fell off them.

I had a feeling Warren was giving me another clue. There was a good story in there somewhere. I rang back the next night to talk to Justin's mum.

Justin's Mum, Lois Marshall: They went next door where they had a plantation of trees. They cut a couple of them down and carried the logs back to this nearby field.

They'd been into Warren's shed and they had saws and axes and all sorts of bits and pieces and they hacked and thrashed at these trees until they got them down.

I saw them wandering past with the trees. Then next thing I knew they were digging deep holes and putting up their own rugby posts.

The neighbours who owned the trees saw what the boys were up to and rang me to complain. 'Your boys are chopping down our trees,' they said.

'I realise this,' I said. 'I've only just seen them myself. I'll deal with it.'

I gave them a bit of a telling off, but there wasn't a lot I could do at that stage. The boys got a lot of enjoyment out of those rugby posts. Justin was about 12 at the time.

They stood there for years, those posts. But then the neighbours started to complain that they were getting too dangerous. So eventually they were replaced with some proper rugby posts. I always thought it was a bit of a shame myself.

Justin: It wasn't just sport for us growing up. I have a lot of memories of going to barbecues at Mum and Dad's friends' places. They'd have kids the same age as us. And we'd play games and swim. Or we'd go out to the local parks.

There were two roads home, one on either side of the river. On one side was the tarseal road and on the other was the shingle road, the back road. Dad used to take the green Holden on the shingle road for us as a special treat. He used to think he was Carlos Sainz the rally driver on that road with Mum in the front beside him and the three boys in the back.

Every now and then on a corner he'd give the pedal a little bit and the back would slide out. Us boys would all be laughing and going, 'Yeah, Dad, you're the man.'

Mum would be like, 'Settle down, Warren. Don't be silly.'

And he'd be grinning away to himself underneath his moustache.

We've been on family holidays to Queenstown or the Marlborough Sounds and we still go on family holidays, where we'll go out for a round of golf or go out boating or water-skiing. That's what it was like throughout my whole childhood. And I'm sure that anybody who's been brought up the way I have would end up successful and happy.

And I'd like to give my kids the same opportunities that my parents gave us when we were younger. If I know I can do this then I'm sure they'll be able to achieve anything they want to in whatever field they set their minds to.

Was there any time when you saw that Justin had a bit of special talent?
Warren Marshall: No.
No time?
What I mean is that while he made rep teams he wasn't any more special than any other kid that made the rep teams.
Why do you think he's got where he has and the other kids are doing ordinary jobs now?
He just wanted to succeed. He loved rugby and he put so much time and effort into it.

Handwritten note found in early scrapbook:

Name: Justin Marshall
Age: 14
Sex: Yes
Birth date: 5/8/73
Girl/boyfriend: —
Food: Chicken — chips
Actor: Eddie Murphy
Singer: John Mellencamp
Hunk/spunk: Samantha Fox
TV progs: Cosby Show
Colour: Black
Enemies: —
Pets: —
Car: Falcon
Films: War films, comedy
Mates: Heaps
Saying: Yes
Family: Mother, father, 2 brothers
Racist: No
Hobbies: Rugby
Animals u like best: —
What do you rate yourself out of 20? 15
Ambition: Play for All Blacks

My brothers and I were sports mad. We played rugby, cricket and squash and we all had a bit of talent. So not only did Mum and Dad have to take us to club games, but also rep games, which took in a broader area.

As kids it never entered our heads that our parents' time was as valuable as ours. They drove us all over the lower half of the South Island to various sporting fixtures. We'd go to Dunedin, Christchurch, Invercargill, Riverton, Lumsden. There wasn't a lot of downtime for Mum and Dad.

You don't get anywhere unless you've got supportive parents and I'm very lucky and thankful that mine set the groundwork so well for the rest of my life.

As well as a free ride, Warren and Lois Marshall also provided the boys with good sporting genes.

Warren was an Eastern Southland rugby representative, while Lois was an Eastern hockey rep.

The boys also had great-uncles on both sides who were All Black fullbacks. On Warren's side there was Lloyd Ashby, who filled in for Don Clarke in the 6–3 loss to the Wallabies in the second test in 1958.

On Lois's side there was Jack Taylor, who played nine games, including six tests, for the All Blacks. He played fullback in the famous series against the 1937 Springboks and toured Australia the following year, playing all three tests. Taylor totalled 45 points for the All Blacks from 15 conversions and five penalty goals.

The good genes were never more evident than one week back when Justin was 18, Paul 16 and Darren 13. After taking part in their age-group rugby tournaments they were all picked for their respective South Island teams.

Tabai Matson: Justin and his two brothers, Mouse and Darren, play this game called Take It Up. Basically, you get the ball, you're in a confined space, and you have to get past the other two people. So nine times out of 10 you have to go straight over the top of them. And when these guys play, it's brutal.

When I was visiting the Marshall family in Mataura two years ago the boys still played it. You haven't seen anything like it. Mouse ended up with a broken jaw!

Chris Rattue, *The New Zealand Herald*, 1998: It was a City v Country thing. Southland style. The batsman, in full gladiator gear, strode to the crease. From close to the boundary at the ground in Gore, the bowler stormed in and ripped a delivery off the synthetic wicket onto the pads. The batsman limped off.

The bowler was Justin Marshall, the eldest of three brothers from the tiny town of Mataura. The batsman — Jeff Wilson, the 'city' boy from Invercargill.

'I don't know if he remembers it,' says Marshall.

'To us they were the flash city types. He had a helmet, arm guard, gloves, thigh pad, box, pads, and anything else you could wear.

'We all had a big laugh about him going off. Too right. They were from the city. We were country.'

School's out

I was out of school by the age of 16. I wasn't really interested during the fourth form. And by the fifth form, I'd lost even more interest.

I took five subjects for School Certificate. Woodwork was internally assessed. I sat Maths, English and Geography. But I didn't even bother with the fifth. I can't even remember what the fifth one was.

My attitude to Geography wasn't much better. I was first out of the Geography exam in the whole fifth form. I had a *Rugby League Week* magazine and I was reading that after about 30 minutes. I got 14 percent. I just wasn't interested.

24

The biggest thrill for me in Geography was taking my colouring pencils and colouring in the pie graph. I think I got good marks for that, probably a decent slice of that 14 percent.

Maths was the same.

I think I passed English. Well, I got about 48 percent, which is about average. I passed Woodwork, so I ended up getting two of the four.

I discussed with Mum and Dad what the hell I was going to do. And we came to the conclusion that I didn't have much option but to go back the next year and be what used to be called a second-year fifth.

So I went back. But it was no good. The teachers sent me from room to room because I was always distracting the other kids. After about two or three months the headmaster called in Mum and Dad for a meeting. And I had to go along too.

'Justin's stopping the other kids from learning,' he said. 'He's a constant disruptive influence in class. He's not applying himself and we feel that he's a bad influence on the other kids. He's either going to have to knuckle down or he's not going to be able to attend this school any more.'

I'm sitting there thinking, 'Oh no. This is no good. Mum and Dad are going to freak.'

But in the end, Dad said, 'Oh well, he's out then.' Just like that!

I remember trying not to grin, thinking, 'This is great. Dad's just said to the headmaster, "Catch you later".'

So I walked straight out of that meeting and out of school. I never went back.

Dad said, 'You're going to have to start working now.'

So I went and worked at two sawmills where I was earning just over $100 a week. I was stacking wood, putting wood on the table to be cut or taking it off afterwards. It was hard, on-your-feet-all-day work with very little at the end of it. Every time I pulled a piece of wood off the table to stack it, I thought about how easy I had it at school.

I had two years at sawmills, one with my uncle, one with another guy. But it stood me in good stead. While the other kids my age were walking about in their shorts and sandals with their schoolbags on their backs, I was doing hard manual labour with men. And I was earning money.

Just because you don't do well in a classroom doesn't necessarily mean you're not intelligent. Some personalities just don't thrive in that environment. And I had one of those personalities.

Anyway, I gutsed it out at the mills and then I went to the Gore freezing works, where I started to earn $350 to $400 net a week, which was great. I was a butcher, doing cattle, sheep and goats.

Mum and Dad worked at the Mataura freezing works. Mum had been a hairdresser. Then she had kids. Now she does a bit of part-time work at the abattoir.

Dad's been there almost all his life. He works down in the chambers, which is down in the cooling floor, every day in the cold, lifting carcasses and stacking them on the chain and pushing them around. I guess that's why everyone calls him Fridge.

Early Southland days

Metropolitan were playing Eastern in a trial match in Lumsden in 1991. This was before I'd even made the Southland team. I was playing halfback for Eastern and Paul Henderson was loose forward for Town.

I was really enjoying myself in this game because it was a great chance to test myself. I was playing against a lot of Southland players and Ginge Henderson was one of them. In fact, he was an All Black.

So anyway Ginge picks up the ball at the base of a ruck. The ruck splits open and he comes charging through the middle. He's running straight at me like some wild, red-haired, Scottish warrior out of *Braveheart*. And as he's coming at me, I'm thinking, 'Uh-oh. Looks like I'm going to have to tackle him. Okay, sweet as.'

But then someone else scrags the back of his jersey and half-tackles him. So he's almost falling as he gets to where I am. So as he's on his way down, I grab the back of his jersey with one hand and give him an upper cut with the other. It catches him square on the jaw and he yells in pain. He also drops the ball, which makes it worse.

'Shit,' I'm thinking. 'This'll be interesting.'

The ball goes backwards and their team whips it out wide. I think, 'I'd better get away from here as soon as possible.'

So I sprint out wide, following play but also getting away from Ginge. And I can hear him behind me screaming his head off. 'I'll get you, you little bastard! I'm going to fuckin' get you!' I turn round and realise he's chasing me across the field.

He doesn't catch me. But at the next breakdown he just gives me a mouthful. He tells me to watch my back because he's going to do that and do this if he gets his hands on me.

I just play it completely innocently, hoping like hell he's not 100 percent sure who hit him. I shake my head and say, 'What's your problem?'

But he doesn't buy it one bit. I think it's fair to say that Ginge and I never hit it off on the right note.

And I reckon he held a grudge, because he always seemed to be pretty hard on me.

Paul Henderson remembers the incident vividly because not many people punched him during his career. But his version is slightly different to Marshall's.

Paul Henderson, Southland stalwart: I was playing this game. I went for a run. And someone punched me in the face. I got up to have a look who it was and there was Marshall, staring me straight in the eye.

Not many people had sought me out to punch me. And here was this young kid of 18 fronting up. When you think about it, it's bloody weird, isn't it?

It was like the young bull and the old bull.

I didn't chase him down or anything like that. But I kept an eye on him for the rest of the game. It was just a bullshit game for me anyhow. I came off the field afterwards thinking, 'This guy could be the next Nick Farr-Jones.' So I started telling people about this kid from Mataura who I thought could be as good as the great Wallaby halfback. And I told Justin that too.

Andrew Mehrtens: Justin didn't come through the system of playing for a 'glamour' first XV. Neither did I really. But he certainly didn't. I first played against him in the South Island Under-18 final between Canterbury and Southland in 1991. We smacked them 27–7, I think. We smoked them. But he maintains to this day that his whole team was terribly hung over.

Justin: When I first made the Southland team in 1992 there was a group of us who used to travel from the Eastern district to training in Invercargill two nights a week: Davin Heaps, Bruce Morton, Drew Reardon, Paul Miller's brother Horrie and myself.

The Southland Rugby Union used to give us $50 each a week for petrol. So we'd all go together to save money and spend whatever was left over at the pub on the way home from training.

Drew was a really talented, hard-nosed, typical Southland hooker. He'd been in age-group teams and could have gone a long way with his rugby. But rugby was just a secondary interest for him. His main interest was partying and having a good time.

So when it was his turn to take the car, he'd always turn up late. The car would be full of beer cans. And he always looked like he'd just had a hard night on the piss. With Drew behind the wheel, the 45-minute drive was always highly entertaining. But one night it got a little too interesting.

Drew decided it would be a great idea if we drank a 40-ounce bottle of rum, which he pulled out from under a seat, on the way to practice. I still don't know why. And I still can't believe that we all agreed. But we did. We started handing it around and swigging and laughing and carrying on until we'd drunk the lot.

Drew was a shearer and I reckon he must have already been on the drink with his shearing gang after work because he was having a great time.

I remember getting to training, looking at everyone getting their gear on and limbering up and asking myself: 'What the hell was I thinking?'

I knew we could all be in trouble if we didn't watch out, although I had the scary feeling that Drew didn't care.

'I'm just going to have to get through this,' I thought. 'I'll hang around in the background and try not to be noticed. I won't go near any of the guys so they can't smell me. And I'll definitely stay away from the coaches and Ginge Henderson.'

Ginge would have gone off his nut if he'd found out I was drunk at training. So I gave him lots of room. And that wasn't too hard. I was mainly a reserve in those days so all I had to do was hold the tackle bags and fluff around. Luckily, we got through the training session without incident.

Paul Henderson: He probably hasn't told you about the time we were getting ready to play Counties in Pukekohe. This was way back in 1992. He'd only played one game for Southland at the time.

He did something stupid the night before and we had a bit of a court session. I said to him afterwards, 'Come and see me in my room.' I think he got the shits about that but he came anyway. And I said to him, 'What are you going to do?'

He said, 'What do you mean?'

I said, 'You could become an All Black . . . or a fuckin' idiot.'

He had it written all over him then. I only ever told two guys they could be All Blacks. One was Jeff Wilson and one was Justin Marshall.

Let's put it this way, there were two of them who'd got in trouble at the court session: Justin and a guy called Drew Reardon. I didn't pull Drew aside and tell him anything. Drew was a talented player. But I didn't think it was worth it. Justin became Southland's greatest All Black.

Creating our own entertainment

As teenagers in Mataura, we either went to the pub or we created our own entertainment.

The big night-time meeting place for young people in Mataura was a car park at the local bakery. It was just a great big empty paddock full of shingle at the end of our main street. It was just before the bridge that went over the Mataura River. So this was an unused space between the water and the end of the shops.

We weren't into racing our cars or anything. We'd just congregate in them at the car park and hang out. If you were out and about and nothing was happening at the pub you'd just cruise around in the car. And if you saw another car at the bakery, you'd just pull in and it was usually a few of your mates. You'd either stay there or you'd go around to someone's house and have a few drinks or whatever.

There was only one pub in Mataura. We used to call it The Zoo because local knowledge was there were quite a few animals that drank there. Having said that, it wasn't rough. It was just a good working-man's country pub.

A lot of people think that I came out of Mataura with a reputation as a mad keen scrapper, which isn't completely accurate. I didn't have a good reputation, but very few people in Mataura do. What I mean is that no one I knew — which was pretty much every guy in town — was averse to getting into a little bit of trouble. It was all part of entertaining ourselves.

A case in point: the caravan story.

There was this guy, about 40 years old, who'd always had a caravan parked on the side of the road outside his house.

Well, one night — well past midnight — the guys and I were sitting in our cars down at the bakery chatting away. And we got to wondering about this caravan. We figured it would be a bit of a hoot if anyone drove past the bakery to see us sitting there with the caravan on the back of our car!

So we went up the hill that I live on and grabbed the caravan and took it down there for a while. When we'd had our fun, we dropped it back off and I don't think the guy ever knew. He was asleep inside his house. He would've woken up in the morning and not known any different.

Well, like I said, there isn't much entertainment in Mataura.

The guys I hung out with in Mataura were Hoff (Grant Harris), Mental (Mark Morton), Spider or Eel (Hamish McKay), Creepy (Kelvin Chamberlain) and Murph (Vaughn Murphy). We called Grant 'Hoff' because he was a big, tall, lanky guy like the former Queensland State of Origin league fullback Paul Hoff.

One night we were sitting down at the bakery. And we thought it would be a great laugh to go down to Hoff's place and grab his father's horse sulky, the contraption the driver sits on in harness racing. It has two big wheels and two long handles strapped to the horse.

So we went out to his place and grabbed it. What we did was put a couple of the boys in the boot with the boot up and they held on to the handles of the sulky. We had someone sitting on the sulky. And someone would drive the car, which was Murph's little Mini. And he had both doors open like the starter in a race. So we drove that up and down the main street of Mataura, taking turns in the sulky.

Luckily, we managed to avoid the local constable, as we did with most of our pranks.

I suppose, looking back on these sorts of things that we used to get up to, we were probably a bit reckless and a bit crazy. I mean it's not what you'd want your own kids doing. But it was just us creating our own entertainment because there was nowhere else to go and nothing else to do. I mean, there were no big bands coming to town. John Farnham came to Riverton once. That was about it.

Let's get ready to rumble

One time Mental, Hoff, Spider, Murph and I went up to Queenstown for the weekend. I took my father's car, Mona the Corona, and we all stayed at the camping ground.

While we were there we had a run-in with some guys. I think they'd been pretty menacing to a few of the people in the camping ground. And we had some words with them ourselves.

It was really funny the way it all worked out.

The worst thing was that before all that happened, we'd been down at a pub to get our big supply to stock up our cabin at the camping ground. And I had gone in.

The older guys said, 'Oh, go in and get us some beer, will you.'

So I went in with Murph's driver's licence and we got about 10 dozen beer and loaded the car up. And just as I was coming out with the last couple of cases, the police turned up.

One of the policemen said, 'You're obviously buying a bit of beer here, gentlemen. Do you mind if I have a look at your licence?'

He said to me, 'Oh, Mr Murphy, what's your birth date please?' And I said, '11/12/71. I mean 12/11/71.'

And he said, 'Oh, which one is it?'

'The first one.'

'This is not your driver's licence, is it Mr Murphy?'

'Yes, sir, it is.'

'It's not, is it?'

'Yes. It is.'

'Mr Murphy, you can make this either easy or difficult. I can take you down to the police station and we can confirm whether or not this is your driver's licence or you can tell me the truth now and save a lot of trouble.'

'It's not mine.'

So they confiscated our beer.

As a result of that I was fined a hundred bucks for trying to buy alcohol under age and also ordered to pay costs for supplying false particulars for evidence.

Anyway, the boys were gutted. That was hard-earned money. And my blunder cost us all that beer. So, obviously we had to re-purchase, which didn't go down that well. And I wasn't allowed to go in any more because I was still only 18.

So anyway we ended up at the camping ground and we had words with these guys. But we also made friends with some of the other campers and had a couple of beers with them.

Then we had another run-in with the same guys. They were driving past in their car and yelled some abuse. When they came back they said something again. So the whole group of us said, 'Bugger this.'

We went up to their cabin and said, 'You guys are being dickheads. You know you are. And if you're going to carry on like this we're not going to put up with you for the rest of this trip. We'll meet you over there for a scrap.' We pointed to a space between all the cabins.

'Okay,' they said, 'whatever you want, if you think you're up for it.'

'Yeah, we're up for it. We'll meet you at . . .' and we appointed a time.

So we went to the grassy space between the cabins just as the light was starting to fade. They put up three of their guys and we put up three of ours.

I think our team was Murph, Mental and me. Murph was quite lean and tall and quick with his hands. In fact, he'd been a champion boxer. And Mental could look after himself too.

It was really bizarre actually. A small crowd had gathered because these guys had obviously been floating around for a couple of days, pissing people off. So it was really strange because this turned into quite an organised fight.

There was nothing spontaneous about it. We almost needed someone to ring the bell. You know, like in *Rocky III*, at the end when Apollo Creed and Rocky are in the gym by themselves. And Rocky says, 'Would you ring the bell?' And Apollo Creed starts the fight by saying, 'Ding, ding.' It almost needed to be like that.

But it wasn't. So we started to move towards them and suddenly it was all on.

Murph just went at this guy and smacked him one. I did the same thing and we all took care of them pretty quickly. Actually, they were staunch-looking big guys. But they obviously didn't have as much fighting experience as we had. We rumbled them up pretty easily and knocked all three of them out, which doesn't sound very good. But we were chuffed and so was the little crowd.

We got one of the boys to take a photo of us straight away. We were all standing there — a couple of us with the odd cut — holding our watches. We'd all taken off our watches so we wouldn't smash them, which seemed to be the thing to do. We always took off our watches before a fight. I think we must have seen it on a Western somewhere along the line.

That night we had a huge party in our cabin. Everyone came along and we were the life of the party, the life of the camping ground from then on.

So we had a good time and fortunately nothing came of the fight, because we'd already been in trouble with the police because of the beer.

Anyway, those guys left us alone from then on and we just stayed out of their way and everybody went on their merry way.

Another time we got arrested and were put in the cells. But nothing happened. They let me out.

We were outside the pie cart in Gore. The pie cart was like a gathering point late at night. And we were causing some sort of trouble and I ended up resisting arrest.

I didn't get charged or anything. I just got put in the cells with a few of the other guys there to cool down and we all got fined 150 bucks.

I think I was just drunk. I wasn't driving but I was in a car. And I objected to the cops pulling me out and giving me the old, 'Put your hands on the bonnet.'

So I turned around and said, 'What are you up to?' And I ended up getting into a slight little scuffle about it.

Were my mates and I scrappers? Well, we didn't all have reputations; we just all did the odd thing that was a bit silly. And when you're doing things like that, every now and then you're going to get caught. And if you're going around trying to create your own entertainment, you're going to bump into some people here and there who don't like it.

The main guys I used to hang out with, like Spider, Murph, Hoff, Mental and Creepy, well, if somebody wanted to have a go at us, we wouldn't be saying, 'Bugger off, we're not into it.' We'd stand our ground. I didn't go looking for fights. But that didn't mean I didn't find them.

A lot of people did get into fights in Mataura and Gore around that time. And it's in my nature to be competitive and confrontational. I don't like to step back. And when you're around your mates as well, that can make you even less inclined to step back. Let's just say I wasn't one to back down from a confrontation. I wouldn't be the one to say, 'Oh, don't be silly, we're all just pissed up, mate. Don't worry about it.' I'd be the first one to say, 'Why don't you do something about it then?'

What I can say is, yes, we had our moments, the odd run-in with local police or a fight or two with local lads who were no different to us, just going a bit far at times to protect their pride and their reputations.

Mataura might not have had movie theatres or lots of restaurants but for me it was a fantastic place to grow up. Those boys I used to hang out with are friends for life and sometimes in big cities you don't get friends that close, as you have other things available to entertain you.

Whenever I see the movie *Stand By Me* about the group of kids who stumble

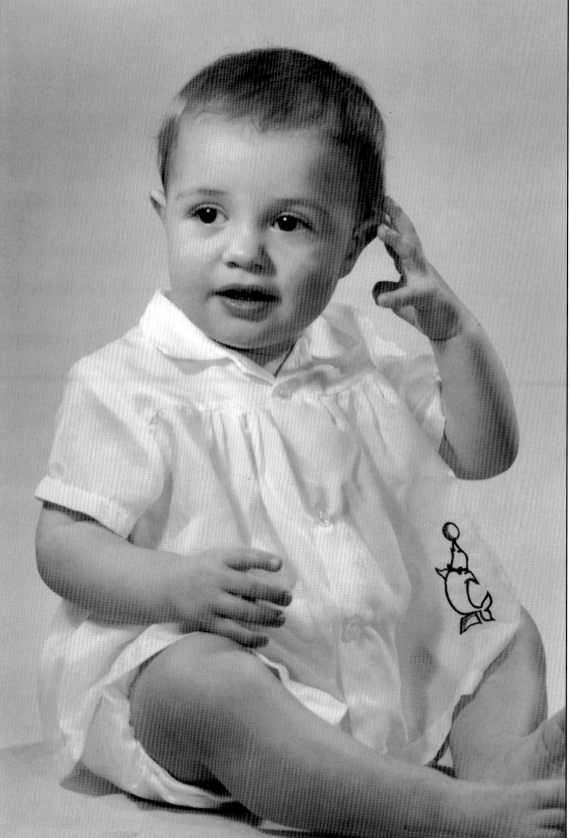

Me as a baby, Mataura 1974.

'You wouldn't like me when I'm angry!' My favourite Incredible Hulk tee shirt gives me the edge in the Mataura School Sports 50 m sprint.

'You want me to do what?' My first day at Mataura School.

'Teeth? Who needs 'em?' On holiday in Christchurch with, from the left, Darren, Paul and Dad.

Where it all began . . . the Mataura School team. I'm seven years old, second from the left in front.

Our three sons. A photo to make Warren and Lois proud. The first of me, Darren and Paul as Southland and South Island rugby reps in different age groups.

We are the champions . . . Southland celebrates winning the Division 2 NPC final against Hawke's Bay in 1994. David Henderson has the trophy. I missed the final with a bad groin injury, but I'm standing right behind him.

The Divisional XV to the Pacific Islands, 1993: Back row: Luke Erenavula, Karl Williams, Glenn Taylor, Mark Cooksley, J.J. Atuahiva, Bruce Hansen, Henry Maxwell. Third row: John Hainsworth, Allen Prince, Con Barrell, Junior Paramore, Mana Otai, Steve Wills, Andrew Roose. Second row: Chas Ferris (assistant coach), David Manako, Justin Marshall, Sam Doyle, Graham Hurunui, Mark Seymour, Simon Culhane, Barry Donaldson (physio). Front row: Darrin Stone, Richard Crawshaw (manager), Steve Tarrant, Jim Coe (captain), Rex George, Peter Thorburn (coach), Michael Scott.

Spot the future All Blacks: the NZ Under-21 side to Australia, 1994. Back row: Scott Lines, Chris Gibbes, Mark Atkinson, **Chresten Davis**, **Jonah Lomu**, Blair Foote. Third row: **Anton Oliver**, Alasdair McLean, Justin Collins, John Pothan, **Tana Umaga**, **Adrian Cashmore**. Second row: Jeff Marr (physio), **Daryl Gibson**, **Carlos Spencer**, **Kees Meeuws**, Boyd Gillespie, **Todd Miller**, Grant Allen (assistant coach). Front row: Shane Carter, Lin Colling (coach), **Justin Marshall**, **Taine Randell** (captain), Brendan Laney, Mike Banks (manager), **Andrew Mehrtens**.

Captain to coach. Above: John Mitchell was an inspirational captain on the Development team's tour to Argentina in 1994. Below: Ten years on and Mitch is still the boss . . . this time, though, the Big Boss.

Taine Randell and I pose for photographers with our new blazers before heading off on our first All Black tour to Italy and France at the end of 1995. My room-mate Zinny would have been proud of my boat shoes, too.

across a dead body together and have all sorts of adventures around their small town, I think of my mates from Mataura and the great times we had.

I believe I would never be where I am now without having experienced growing up in a small town. Learning to take the knocks, sticking up for myself, my family and my friends because they were important to me, and most of all being creative, because you had to be, and that is how I like to play my rugby.

Taine, Mehrts and George

Taine, when did your path first cross with Justin's?

Taine Randell, former All Black captain: The year was 1992, New Zealand Under-19 trials at the Police Academy in Porirua.

How did you two get on?

Justin and I seemed to hit it off straight away. We were in the same New Zealand teams from that point, Under-19s, Colts and finally the All Blacks. And we developed a strong friendship over the years.

How did he strike you early on?

Yeah, well, he could only pass with one hand . . . one way.

Is that right?

Yeah. If it came to passing the other way, he either had to turn fully around and then pass or he just ran it. Most of the time he just ran it.

Have you ever seen that movie *Zoolander*?

Yeah.

Ben Stiller played the male model who could only turn one way on the catwalk.

Yeah, that's exactly what Justin was like. He always seemed a bit cocky. But I've always found him very, very amusing.

What about his temperament? Did you find that amusing at times?

I found that very amusing. You'll obviously have to clear this with him, but I remember him being involved in a massive scrap when we were in the Under-19s. We were playing South Canterbury in Timaru. We all went out that night, a bunch of 18 year olds. Next thing I know there's been this big scrap. I look around and there's Marshall sitting at the bar with a ripped shirt and blood all over him. He'd been fighting two other guys. They were worse off than him. So he did quite well.

No two rugby players have had a bigger influence on Justin Marshall's career than George Gregan and Andrew Mehrtens.

Gregan was his opposite in the Wallabies and his nemesis in so many close Bledisloe Cup losses.

Interestingly, his first big game alongside Mehrtens was also his first game against Gregan, a New Zealand versus Australia Under-19 clash in Dunedin.

Justin: We were all over Australia that day so we had no problem beating them. But I remember George caught my attention because I thought, 'That guy's a bloody good halfback. I wonder if I'll run across him again. He's got a nice healthy head of hair too. He should look after that.'

George Gregan: What I remember about Justin from the match was that his attitude was super-competitive. Then, post-game, the Australian and New Zealand teams had a meal and a drink together. There were drinking games and he was right in the middle of them and he was a real character. He always had something to say. And I think it's pretty much been that way ever since really.

Justin: Funnily enough, next time I saw him he was playing for the Wallabies. He pretty much bypassed the Colts and went straight into the big time.

And when I saw him playing for Australia, it was the first time I ever thought that age-group rugby could actually be a stepping stone to the top.

I remember thinking, 'Now he was a good player. But he didn't outplay me on the day. If he can get there, maybe I can get there too.'

So I started working towards the day when I'd be playing for the All Blacks against George Gregan and the Wallabies.

Before I got there, George had already been involved in an incident that would haunt New Zealanders for years to come. It was in the dying moments of the one-off Bledisloe Cup match in Sydney in 1994. My old Southland team-mate Jeff Wilson was in mid-air about to score in the corner. But George seemed to come from nowhere with a desperate covering tackle that jolted the ball from Goldie's hands.

It felt terrible watching George and the Wallabies steal the Cup away from the All Blacks like that. And I was to find out the hard way that no matter how often it happened, you never got used to it.

The other memorable thing about that incident, of course, is that George still had hair then. Next time they replay it on TV, check it out.

Taine Randell: I remember we were playing for the Colts up in Auckland one year. So in our spare time, Justin, Andrew Mehrtens and I went for a game of golf. I can't remember which golf course it was. But we got a golf cart and they said, 'As long as there are only two of you on it.'

'Yeah, no problem.'

So the three of us are going round in this golf cart, having a great time. We're coming up the eighteenth fairway and the club captain, who was a guy of about 50, comes over to give us a rip.

By this time Justin's gone off to get his ball, which is in the rough. And we're talking to this guy and he's saying, 'You guys have been going round with three.'

And Mehrts is saying, 'No, no, mate. There have only been two of us. We've only had two the whole time.'

'No, no. There have been three. People have seen you.'

Anyway, we're talking away and Mehrts is doing quite a good job of smoothing things over. He tells the bloke we're preparing for this big Colts game and we're not off the hook but we're making progress.

Then all of a sudden this ball goes whizzing by this old guy's head. And Justin comes up. The guy goes bananas at Justin. And Justin absolutely serves it to this guy.

Mehrts and I just sat back and went, 'Ooh, jees.'

Justin is yelling at this guy. 'You don't know what you're on about! There's only been two of us on this cart the whole time.' That was a lie, for a start.

Anyway, in the end the guy wished us well for the game and told us never to come back to the course again.

It was a difficult moment at the time but it was hilarious afterwards.

Charged with assault

In 1993 Marshall made a mistake that had the potential to change the course of his life. He beat up a man named Hemi Mathias at a pub in Gore. The 19-year-old freezing worker and Southland representative halfback pleaded guilty to common assault and not guilty to assault with intent to injure. His destiny was literally in the hands of the court. A guilty verdict on the second charge could easily have meant jail time. That would have meant no All Black career for Marshall. And up the road at Otago Boys High, a 15-year-old Byron Kelleher would have been skipping down the street with a huge smile . . . wondering why, all of a sudden, he felt so happy.

Why do you think he went off the rails there for a while?

Warren Marshall: I wouldn't say he went off the rails. Did he tell you how that situation eventuated? He was just walking out of the pub and some guys from a rival team hassled him. I don't think he was that bad, really. It's sort of a thing down here.

To fight?

Not so much fight, just booze and cruise.

So you weren't too worried about him?

I was then. But it was a good chance for him to take stock. He was pretty devastated when he heard how badly Hemi was hurt.

While a judge ruled the trial notes could be released for use in this book, the Gore District Court later found that the notes had already been destroyed. So the *Southland Times* was called to see if they'd run anything. They had: one story, two paragraphs long.

Southland Times, **9 September 1993:** Fine of $1000: A man was fined $1000 when he appeared on an assault charge before Judge Phil Moran in the Gore District Court yesterday.

Justin Warren Marshall, aged 20, labourer of Mataura, was charged with assault at Gore on July 11. The fine is to be paid to the complainant.

It's fair to say, a local rugby rep found guilty of assault is big news anywhere in New Zealand. So either someone managed to keep this story reasonably quiet or the court reporter that day didn't know much about Southland rugby. Whatever the reason, Marshall got off lightly in that regard.

So in the absence of any real official record, we've relied heavily, in the telling of this story, on the faded memories of the two protagonists, Justin Marshall and Hemi Mathias, Marshall's mother Lois and his lawyer, Kevin Phillips.

Bar-room brawl

Kevin Phillips, Marshall's lawyer: He had left the Mataura Ruby Club to join Woodlands. Now the Mataura Rugby Club, you don't leave there unless you're dying or you've got broken legs and you can't play rugby any more. When he did that a lot of the people in Mataura were angry with Justin. He wanted to play a higher standard of rugby but he took a lot of flak about that.

Justin: I'd always played for the Mataura club. But one year an Invercargill team called Woodlands asked me to play for them. I said okay.

But I wasn't just leaving my club. I was also leaving the Eastern district, which covered the Mataura and Gore area, to join their city cousins. Effectively I was turning my back on Eastern. And some people didn't like one of their up-and-coming players doing that.

As for me, I was in Southland's NPC squad for the second division and I felt I needed to play in Invercargill if I wanted to keep my place.

I still lived and worked in the Eastern district and socialised there in the pubs. And a few people really got into me for choosing town over country. My Mataura mates were all right about it. They understood what I was trying to achieve. But some of the guys from the other Eastern clubs were thinking, 'Who does he think he is?'

So whenever I went into Gore drinking, I'd get people making smart comments. It pissed me off at first but then I started to put up with it.

But one particular night this guy hit me in the thigh and I went haywire. Well, that's what it seemed like.

Looking back, though, it's all a bit blurred. The guy I'm talking about is Hemi

Mathias. He's a big Maori guy who played for a club called Pioneer. I didn't know him. But I knew quite a few of his Pioneer team-mates.

He wasn't doing much to be honest. We were in a bar in Gore and I thought he said something to me. But really I'm not sure whether it was even him. It might have been someone beside him or around him.

I think, basically, I'd just had enough of the shit I'd been getting. And he happened to be the person that was there. And like I said, he probably didn't even say anything to me. But something in me just snapped. I don't know what it was. And I just hit him. And I hit him pretty good, knocked him over in the bar.

Do you have much recollection of what happened that night?
Hemi Mathias: Well, I was pretty full. No, I don't really have a great recollection of it. I do remember seeing Justin at the pub that night. But all I know is that it was totally unprovoked. As far as I know I did nothing to provoke him.

One prime witness said, 'He just turned round and hit you for no reason.' So he did turn around and hit me so maybe that suggests he did think I said something to him. But from all accounts I didn't say a word. It was a big crowded bar. Somebody could have had a go at him.

Justin: I was drinking with two girls I used to hang out with. They said, 'My God, what have you done? We've got to get out of here.' Which was a fair call. You just don't knock someone over in a pub.

So we got out of there pretty quickly. And they were saying, 'What the hell did you do that for?'

I was going, 'I don't know. I thought he said something to me.'

'You shouldn't have done that. We've got to get out of here.'

By now, I'm like, 'Oh no. I've got to go back in. I've got to go back in and say sorry.'

'No, no. We've just got to go.' And we're heading towards the car.

But in the meantime he's obviously got up and realised what's happened so he's coming out after me.

We're getting close to the car and the girls aren't far away from putting me in, when they see him coming. He's running towards me through the car park, charging at me. And one of them cries, 'Look out!'

I manage to evade him. But he's just enraged, obviously, as you would be. He's thinking he's been punched in the bar for no reason, which is more than likely what happened. I don't know, because I'm really not sure whether it was him that mouthed off at me. But I admit to being wrong about all that. I always have done.

Anyway, he's back on his feet by now. And he's in a complete blind rage. He's just out to get me, to nail me. And he keeps coming at me and I can't get away from him. I can't get him off me.

I'm going, 'Nah, nah. Stop mate. I'm really sorry. I didn't know what I was doing.' But he's throwing punches and moving towards me. I'm backing away, getting away from him. But in the end I can't get him off me. So I hit him again. I have to. Otherwise he's going to bloody destroy me. He's much bigger than I am. He's basically chasing me. And there's no way the situation's going to be diffused. I have to stop him.

Look, if I'd been in his position, I'd be feeling exactly the same way. But I could tell he was pretty drunk and dazed because he was coming at me and swinging wildly with a glazed, unstoppable look in his eyes.

Hemi Mathias: My nose was broken after the first punch. So one guy was taking me to the hospital. I was heading outside holding on to my nose. I can't recall this either. But by all accounts, Justin, he could have been coming to apologise to me, I don't know, but the guy who was with me, Stu Henderson, said Justin came over and I took a swing at him. And that's when it started up again.

Justin: After I hit him we jumped in the car and took off. My mates were there and his mates were there, and people were starting to pour out of the pub. By that stage we just needed to get out of there because it was a bad scene.

And it just escalated from there. I went home, while an ambulance came to the pub and took him to Invercargill Hospital.

'Don't leave home, pal'

Hemi Mathias: I suffered a broken nose, a fractured eye socket and stitches on the chin. I had to get the eye socket rewired. And getting the broken nose fixed was about the sorest thing I've ever had done. The recovery time wasn't too bad really. But it takes about six to eight months before you mentally come right and can do things like play rugby again.

Justin: Anyway, the girls took me home and I went to bed. I didn't know this whole other machinery was already set in motion involving an ambulance, surgery and a police investigation.

So I woke up and people started calling me, saying, 'You're going to get it, Marshall. We're going to get you. You're dead. Don't leave your house.' I guess it must have been Hemi's mates. 'You're not safe. You're going to get a hiding. Don't leave home, pal.'

Hemi Mathias: I refused to press charges. I've always been a big fan of any sport but particularly rugby. And I knew Justin had a lot of talent. I didn't want to ruin his rugby career and I didn't see any point in stopping him. I wasn't very happy about what he'd done. But I didn't really see what I'd be proving by stopping his career.

I'm not the type of person who'd press charges over something like that anyway. I'm a bit old school when it comes to that sort of thing.

The Invercargill police came and saw me in hospital and asked me to press charges.

Then when I got home the Gore cop came and saw me and he also wanted me to press charges. He said, 'We've been after him for a while.' I know, and Justin will admit, that in that six- to 12-month period leading up to my incident he did assault quite a few people. So the cops wanted to get him because he'd got off on the other ones. They saw it as an opportunity to get him. That's what the cop said to me anyway. But I said no and in the end they pressed charges themselves because they had plenty of witnesses.

Some prominent Southland rugby players came and saw me too and pushed me to press charges. One of them was the former Southland lock Alan Byrne (a stalwart of the Pioneer Rugby Club).

These guys had been Southland team-mates of a hooker called Bain McCall. Bain had played for Edendale and the Eastern district and he'd been a New Zealand Junior. About five years before Justin came on the scene, Bain was banned for 18 months for assaulting one of the managers of the Ascot Park Hotel. The Invercargill Licensing Trust was one of the big sponsors of Southland rugby, still is.

A lot of Bain's old team-mates were upset that the rugby union didn't back Bain at the time. They felt it was a double standard when the Southland union didn't take any action against Justin.

So the guys who were in the team with Bain wanted me to press charges on Justin to get back at the Southland union. They wanted Justin's assault to be out in the open, just as Bain's had been. They didn't like the way the union hung one guy out to dry and protected the other.

Justin: Hemi refused to press charges against me. I can think of only two reasons why he would do that. One, he couldn't be bothered going through the whole process. Or, two, he thought he'd get me back in his own time.

But the police pressed charges against me anyway.

I must admit, Hemi's never tried to exact revenge. But I can't imagine him just wanting to move on and get on with life. Surely, there's no way he'd think that.

I can understand him not pressing charges. I wouldn't do that. But I'd definitely hold a grudge.

Photographed, fingerprinted, charged

The really freaky thing was the way that the police came and got me from home that morning. I'm a big movie-watcher. And the whole thing felt like I was in a movie. It was quite surreal. There was a tap on the front door. And we could hear from the other side, 'Hello, it's the police.' We all looked at each other. Mum and Dad were obviously wondering what was going on. I hadn't told them anything. I'd been hoping it was all just going to go away.

Mum said, 'What's all this about?'

'I think it's about me, Mum,' I said. 'I got in a fight last night at the pub.'

The police came in and told Mum and Dad what had happened. The extent of Hemi's injuries was news to me too. We all knew immediately that this was different from all my other little skirmishes with authority. This time, it was serious.

The police told me I had to accompany them to the station. And that feeling of being in a movie took hold again. They put me in the back of the police car. I sat in the back seat alone.

Cut to shot of the back of the two police officers' heads. The one in the passenger seat turns slightly. 'You're in a lot of trouble, Mr Marshall.' It was a 10-minute drive to the Gore police station. Cut to shot through the window of the countryside whizzing by. The scene ends with a wide shot. You can see a blond mullet through the back window as the police car disappears around a corner. The camera tilts up to a grey and claustrophobic Southland sky.

I don't know why my mind was reacting like that. But the movie continued at the station. I was photographed and fingerprinted and then the police took me to an interview room and gave me instant coffee in a styrofoam cup.

I'd been put in the cells and handcuffed on other occasions. But those times I'd been in the wrong place at the wrong time and got caught up in scuffles. This was an investigation. It felt completely different. And I was worried.

They asked me my version of events. I told them what had happened.

I admitted to assaulting him. I said, 'Look, it was my fault. I don't have any excuse. I'm not trying to look at legal loopholes to try and get out of it. I feel terrible. I actually assaulted him, and I'm prepared to plead guilty to that.'

But they said, 'We're also going to charge you with assault with intent to injure.'

'Well,' I said, 'I've told you what happened. I was acting in self-defence. I couldn't get away from the guy. I didn't chase him. I didn't hit him and then go back to the bar to finish him off. He came after me. I told him I didn't want anything to do with it and the people who were around me will verify that. But he was just in a rage and I couldn't keep him off me.

'I didn't have any intent to injure him. I just wanted to get out of there. I knew I was wrong in the first instance because I said to the girls, "I think I should go back," and all that. And they said, "No, don't be stupid, that's the last thing you want to do." Look, in the finish it was self-defence.'

And they said, 'Well, we don't think so.'

'Why not?'

'The story you've told us isn't the story we've heard from the witnesses at the pub and particularly in the car park.'

'Well, I think you might have a problem with your witnesses.'

'I don't think so, mate. I think you're the one who has a problem with our witnesses.'

So I said, 'Well, I can't plead guilty to that second charge I'm afraid.'

'Well, you'd better get a lawyer.'

So I did.

I've been told since by friends in the police force and in the legal profession that I shouldn't have admitted to anything. But I was a bit naïve. I'd always come clean over anything I did wrong. I just stayed true to type.

Lois Marshall: It was pretty scary when it happened. It was like, 'Okay, this is really serious now. You've really got yourself into quite a bit of trouble.'

What he was doing before was what all the kids round here do. They played rugby. Then they drank. And they'd end up doing something stupid. There'd be the odd fight. All the parents' kids were like that. But this was a bit more serious and he was very scared. He didn't know what was going to happen.

After his surgery in Invercargill, Hemi was taken to Gore Hospital. Justin tried to go and see him that day, the day after the incident. He rang the local police officer and said, 'You've probably heard what I've done last night. I'd like to go and see the guy.'

The policeman said he'd see what he could do. But he came back and said Justin shouldn't go down there. There was a lot of bad feeling towards him.

There's a whole lot of rivalry between Gore and Mataura in the rugby. And the fact that a Mataura player hurt one of their mates would have made it worse.

Fear of prison

Justin: After the charges were laid it was a case of the police going about and getting their case together and of my lawyer and I doing the same.

I remember having a really full-on conversation with Mum and Dad either the night or two nights before I was to appear in court. And I ended up in tears.

I was standing by the fire in the living room. And I don't usually open up too many times to people. I'd been keeping everything bottled up. But as D-day loomed, I realised I needed to talk to them about it, to say that I was really scared and that this wasn't the way I'd seen my life going. I basically said all those things you say when your back's really against the wall and you're stuck in a corner and you've got nowhere to go and there are a lot of feelings you've been keeping to yourself.

I told them I was embarrassed because I'd let them down, and because it had got to the stage that my court case was one of the most talked-about issues in town.

There wasn't a lot they could say to me because they weren't sure what was going to happen. But basically they were very supportive. They were hoping that I'd be spared a jail sentence. But more than anything they were hoping that I was going to learn my lesson.

I knew I was going to be in trouble no matter what. I was quite prepared to take whatever punishment was meted out. But whether or not I could have handled jail, I'm not sure. I don't know if I was man enough to go to jail actually because I was really only a kid.

I had a fantastic upbringing with really supportive parents, who put a lot of time into us three boys and who gave up all of their spare time to drive us all over the place.

And in one fell swoop on one stupid night I almost wrecked it all.

Lois Marshall: Justin thought he was going to jail and he was really scared about that.

I said, 'Well, I think we need a good lawyer for a start off.' So I rang a guy I knew through playing squash, Kevin Phillips, in Queenstown.

We drove through to see him and it was a very quiet trip. Kevin was very good. He told Justin, 'You're in serious trouble.' And he spelt it out. Then he said, 'Tell me the truth and we'll deal with this.'

He came down to Croydon Lodge, where it happened, to have a look. The Lodge is where everyone meets and anything can happen. It's always packed on Saturday nights and has a band playing. Everybody seems to end up there.

Kevin was actually from Gore. So he knew a bit about the town and why it had happened and how it had happened, because he knew what it was like to live down here. There's not much to do. So the boys play rugby. Then they drink. And that sometimes can lead to trouble.

Justin: I remember walking into court and knowing that there was a strong possibility that I might not be going home at the end of the day.

I was wearing a pair of grey zip-up loafers that Dad had lent me. I'd given it my best shot at looking comfortable in a suit. And I was wearing one of those thin liquorice strap leather ties.

It wasn't a jury trial. The case was heard and decided by a judge at the Gore District Court.

Once again, I felt like I was in a movie. I put my hand on the Bible and swore to tell the truth, the whole truth and nothing but the truth. Even the feeling of standing in the witness box was somehow unsettlingly familiar, even though I'd never been in one before.

I pleaded guilty to the assault charge straight away. But my lawyer was adamant that my actions in the car park as I described them did not constitute assault with intent to injure. I still wasn't confident of being found not guilty, though. Because the police had pressed charges themselves, I knew they'd be determined to get that second conviction too.

The trial was over and done with in one day. The only witnesses I had for my defence were the two girls with whom I'd been drinking. But their stories were simple and consistent.

The thing that really upset me about the whole episode and, looking back on it, still upsets me is that the police witnesses' statements were so inaccurate my lawyer was able to discredit their version of events by picking holes and finding discrepancies.

Now I can understand them being unhappy with what happened to their mate. But they were obviously going to get an opportunity to get me back for that at some stage. And I was fully expecting that, after all the threatening calls they gave me.

But to go out and accuse me of doing those sorts of things that I certainly hadn't done was a form of revenge that caught me off guard. The stories they were telling could have put me in jail. That was pretty scary.

The judge obviously considered the two girls with me to be more credible witnesses than those for the prosecution. He found me guilty of assault and not guilty of assault with intent to injure.

It was pretty much the worst day of my life.

Hemi Mathias, the victim, didn't have to get up and give evidence. He was at the courthouse following proceedings with a lot of his friends and family from the Pioneer Rugby Club. But because he hadn't pressed charges I guess he just wanted to stay outside the whole process.

Kevin Phillips: It's a long time ago, but my memory of the case is that there was a band at the Croydon Lodge. Justin and his girlfriend went there. This guy Mathias picked on him and was saying things about how he'd gone to Woodlands and started jostling his girlfriend. Justin was concerned about it and hit him. Justin hit him, we argued, and as I remember, in defence really of his girlfriend.

As I remember it, he was charged with an offence under the Crimes Act of injuring with intent. It's a serious offence where if it's unprovoked violence the court's looking at imprisonment. The judge, Phil Moran, reduced it from that. He convicted him on a lesser assault charge and fined him.

No animosity

Hemi Mathias: I bear Justin no animosity over what happened. I know his parents and a lot of his friends. So there's no point in holding a grudge.

He was always under the impression that you were out to get him.

Yeah, well, I was for a start.

So if you'd seen him in the pub you would have had another go?

Yeah, I was for a start, probably for the next 12 months, once my face healed and I felt I could have another go. Plus the media hype doesn't help either you know. He was doing well with his rugby and you'd be reading his name in the paper just about every week. I don't begrudge him his career but when you see his photo in the paper every week, it was always a reminder.

What was the turning point that made you decide there's no point in holding a grudge forever?

I don't know. As time goes by things heal, I suppose. Plus one of my best friends is also a best friend of his parents, Lois and Warren. So we cross paths a bit. I worked at the Mataura freezing works with his parents and I worked quite closely with his mother. Since then I've talked with his parents. We'll bump into each other and yarn. Yeah, good as gold.

The incident never comes up, though?

No, the incident's never come up.

He said there were a lot of threats from your mates when he woke up in the morning.

Yeah, I heard that, yeah.

So he had to lie low for a while?

Yeah. But I don't think anyone got him.

That's right. He's an elusive runner, isn't he? He said he kept waiting but nothing happened. He was fully expecting to get done over.

I knew a few guys had rung his parents' house.

He reckoned some of the guys made up a story in court about him getting a wheel brace from the car.

When I went outside, Stuie reckoned he had something in his hand.

Was Stu Henderson one of the witnesses?

There were three witnesses. He was the main one because he came out to the car park with me.

Was he one of your Pioneer team-mates?

Yeah. He was also a New Zealand boxer at one stage.

Right. And he reckoned Justin had something in his hand like a wheel brace or he got something out of the car?

Stuie reckoned he had something in his hand. I think the wheel brace was just something that people made up.

Yeah.

I don't think he did.

Yeah. Were there a couple of people saying he had a wheel brace?

At that early stage there weren't many people outside apparently because the bouncers had erupted inside, you see. After the first incident a lot of guys that had seen what went on started jumping on Justin. So the bouncers broke it up and they actually put Justin outside to stop it erupting because they knew a lot of people were aiming at him. So there weren't a lot of people outside when the second incident happened. Not a lot of people saw what happened outside I don't think.

So Pioneer's a Gore club is it?

Yeah. There was a lot of shit went down there too because they banned Justin from their clubrooms for after-match functions and things like that.

He'd be mad if he ever walked in there, though, wouldn't he?

That's true.

What position did you play for Pioneer?

Seniors I played fullback. But I put a bit of weight on and slowly worked my way into the forwards.

Did you play rugby again after the incident?

I was about 30 when it happened. I hadn't played seniors for about a year at that stage. And it was about another year before I started playing senior social stuff.

Are you still at the works?

No, I'm at Fonterra, Edendale now.

Big milk factory is it?

Yeah.

Aw, okay.

The only other thing that came up in the court case and this is probably the thing that hurt me most . . .

Yeah.

. . . and I wasn't even told this. This came up in the court case. There was a bit of racism outside.

Aw, is that right?

Yeah. And that's the thing that hurt me more than anything.

What was the racism? From his mates? Or from him?

From Justin, yeah. I don't know if Justin will admit to that. But Stuie's a pretty honest guy, the guy in the witness box who said it.

What was it like? Do you remember the words?

Well, Stuie said in the witness box it was before the cops got there . . .

It doesn't sound very apologetic if he's being racist outside, does it?

I know. Well look, all the bar patrons flooded outside afterwards and there were scuffles and all sorts of carry-on apparently. There were Mataura groups scuffling with Gore groups in the car park. And if I recall right, in the court, Stuie said there was racism coming from Justin. And he said, 'That'll teach you, ya black bastard.'

Is that right? Far out . . . because he said to me he wanted to go in and say sorry to you because he realised he'd mucked up.

I know Justin's not racist. You can't be racist coming from Mataura. It was probably just a lot of things had built up and he'd had a few to drink, I suppose.

Yeah. I wouldn't say he's racist from what I know because a lot of his mates are Maori guys or Island guys. And it's amazing what stupid things people say when they've had a few.

Exactly.

Well, that's excellent, mate. I'll make sure Justin sends you a free copy.

Yeah, keep him honest, mate.

Lois Marshall: I thought, 'Surely, he'll learn his lesson from that.' I think he was so petrified that he would have had to.

He had one way to go. He could choose rugby or he could muck around and live the next 20 years doing what he was doing that night. He could spend his life playing club rugby, having a few rep games, getting on the alcohol afterwards and not going anywhere.

I think that whole experience made him realise how much rugby meant to him, how much he loved the game and that he did want to succeed at it and that there were certain things in his life that were stuffing him up.

I don't know whether he's told you this. He didn't drink for nine months after that. He was too scared to drink. He was too scared of the consequences, because he started to think, 'Perhaps this is what my problem is.'

Justin: I really haven't been in a great deal of trouble since that day. I've had my moments. But nothing that serious again.

It's not something that I enjoy talking about. In fact, as a rule, I don't talk about it. But the reason I wanted to tell that story in this book is because I've always regretted what happened and I've always regretted what happened to Hemi.

In a strange way I've got a huge amount of respect for him for the way he handled himself after the fight.

He could have pressed charges. But he didn't. He could have got revenge. But he seems to have moved on. I live in hope, anyway, because Hemi Mathias is a big guy. You wouldn't want Hemi Mathias coming after you.

Hemi and I have never really run into each other since then. I don't know what he thinks of me. I wouldn't imagine he thinks much of me to be honest.

But, as I say, I have full respect for the guy and I'm sorry about what happened.

The other reason I wanted to recount the story was because I believe it was the turning point for me in my life. It forced me to open up to my parents for the first time in my whole childhood. It was that scary and surreal and powerful to be staring straight at a life in prison that it really freaked me. And I didn't drink for most of the next year. I had a quiet existence, apart from that spot of bother on the Divisional Tour.

The Divisional Tour

I was 20 when I toured the Pacific Islands with the Divisional team in October and November of 1993. I was still with Southland. We were all second and third division players. It was my first tour ever.

And it wasn't an easy tour. They're not easy countries to tour, the islands, at the best of times. It's hot and the facilities aren't that great.

We started the tour in Nadi, Fiji, at a ground where the people watched the game from up in the trees but out on the field it was almost unbearably hot and sunny. We won 31–29 and I scored a try.

Next stop was the Cook Islands. That was pretty much the same. We won 26–15 in the incredible heat and I scored another try.

I was younger than most of the others on the tour. Guys like John Hainsworth and Bruce Hansen from Wanganui had been around a bit. And they used to tease me, which is good. It's all part of it.

Bruce Hansen brought these videos along for people to watch. They were all of him and his brother Scum — that's all I know him as — blowing up stuff with dynamite. They were blowing up all sorts of things around their farm. Bruce would be holding the camera. So you'd see Scum running down to burn something. Then you see him run up. And big, big explosions. And so on and so forth.

I got on particularly well with Bruce Hansen, but they were all really good hard-case guys on that tour. There was great camaraderie because we were the second and third division boys from the provinces. We drank a bit of piss together and got to know each other and we played some good rugby actually.

There were these spiders over there in Rarotonga. And Bruce would always grab them and put them in my face. They were massive spiders, as big as my hand. He'd let them crawl all over his face and down his arm and all that. They can't have been poisonous. But I found that as creepy as hell, because they were so big. I'm quite phobic about that sort of thing. And he was always threatening to get me with one.

'I'm going to put it in your suitcase. Or maybe in your bed.'

So every night I'd be checking underneath the bed and between all the sheets and blankets and under the pillow. Every time I felt a tickle or an itch in the night I was sure it was a giant spider Bruce had left there for me.

I actually didn't sleep very well for the rest of that tour.

So we got to Apia in Western Samoa. We beat the President's XV 35–26. And it was all downhill from there.

The last game of the tour, against Western Samoa, was called off after an all-in brawl at the Tusitala nightclub in Apia. Justin Marshall's story of the night has changed slightly over the years. But in both versions, he was the Divisional player at which the first blow was aimed. Twelve years on, the differences to the story and why they're there (whether it's because time has softened the details in Marshall's memory or whether he feels he can now tell the truth without fear of hurting his career) probably don't matter a hell of a lot. We'll just tell both versions, the first via an article by Roger MacPherson written soon after Marshall arrived home to Mataura.

The Gore Ensign: Marshall keen to set record straight about team's return: The New Zealand Divisional XV's rugby tour of the Pacific Islands was not abandoned because of the ugly assault on two of their members.

That's according to a central figure in the affair, Southland halfback Justin Marshall. And the talented Mataura player is keen to set the record straight.

Apia's National Stadium is being resurfaced and the alternative venue left a lot to be desired security-wise, Justin said.

He was also adamant the incident, which left him sporting three stitches to the head and a black eye, was a completely unprovoked attack and the only sad point of what had been a happy tour by 'a great bunch of guys'.

Wanganui loose forward Bruce Hansen suffered a nasty cut to the face, which needed 10 stitches after he went to assist Marshall.

Neither player is facing charges, a fact Marshall said exonerates both men.

'The whole thing only lasted about four minutes at most and was initiated by a Western Samoa supporter. Reports have been greatly exaggerated,' he quickly added.

'We were standing in the bar at our team hotel after Thursday's game against Western Samoa Country. I was talking to Sam Doyle when all of a sudden I was punched from behind and struck on the head with a bottle. I'm not sure what followed because I was taken out and attended to.'

The only reason Justin can recall for the attack was a brief exchange of words immediately prior to being struck. This came after a racist remark was directed at him.

After attention the injured parties made statements and were taken to hospital to have their wounds stitched. Two Western Samoa supporters are facing assault charges as a consequence.

Here's the version Marshall offered in 2005.

If I was into omens I could've guessed the night was going to end up leaving a terrible taste in my mouth. Like I said, being the gullible youngster on tour, I was the butt of a few jokes. On the team bus a couple of the guys handed me a bottle of something and said, 'Here, have a sip of this.'

I didn't know what it was. I thought it was probably some sort of liqueur or spirit or something. It was actually Tabasco chilli sauce. And it burnt out the inside of my mouth. Being a meat and three veg kid from Mataura, I'd never experienced anything like it. 'Fuck!' I cried. I was gulping in air. My eyes were watering. It was awful. As soon as the bus stopped, I jumped off and ran straight down to the pool and started sloshing water around in my mouth.

Later on we went to the nightclub and hung out with the locals. We were due to play Western Samoa, which was our biggest game on the tour. But, in the meantime, we were having a few drinks and a good time.

I guess I must have had a few drinks because I'd managed to get myself out onto the dance floor and, you can ask my wife, that's pretty rare.

I was dancing with this particular girl, and having a good time. The problem was she was the girlfriend of one of the local rugby supporters. And apparently dancing with someone else's partner isn't the thing to do over there.

So you can imagine it. Everyone's on the dance floor. I'm dancing. They're dancing. I start dancing with his girlfriend. And he comes up to me and says, 'You're dancing with my girlfriend.'

I've got a few beers in me and I'm pretty relaxed. I say, 'Oh, okay, I won't be long.' And next minute he cracks me with a bottle, just above the eye, splits me open.

I was bloody lucky, actually.

Well, the boys see that and they're all in there. It starts a massive brawl.

I don't get involved in that. The cut above my eye is quite sore and bleeding like anything. So I manage to make my way outside. But it's a full-on fight. Bottles and fists are flying. Just like a saloon bar fight in a Western. They go pretty nuts when they fight over there. They certainly don't hold back.

Eventually it died down and as far as I know there weren't any major injuries, just cuts and bruises.

The team doctor took Bruce Hansen and me to the hospital to get stitched up. Then the police got involved and I had to make a statement.

It was difficult for me because the police were contemplating pressing charges. And I'd just been fined a thousand dollars two months before this for assaulting Hemi Mathias. I was going through a bad period.

I'm thinking, 'Man, this is not what I need.' And I'm weighing up, 'Which way's it going to go for me, left or right.'

I told the police, 'Look, I didn't do anything wrong. The guy cracked me. Here's my eye. Have a look.'

The police took notes and left. I can tell you, we weren't very popular in Apia that night. They don't like guys coming into town and fighting the locals. The police left to get the other side of the story. And I was left wondering how it was all going to end up.

I ended up going back to the hotel and we had a meeting about it the next day. Peter Thorburn was the coach and the late Richard Crawshaw was the manager. Peter Fatialofa was there from the Samoan team.

Now Fats has got a lot of mana over there but even he couldn't do anything to quell the bad feeling against us. People were really angry. And the boys in the team were quite worried.

Fats was trying to reassure us. He kept telling us everything would be fine and not to worry. But we'd already heard that the people involved in the fight and their supporters intended to come and get us. Things were definitely not all right for us in Apia.

We had major concerns about the security at Apia Park, where we were going to play Western Samoa. Basically, there was no security.

We'd be training and the locals would be walking down the road, having just finished working in the fields, and they'd be carrying their machetes. They were just walking down the side of the road next to where we were training. And we were starting to get really paranoid.

'Don't worry about it,' Fats was saying. 'You're overreacting.'

But the guys who'd been in the fight said, 'Fats, we know you've got a lot of power and influence over here. But you were at the nightclub. And you were trying to break up the fight and calm down the crowd. But you couldn't, Fats. It was even beyond your control.'

Then we started to contemplate whether or not we should even play the game. We did some research into the security and we decided it was pretty non-existent. We pulled out of the game and headed home.

Second chance

Despite all the hullabaloo over the Divisional team's tour of the islands, Marshall was picked four months later, in March 1994, for the New Zealand Development Team's tour of Argentina.

The late Lin Colling, a former All Black halfback, coached the side while All Black coach Laurie Mains toured as a kind of observer-cum-overseer.

Mains has been criticised by some commentators over the years for being too much of a disciplinarian. But he was the right coach at the right time for Justin Marshall. In some ways he was the making of him. He helped him manage the wilder aspects of his nature, gave him a glimpse of a future with the All Blacks and, basically, set him on the road to rugby greatness.

Laurie Mains: I first selected Justin in that Development team because the game was moving in the direction of needing more robust-type halfbacks and he certainly had that. And he was a player who looked to me, when he was playing for Southland, as if he had a lot of ability, lots of grit and a really competitive nature. So I took him on that tour.

You see, Justin had a reputation for being a bit of a hothead off the rugby field and a bit of a hard diamond. So I spoke to him on that Argentine tour. I spoke to the team in general about how behaviour was an important part of it. And my recollection is that he trained damn hard and didn't put a foot wrong. And he continued to improve and develop in his play and that's why we selected him in the All Blacks in 1995.

Marshall believed he'd been given a second chance by the rugby hierarchy and he was determined to repay their faith in him.

Justin: When I got named for the Development tour, everyone was going, 'Who?'

The few that weren't wondered what the hell the selectors were up to. It was a real gamble. I know Laurie was told, 'Don't touch that guy, he's trouble.' But he still took me on.

Laurie Mains: There is a degree of truth in that. And my response to that in his case and in the cases of any players with the same reputation is: 'Let me see how he responds in my terms.'

I like to give everyone a chance. And I like to give them the opportunity to meet my standards.

Norm Hewitt was another one, incidentally, who caused mayhem in Dunedin at one stage. And we basically denied him selection into a team. It wasn't the All

Blacks. It was another team. And then the following year I spoke with him and I said, 'Look, here are the guidelines, Norm. If you can stick to those guidelines, we'll put you back in the firing line.' And he never put a foot wrong with me again.

And I found this with a lot of players. If you were honest with them and straight and you took no nonsense, then they wanted their rugby careers and they were happy to comply with the rules.

How 'make or break' was that Development tour for Justin?

Laurie Mains: Let me put it this way, players behave differently in different teams and circumstances, depending on the level of discipline that is applied. What I was doing on that Development tour was applying the levels of discipline that I expected in the All Blacks and I watched players to see how they handled that, to see if they were prepared to have the discipline needed to take their game to the next step. Now, to my knowledge, nobody put a foot wrong on that tour to Argentina, including Justin.

In many cases, this is all it requires. Players know what that line is that they can step up to, and it varies from coach to coach, from team management to team management.

Justin: I was playing to redeem myself on that tour of Argentina.

So I told myself, 'No drinking this time, Bud. They're obviously interested in you. They keep giving you opportunities. But you're going to have to be a bit careful about the way you go about things. With everything that's happened in the past, they're going to be keeping an eye on you. They'll be keen to see how you respond. So it's time to knuckle down and show people you can behave yourself when you want to.'

A lot of All Blacks were in that side. John Mitchell was the captain and there were players like Norm Hewitt and Blair Larsen. So it was a real stepping stone for me. I just wanted to have a good tour and get through it nice and clean, which I did.

John Mitchell, Development team captain: Justin Marshall is probably the most competitive player I've ever met in my playing and coaching career. I guess the first time I saw that aspect of him was at the start of the Development tour.

We'd just arrived in Rosario after a long bus trip from Buenos Aires and we'd had a big meal at the hotel. Most of the guys were sitting around letting their meal settle. But Justin and a couple of the others were nowhere to be seen. I heard a strange racket coming from one of the rooms so I went to investigate.

I opened the door and popped my head in. Justin, Jeff Wilson and Slade McFarland were playing cricket. And they were absolutely drenched in sweat. It was dripping off them. Jeff was bowling to Justin. They were playing on a wooden tongue and groove floor with a taped-up tennis ball. And that's why it was so noisy.

Jeff had already been an all-rounder for the Black Caps and he wasn't holding back. But Justin and Slade were just as serious and Justin had that look of grit and determination.

I'll never forget the sweat and the deadly seriousness. I thought, 'Hell, we don't have to worry about these boys' attitudes.'

Off the booze

As far as the drinking goes, I don't think I had a major issue with alcohol. I wasn't a young alcoholic or anything like that. But like a lot of young Kiwis I was prone to the odd binge, especially when I was out with my team-mates.

I knew I had a tendency when I drank too much to get myself into the wrong situations. And having gotten myself into those situations I tended to compound things by making the wrong decisions. In other words, I'd end up in trouble.

The common denominator every time was alcohol. So I just thought the best thing for me, to get me through this tour, was to take booze out of the equation. Just stay away from it, learn and see whether I could actually go a bit further.

So it was my decision but I also knew that the likes of Laurie would have thought it was a good decision.

Laurie Mains: Look, I loved coaching the kid because I found with him a really fresh, honest young player who just wanted direction. And when he knew what the boundaries were he was happy to stay inside those boundaries. He'd push the boundaries to the limit. But you'd expect that from a halfback, as you would with a loose forward.

As far as I was concerned, he came back from that Development tour with a reputation among us that we could select him with confidence and know that we wouldn't have a problem.

Justin: The Development XV was a big step up from the Divisional side. It was effectively New Zealand B. But I think I handled myself well. I played in three matches. We won them all and I scored three tries. But I also picked up a niggling groin injury.

Career at risk

Marshall got another break in 1994 when Southland's first-choice halfback Bobby Murrell retired. Marshall had already spent two years in and out of the Southland team,

overshadowed by Murrell. Now he finally had the chance to make the Stags No. 9 jersey his own in the NPC second division.

He was also picked for the New Zealand Colts and scored a try in the 41–31 win over the Aussies in Sydney. But he tore his groin muscle during the match.

Nevertheless he turned out for Southland the next week. Having waited so long for that jersey he was reluctant to give it up.

All of a sudden I started having this problem with my groin. It caused me pain up in that area you associate with a hernia, just above your pubic bone. And it got to the point that the pain just kept getting worse and worse the more I played and trained.

By the time the NPC was in full swing, the groin injury had really flared up and I was getting two or three painkilling jabs every time I prepared to take the field and I'd only make it through to halftime anyway.

Even the easiest tasks became a mission to accomplish. I had to sit with my legs out straight in front of me before I could lie down in bed. It was a shocking injury. There was a lot of pain. I couldn't get out of bed in the morning. I couldn't even lift my upper body. It was a really bad time for me. No one knew what was going on.

It turned out that there are two bones in the pubic area and they were out of alignment. One of them was higher than the other. And it shouldn't have been. That resulted in an imbalance in muscle development and subsequent weak spots.

One specialist I went to wanted me to have the bones fused together with a metal plate to keep them level. I was a bit skeptical about that. Another suggested quitting rugby for two to five years. I was even more skeptical about that.

I had a period of rest for about two months and it didn't make any difference. I kept wondering: 'Am I doing everything I possibly can to get myself fit again. There must be some way I don't know about to heal this injury.'

Then out of the blue I got a call from Vance Stewart, who was coaching Canterbury. He'd also coached me in the New Zealand Under-19s and he'd been following me through the Colts. I'd mentioned to him a couple of times that I was interested in moving to Christchurch at some stage. He said, 'I just called to ask if you'd consider coming up to Canterbury to play your rugby. Graeme Bachop's off to Japan and while there's still some pretty tough competition at halfback, I think you should give it a shot.'

Canterbury had the Ranfurly Shield as well, so that was another drawcard for me.

I was pretty chuffed Vance had called to tell the truth. I'd been talking to Otago and Southland, but neither seemed interested in helping me out with my injury. Southland's attitude was pretty much that I wasn't in very good shape so they were looking to fill my shoes. I even heard on the quiet that they'd lined up Brett McCormack from Otago in case I wasn't right. They were pushing me away.

Paul Henderson: I was put in a bad situation in Southland just before Justin went to Canterbury. It was the start of professionalism. A group of businessmen put up some money for us to buy some players. And I was asked my opinion on how it should be spent. Justin could hardly walk at the time and I didn't put him forward as someone they should invest in. I think Justin probably thinks I had it in for him. But I didn't at all. I've always really rated him and I admire and respect what he's achieved.

And if you look at the big picture, the move to Canterbury was the best thing for him and for New Zealand rugby. I'm glad it worked out for him.

Justin: I said to Vance, 'Look, I'd relish the opportunity to come and play for you but I'm stuffed right now. I've got this terrible groin injury and I'm not sure if I can fix it. It feels a bit funny talking about moving to a new province when I can hardly walk. There's no way I'm coming up to Canterbury to play rugby unless I can do it. And at the moment, I can't.'

His answer to that was: 'I know a guy up here who specialises in groins. Why don't you come up and have a yarn to him?' Vance wanted to help me with the injury, which was now my main priority. And in a nutshell his concern won my loyalty.

Vance Stewart introduced Marshall to Christchurch sports doctor David Burke. After checking him out, Burke sent the halfback to Sydney specialist Neil Halpin for an operation. He travelled over with Canterbury flanker Angus Gardiner, who had the same injury, but not as bad.

Dr Halpin had made a specialty of this particular groin operation, having performed it 430 times. He'd done it on league stars Ian Roberts and Ricky Stuart and cricketers Wasim Akram and Craig McDermott. He'd also worked his magic on Kiwi league halfback Stacey Jones. But Marshall was still worried.

Before the operation, Dr Halpin told me my chance of playing again was 80 percent. It might seem like pretty good odds. But think of it this way. That's a one in five chance of my rugby career taking a bullet. If you play Russian roulette your chances are one in six.

The surgery involved, in short, cutting the inductor tendon to ease the pressure and tension on it. It was considered quite a simple operation. But Marshall's condition was

apparently the worst, the most extreme, the surgeon had seen. So he spent an hour and a half under the knife compared with Angus Gardiner's 20 minutes.

The Canterbury Union paid for Marshall's trip to Sydney and for the operation. After being virtually ignored by his home province, Marshall had no hesitation in signing with Canterbury for the 1995 season. He knew Southland weren't going to be happy. But he was willing to wear that.

The next thing he had to do was get fit again. He wasn't allowed to play rugby for six months after the operation. The injury cost him his place in the New Zealand Divisional team to tour Canada, Fiji and New Zealand and denied him a chance to play for Canterbury in the Super 10 series.

As always, Marshall was aggressive in his rehabilitation. Within a week of surgery, he was in the swimming pool. A couple of weeks later, he was doing weights. After about six weeks, he was running.

He also played a lot of golf. It became something of a passion, if not a special skill. His playing partner more often than not was Andrew Mehrtens.

The Brock Car

I was working on my rehab. But there were occasions when I felt like a bit of a burden and a waste of space for my new province. Having said that, the months sitting around literally waiting for my groin to heal made me keener than ever to show my thanks to Canterbury when I finally was able to get out on the field.

When I arrived in Christchurch I stayed with my old rugby mate Simon Forrest and Tabai Matson's girlfriend Nadia. That was useful because I hardly knew anyone in Christchurch and it took me quite a while to adjust to city life. I wasn't even used to traffic lights. We never had any in Mataura. Three cars were a jam where I came from. We had one railway crossing and a roundabout. And that was it.

But the hardest thing for me in Christchurch was the one-way system. It did my head in. And I did a really bad thing.

Canterbury gave me a car. It was a sedan. I can't remember what make. But the thing that was unique about it was that half of it was white and half of it was black. All the way from the hood to the back of the front doors was painted white, and the whole back half was black. So it looked a bit like a racing car.

When I received it I rang Mum and Dad all excited and said, 'They've given me a car like Peter Brock's. I'm calling it The Brock Car.'

I thought it was great because my car down home was a lowered XB Falcon with mags and twin pipes. It was a real bogan car, my pride and joy. But I liked the one Canterbury got me as well.

But it was really recognisable.

It wasn't just like a run-of-the-mill car that everybody's driving around. It didn't have any signwriting or anything on it. But the two-tone paint job was unique. And when I first arrived in Christchurch a lot of people said they'd seen me out and about driving the wrong way down a one-way street.

I mean going to the city for me was pretty much Invercargill. I'd been to Dunedin a couple of times. But I didn't really drive there. And they didn't have many one-way streets anyway.

But they're everywhere in Christchurch. And I was constantly turning into them the wrong way. So I'd have to brake, pull over onto the footpath and spin around again. I'd get caught out quite a few times.

Anyway, I remember one time I was going down this big main road and there were two lanes either side: two lanes heading towards town and two back the other way. I was heading towards town, and I thought, 'Oh no, I'm in the wrong lane, I need to be in those other lanes heading the other way. I'm going to have to do a U-ie.' So I pulled over to the side of the road. And I looked in my rear-vision mirror. But I was still sort of watching all the traffic going the other way because I wanted to dash across my two lanes and merge into that flow. Spotting a gap, I pulled a sharp U-ie. But I clipped a car that was just going past me from behind. I just clipped the back, but I knew I'd clipped it. And the guy hit the brakes. And I hit the accelerator.

I'm thinking, 'I don't know what's gonna happen here.'

Then all of a sudden he spins around as well. So we were in a chase.

I'm thinking, 'I don't want this. I don't want anything to do with this. I can't have the Canterbury Rugby Union finding out about this. Here I am, I'm injured. I haven't even played for them yet. They probably already think I'm a gamble, an injured guy who has a reputation for attracting trouble. And they've just given me this car.'

So I pretended I didn't know that I'd clipped him. And I just kept driving. I just took off. So we had a bit of a race around Hagley Park in Christchurch. And I lost him down a side street. I thought, 'Sweet, I've got away with it.'

I figured if he followed it up with the police or the insurance and it came back to me, I'd just plead dumb and say, 'What crash? I didn't even know I'd hit him. What are you talking about?' I was pretty naïve about the whole thing really.

I was thinking, 'Christchurch is a huge city, how are they going to find out it was me among all those people out there?'

So I got home and I was sitting on the couch that night watching TV and I started to get the guilts real bad. Plus I started thinking about the black and white Brock Car being so recognisable and easy to trace. I knew I was in the wrong because I'd done a runner and I was wondering what Vance Stewart and the rest of the Canterbury management would think of me if they found out. Just as I figured Canterbury would, I was taking into consideration my assault of Hemi Mathias in Gore and the all-in nightclub brawl with the Divisional team in Samoa. I was sure they'd be thinking, 'What sort of person have we got here? The guy's totally unreliable.' I just had an awful night. Before long I was convinced Canterbury were going to send me back down to the Deep South when they found out.

So I went down to the police station in the morning and I filed a report. I said to the cop on the front desk, 'Look, mate, something happened yesterday and I'm not sure whether or not I might have clipped this car. But just in case I did, I'll give you my details.'

As it turned out the guy went to the police that morning and told them about being hit by a blond guy in a distinctive black and white car. But it was all sorted out above board and Canterbury were okay about it. They just said, 'You've done well. You've reported it. You've done the right thing. And that's all we can ask.' So that was a huge relief. And there was very little damage to the cars so the repair bills were pretty cheap too.

Culture shock

Even when Marshall was sitting around waiting for his groin to heal, the name Justin Marshall just kept making headlines. The reason: a player with the same name who played in the same province.

The other Justin Marshall was a talented sevens player who represented Canterbury at the South Island and New Zealand Sevens tournaments. He was also a flanker for the Canterbury Colts and played his club rugby for Old Boys.

Guess which club the injured Justin Marshall had signed up for in Christchurch. That's right, Old Boys.

So how did Old Boys plan to get around any confusion? To differentiate, the flanker would be referred to by his commonly used nickname of 'Jud' Marshall.

When I arrived in Christchurch I didn't really know what to do with myself to be honest. And I was particularly lost those few times I went out with girls on dates. I'd take them to a movie. But, when you think about it, that's not the greatest place to get to know a girl on a first date. So the movie would finish and I'd drop them off. Understandably, those dates never developed any further.

It took me a while to cotton on that what you should do is go out and have a drink somewhere. Then you go and have a glass of wine or a beer over dinner and a bit of a chat. And after that you go and have a coffee and a bit more of a chat.

All I knew was how it used to be in Mataura where, as I've said, the only entertainment around is the entertainment you create.

You don't go out to a restaurant for dinner. You don't go to the movies. You don't go ten-pin bowling. You don't do any of those things you take for granted when you're bored in the city.

Tabai Matson: When Justin Marshall first arrived in Christchurch he was a downright bogan. He used to wear these terrible mutton-cloth shearing tops.

He was fresh off the boat. That's the only way to describe him. He was white and he was from the Deep South. But as far as the city went, he was as fresh as any Pacific Islander arriving in the big city for the first time.

My wife used to flat with Justin when he first turned up in Christchurch. He'd never lived away from his mum before. She's a lovely lady by the way. She runs around after those three boys like you wouldn't believe. But poor old Justin couldn't cope without her. He couldn't clean. If you came home late there was never any food on the table because he couldn't cook. He was always in and out like a yo-yo: 'Oops, I forgot my boots. Oops, I forgot my shirt. Oops, I forgot my gear bag.'

Christchurch Press: Marshall elated to be back in thick of action: Highly rated New Zealand Colts halfback Justin Marshall played his first rugby match for seven months on Saturday and was all smiles afterwards in spite of not completing the match.

He appeared for the first time for his new club High School Old Boys against Otautahi at Rugby Park. Marshall retired midway through the second half but it was more a precautionary measure than through any signs of discomfort.

Mike Anthony, former Canterbury and All Black trainer (now works for the Gloucester club in England): When Marshy first arrived at Canterbury in early 1995 he was one of the first guys that I worked with. I remember him wandering down the corridor. He had his rat's tail blond mullet at the back and his checked shirt and his fisherman's jersey and super-tapered bloody Hallenstein's jeans. I wondered who the hell this was coming walking down the corridor. I thought he was lost.

He introduced himself and we went from there. He was an interesting character. He thought he knew what he was doing training-wise. He had a couple of dumbbells in his garage back in Mataura and he was throwing them around. I think his main concern was looking good on the beach.

The game wasn't even professional then. Marshy was pushed my way to make sure he kept on the straight and narrow.

Early on we had an interesting relationship. I gave him a programme but he didn't agree with it. Having a trainer was all a bit new to him. But nowadays he's a phenomenal trainer.

David and Goliath

Once I'd recovered from my groin injury, I began to train with Canterbury for the 1995 NPC. And I made my presence felt at one of my first sessions.

We had a good strong pack but we were having a few problems getting the ball out the back of the scrum. It was thought that the ball was taking the wrong channel from the front to the back. So could it be that the hooker wasn't hooking the ball properly? No, it was decided that the halfback must be putting it in wrong.

So we spoke about it and tried different things and it came up in team reviews a couple of times.

And I said, 'Come on, guys. Do you really think that me not putting the ball in exactly the right place is going to make that much difference? The fact that I'm not putting the ball in properly doesn't make the scrum wheel around or force it to get shunted the wrong way.'

As far as I could see that was a weight or a timing problem. The ball was getting to the back of the scrum okay. But the pack was wheeling from that point.

So we're having this team run and All Black hard man Richard Loe and Stu Loe, the two props, and Matt Sexton, the hooker, kept having a go at me about it.

And in the end it must have been enough to crack Richard Loe because he rose up out of the scrum like an Orc from *The Lord of the Rings* and yelled, 'Fuckin' hell, Marshall. What's wrong with you? Why can't you put the ball in properly? It's a simple thing to do! If you can't manage it, then you must be a fuckin' idiot! And you shouldn't be here.'

I'd just had enough of it by that stage. We'd been talking about it for ages. And as far as I was concerned it had nothing to do with me. So I actually cracked back at him. I said, 'Oh, for fuck's sake, Loey, if you actually pushed in the scrums in the first place we wouldn't have this issue!'

Then I popped the ball in and got to the back of the scrum as quickly as possible.

All the boys went, 'Uh-oh, here we go.'

But Loey didn't say anything to me. I could hear him swearing and cursing in the front row. But the scrum had already gone down. So he was stuck there.

I was just waiting for him to come and smack me from behind for the rest of training actually. But he didn't. He just grumbled away and moaned and that was it. He didn't really say much to me for the next couple of weeks. And we were fine after that.

I think the moment I stood up to Richard Loe is probably the moment I was fully accepted as a Canterbury player and a person to be reckoned with.

Aussie McLean, Canterbury NPC coach: You know what made Justin stand out and gave him the edge in those early days? The same thing that does it now: his work ethic.

When professionalism first came into rugby, none of us knew how long it was going to last. So all the players carried on with their day jobs.

Justin was working as a carpentry apprentice for the Christchurch City Council, which is quite a physical, tiring job. There were some long days for the players. They'd have to do their gym sessions before work, at 6 am. After work they'd come to training, which was always tough. The guys would be shattered at the end of it.

The thing about Justin, though, is he'd always ask me to leave the lights on. After everyone had gone we'd still be out on the field and I'd just stand there and catch passes for him.

Selected for the All Blacks

In late 2004 I accused the All Black selectors of devaluing the All Black jersey because they picked three other halfbacks and rested me, the incumbent, for the Northern Hemisphere tour. But if I think about it I was a virtual unknown when Laurie Mains first picked me in 1995. It was just after New Zealand had lost the final of the World Cup to South Africa, a tour of Italy and France, and it was Laurie's last job as coach.

I came into the All Black squad off the back of my first season with Canterbury. We had the Ranfurly Shield until we lost it in our last game against Auckland.

That game was an eye-opener to me about the level that was needed to step up. The Auckland team was stacked full of All Blacks and they came down to Christchurch and gave us a hiding.

At the end of the NPC, I felt I'd done quite well, but still had a bit to learn before making a push for the All Blacks.

I'd been through the process, though. I'd been in the New Zealand Under-19s and the Colts. I'd toured with the Divisional XV. And Laurie Mains had seen me on my best behaviour with the Development team in Argentina.

His performance on the Development tour, did that have any direct relation to him being picked 18 months later for the All Blacks?
Laurie Mains: Well it did in that we had an understanding how he was as a person. We also knew a bit more about his play. And we knew that his time would come.

I haven't got my notes now that I made on that tour. But I can clearly remember that he was one that had a tick, that when the opportunity came we would be comfortable about introducing him to the All Blacks. But he needed a bit more experience.

Now the reason the opportunity came was that Graeme Bachop was going off to Japan and they wouldn't let Graeme tour at the end of 1995. So that was an excellent opportunity to take Justin on that tour.

And he was just sensational in two ways. One, he was just such a damn hard worker and he was like a breath of fresh air around the place. And the second one was that he actually, as he's done all of his career since, stepped up to every challenge that was put in front of him.

Justin: I remember the first time I assembled for the All Blacks. It was at the Poenamo Hotel on the North Shore in Auckland. I was shitting myself. I was practically unknown, had just been a New Zealand Colt and hadn't really mixed with any of the top New Zealand players apart from the Canterbury boys. And if you think of the All Black team at that time, it was crammed with legends. Just in the forwards, you had the likes of Michael Jones, Ian Jones, Sean Fitzpatrick, Olo Brown, Craig Dowd, Zinzan Brooke, Robin Brooke. My saving grace was that Taine Randell and my Canterbury team-mates Tabai Matson and Mehrts were named too, because they were taking a big squad away. But I was thinking, 'Aw man, I'm out of my depth here.' I was really thrilled to be involved, but also really worried about what the other players thought of me. I remember going through the reception at the Poenamo and thinking, 'Please let me be rooming with Mehrts or Taine or Tabai or one of the other Canterbury boys, even Richard Loe for God's sakes.' I just wanted someone I was familiar with. Not only am I going into an environment I'm not comfortable with, I'm still in awe of a lot of these players.

So I rolled up to the reception and I just had my fingers crossed thinking, 'Please, please, please, please.' The keys were all on the desk and each person's name was written down next to the name of their room-mate. I found the list and, sure enough, about midway it said Justin Marshall, and I looked across and it was Zinzan Brooke. I thought, 'Of all the people! Zinzan Brooke!' He was one of the people I loved to hate. Growing up down south, I just assumed he was an Auckland wanker. This is what happens with players and criticism: you get fed what everybody thinks of somebody. And what people down south thought of bloody Aucklanders . . . 'Boat shoes' was the big phrase in that day. They wear boat shoes and they drink lattés — yet here I am right now telling this story and having a latté — and they're all up themselves. They were obviously successful, very successful, so they were just loathed, particularly down south and at that time when Auckland was so dominant.

But the thing is I didn't form my own opinion about them. I just jumped on the bandwagon. And when everyone would say, 'Argh, Zinzan Brooke, Sean Fitzpatrick,' I'd just go, 'Yeah!' and just go along with it. If someone said, 'Dickheads,' I'd say, 'Yeah, I reckon they are too. Look at them.' But I never really formed my own opinion from it. I just went along with the flow.

So it was a shock to see his name on the list, especially as the only other encounter I'd had with him was in that game when Auckland wasted us to take the Ranfurly Shield. And they were into me, particularly Fitzy and Zinny and those guys, because I was a fresh-faced new player and I'd had a bit of a dream run throughout the Shield campaign and then they thought, 'Aw yeah, we'll see what he's made of.' There's a really good photo actually. It's in the first 10 minutes and Fitzy's just given away a penalty at a ruck and he's just getting up and I'm standing there patting him on the back. And he's turning around half to look at me and also talking to the ref. And that was probably the only word I got in all day from about then on, because everything went downhill. We didn't get any more points for the rest of the day and they just sledged the hell out of me. They were saying, 'You're out of your depth.' Whenever I did something wrong they'd say, 'You shouldn't have done that. Go back to school and learn how to play properly.' They were just reminding me that I was out of my depth. 'You're out of your comfort zone and we're just going to let you know and every time you do something wrong, we'll be on your case.' And they didn't miss a thing, not a single beat. I particularly remember Fitzy, Zinny and Robin Brooke being the most vocal and I think Robin Brooke clouted me one in that game too.

Rooming with Zinny

So my second encounter with Zinny was going to be rooming with him in the All Blacks. Now, I'd already been conditioned down south to hate Aucklanders like Zinny, and I'd also just recently been sledged and beaten by him in a Shield match. So anyway I grab my key and go round the back and up the steps at the Poenamo towards the room. Now the only contact I'd had with him was to shake his hand. I never said anything to him after the Shield match.

So I was absolutely crapping myself. I was going up the stairs. I had my suitcase and my bags. I'm thinking, 'Oh God, what am I going to say? I don't want to come across as being really young and immature and green.' And I thought, 'Maybe I just won't even speak. Maybe if I don't say anything, just give him a nod when I go in.' I was thinking about all these things I could do. And then I thought, 'Maybe I could try and be funny, but then that might not go across very well. I don't know his personality.'

Anyway, I got to the door, hesitated a bit, then in I strode with all my gear, banging and crashing through the door.

Zinny was across the other side of the room lying on his bed and he just sort of looked up at me as I walked in. I sort of kept my head down a bit and then looked at him and gave him the old Kiwi hello, the raised eyebrows. He raised his eyebrows back at me and when Zinny raises his eyebrows the room suddenly seems a little smaller, he's got such a big melon. He's got a real big head on him. So I was well aware he'd acknowledged me and that was a bit of a relief.

He'd already commandeered the double bed and I was thinking about letting him put his suitcases on my single bed. So I said, 'How ya goin? I'll just put my things over there, in the corner . . . and sleep on the floor.' I was saying it half-jokingly, but I was also prepared to defer to the experienced All Black and start going about what I considered would be my initiation.

But as soon as I said that he sort of looked at me and said, 'Nah, nah, sweet, you're all right, Marshy, don't worry about it. There's your bed. Just make yourself at home.'

He jumped up and shook my hand and said, 'Congratulations, good to see you.'

After that we just hung out and talked like we'd known each other for ages.

But it taught me a simple but valuable lesson that day and it's a lesson that I've taken with me ever since and that is not to judge a book by its cover and not to form an opinion of people or persons that you don't know. You see, I became great mates with Zinny and had I not become an All Black, I would have gone through my life despising the guy for absolutely no reason at all.

If I look back on a lot of things that went right for me when I first made it into international rugby that would have been the first thing, rooming with Zinny. It was the best thing that could have happened.

If anyone knows Zinny, he's a super-competitive guy. And he'd sit in the room scribbling away with a pen and paper working out all these scrum moves and he'd ask my opinion. Here's me, I've just turned 22 and he's asking me: 'Whadya think? Ya think this'll work?'

I didn't say much initially. But he was so enthusiastic with his little arrows and circles and crosses that he drew me into it and made it fun. He was like an inventor or a scientist. I've never come across another player like him in that regard. And it's something I've picked up off him, because I always like working out new moves myself now. They're like puzzles.

He did it all for himself, though. It was all to keep him in the team, at the top and to give him an edge over his opponents.

Leading into it I'd heard all the stories about how the experienced All Blacks treated the young players. But they just weren't like that, those guys, and that was great.

Professional rugby player

The tour of Italy and France was the first professional tour the All Blacks ever went on. Each player got paid $30,000. And it was really bizarre.

$30,000 was more money than I'd ever seen. The most I'd ever earned in a year was about $26,000 at the freezing works in Gore. And here I was, in a situation where we were away for five or six weeks, and I was earning all this money.

Shield fever: The chance to play Ranfurly Shield rugby was a big motivation for me to move to Canterbury. In my third game, in 1995, we beat Marlborough 79–0.

Happy and relieved — with Mark Mayerhofler and Andrew Mehrtens after a successful Ranfurly Shield challenge, this time against Waikato in 2000.

I'm sure I was trying to punch the ball out of Keith Lowen's grasp. We won this 2001 Ranfurly Shield clash with Waikato 52–19.

Making the most of a photo opportunity after Ben Blair's last-minute try in Canterbury's 31–29 Ranfurly Shield win over Wellington in 2001.

Follow the leader. I run out on to Jade Stadium moments after Todd Blackadder gets an ovation for his last game. It was the 2001 NPC final. We beat Otago 30–19, the perfect send-off for Toddy.

'We did it!' Chris Jack and I get quite emotional after scraping home 16–13 in a Ranfurly Shield defence against Otago in 2002. I scored a try and a rare dropped goal in the win.

What happens on the field, stays on the field. I share a joke with Matua Parkinson moments after we've been sin-binned for fighting. North Harbour won the 2001 NPC match 20–9.

'Not up my nose, Mehrts.' Celebrating Canterbury's 40–27 NPC final win over Wellington at Westpac Stadium in 2004.

Running in a try against Wellington in the 2004 NPC final.

With my good friends (from left) Robbie Deans, Mike Anthony and Eroll Collins on tour in South Africa, 2003.

I thought that was just brilliant and it was also strange.

I couldn't have cared less about the money. If they'd said to me, 'You can't have any money but you can come on tour with us,' I would have been just as happy. I just wanted to play for the All Blacks and represent my country. That had always been my dream. The money just made the realising of the dream even sweeter. I would have just been happy to get all that gear that you see the All Blacks running around in: nice clothes, training gear, bags and boots. That would've done me.

I remember thinking, 'Wow, if this is the starting point, where does the money go from here?'

But although that was the first professional tour, similar to what the tours are like nowadays, it was still an old-fashioned tour in the sense that there were midweek games as well as the three test matches. And we took quite a large squad to cover the midweek games. I got to play in the first game against Italy A in Catania.

But what I remember most about the trip to Italy was a couple of the older players taking a few of us new boys aside. They sat us down and solemnly warned us: 'Whenever you're walking around here in Italy, if you see a man walking towards you with a hat on, don't look him in the eye, he's Mafia.' And I got really paranoid about that.

I've been sucked in by things like that, being really gullible, ever since I can remember. When I first started working on the broom at the freezing works the butchers used to call me over. They'd say, 'Hey, Justin, Justin, come here mate.'

'What is it?'

'Can you whip down to the store and get me a left-handed knife for this job that I'm doing?' And off I'd go to the storeroom.

I was always like that. If someone told me something I didn't really think about it. I just believed it and followed the instructions.

So I took the Mafia comment hook, line and sinker. And I didn't know where to look the whole time I was in Italy because over there almost every man wore a suit with a hat.

Obviously that game against Italy A was my first for the All Blacks. We hammered them 51–21. I was really nervous but the good thing was that I was playing alongside a few other guys who hadn't played for the All Blacks before either. I'd also worn black jerseys in age-group teams so I wasn't that daunted. The main thing for me was that I didn't let anyone down and I was able to prove that I deserved my selection.

The test team thrashed Italy, and we headed on to France.

My second midweek game was a 34–19 win over the French Barbarians in Toulon. But I did a bit more on the ball, a bit much actually. I was trying to speed the game up with quick tap kicks and getting involved at every opportunity and I overcooked it. After the midweek games me and my dirt-tracker mates tended to overcook the social side of things as well. We'd play our game then go out and have a few drinks. Then we'd go and watch the test team on the weekend and go and have a few drinks. And a bit of a pattern started to emerge.

We didn't play that well in the second game and Laurie called a big meeting afterwards. A few of us were singled out in front of the whole squad. Laurie ripped me apart. 'As for you, Marshall,' he said, 'you're too headstrong for a young All Black. You're just finding your feet and you're taking quick taps out there. Just pull your head in.'

I wasn't the only one to wear it, though. Taine Randell, Tabai Matson and a couple of others got a good bollocking. 'You younger players on this tour are drinking too much piss! You need to recognise what we're here for. We all like to have a beer but you guys are going overboard.' There were about half a dozen of us that he ripped apart. And we probably deserved it too. I'd started to cruise into the playing on the field, playing off the field routine of the tour and Laurie woke me up to the fact that I couldn't cruise; I had to knuckle down because he was watching us closely.

Laurie Mains: Well, it wasn't a matter of pulling him back into line. It was talking to him about what his main function was as a halfback. There's a list of about four or five jobs that are the most important things for him to do. There's his clearing of the ball, his kicking when it's required, his once or twice per half running and his communication with the forwards. Now I didn't want him doing anything else because when a halfback starts getting too busy he neglects his main jobs. And it was just enthusiasm. It was nothing else. That's all part of learning. And what I liked about that was that he listened and he performed. He did exactly what he was asked to do.

'Timber!'

Justin: The main focus of the tour was the two tests against France. The All Blacks lost the first test and played poorly. We were having a meeting in the team room a couple of days later. Laurie Mains said a few words and then Colin Meads, who was manager, decided he had something he wanted to say. And he must have been stewing on it for quite a while.

All Black flanker Liam Barry's brother Tim was in the room. He worked for Lion Breweries so he was travelling with the team as the sponsor's rep. Pinetree said, 'What the hell are you doing here? You're not part of the team. You're just here to look after the team. Get out of here.'

'Sorry, Pinetree.' Tim skulked out of the room and the rest of us shrunk down into our seats as much as we could. I always knew Pinetree was a mountain of a man. But I'd never realised the mountain was volcanic.

'Right, you pricks,' he started. 'You need to be told some home truths.' Well, that's how I remember him starting. And the rest is all a bit of a blur. Pinetree's anger was like a devastating force of nature. And the All Blacks just let it batter against them.

The senior All Black forwards took the brunt of it. Pinetree just chewed them up. Guys like Fitzy, Olo Brown, the Brooke brothers, Craig Dowd. Tough characters. 'You're an absolute disgrace!' he told them. 'You're soft! You're walking around with your heads stuck up in the clouds, prancing around, thinking you're something that you're not. Call yourself All Blacks?'

Then he started getting stuck into individuals. He was questioning them one by one whether they should even be on an All Black tour. Even Fitzy and Laurie Mains weren't spared. He had a go at Laurie about his attitude and how he was preparing the team.

He was hitting us all in one big attack and no one was able to escape because the thing was, he was right. We needed a good hard kick up the arse and Pinetree had no problem giving it to us.

Now, Pinetree's a big man. But among All Blacks, he has an aura that makes him a couple of feet taller and twice as broad. And he's intimidating. He points a finger the way some people point a bone and others a gun. And once he got angry, which was pretty much straight away, there didn't seem much room or even much air for anyone else. He swung his fury around like a black cat he had by the tail. And every time he turned your way, you'd retreat into the wall away from the extended claws and the hissing teeth that slashed past your face.

He was as serious as I've ever seen him. And he was just giving it to us. And I just remember sitting, watching his face, feeling flat-out uncomfortable.

You've got to remember that this was the first All Black tour of the professional era. His generation had made huge sacrifices every time they went on tour. Yet here were we being paid previously undreamed of amounts of money and we weren't earning it. He told us all that we were being pampered, that we thought we were better than we actually were, and that we were getting on the piss too much. As far as Pinetree was concerned we were degrading the legacy of people like him and just not being All Blacks.

This went on for 10 to 15 minutes. Then he just sort of mumbled something and that was it. He walked out. We just all sat there stunned. No one really moved or said anything for a few minutes. Everyone was just sitting there either taking it in or thinking about it. I couldn't wait to get out of there and go back to my room. But I couldn't move.

Eventually people started to sort of shuffle about and then we just all got up and left the room one by one. No one said anything.

From that moment on there was no way we were going to lose the second test to France.

Now, I'm not a fan of people blasting the players willy-nilly. Usually it doesn't work. But what Pinetree did at that meeting worked. And for something like that to work it needs to be the right person at the right time saying something that needs to be said. And it did need to be said.

The other powerful factor was the delivery: the way that he said it and the person that he is and the way that he just went about the whole thing. How could I describe it? I don't want to seem cruel. Colin Meads is certainly an intelligent man. But he's not an academic. He's a typical farmer. So he doesn't say, 'Righty-o chaps, if I could have a civilised word about a few important issues.' There's no trying to put it across in a nice way. You're a bunch of arseholes and that's it. He was just saying how it was and that was good because he just let it come out as he thought it should come out.

I also think it made a difference that it wasn't the coach going off at us. Sometimes a coach can give you a bollocking and you're actually trying bloody hard. But on this occasion we weren't. I don't think we were. Well, I know. We weren't trying and doing the little things as much as we could have. And that's why we lost that first test.

Pinetree's blast did another thing for me that I'll always thank him for. It acted as a bridge from me to the All Black teams of the amateur era. It gave me a real connection to and an awareness of the history of the All Blacks and the legacy that we as players carry around with us at all times. I realised that we have a huge responsibility and we have to honour and respect that tradition.

A whole new ball game

The All Blacks as a group have changed a lot over the years. In the old days they were seen as strong, aloof and emotionless. You had TV adverts celebrating Griz Wyllie's inscrutable lack of emotion at a rugby match, Colin Meads lugging fence posts around and Sir Brian Lochore grunting non-committally about his Toyota Camry. Nowadays Ma'a Nonu's wearing eyeliner on the field and in the TV adverts Mils Muliaina's mum comes out to the team bus with a cuddly toy Kiwi and tosses it to him, saying, 'Don't forget Zinny.'

To me the issue is the transition that's been made from amateur to professional. I had a bit of time in the amateur ranks, and when you become a professional rugby player, you're playing 10 or 11 months of the year. You're in the spotlight for too long these days to get away with what the likes of Olo Brown got away with. Olo was a regular All Black and Auckland player who never did interviews with the media.

But when you go into any professional team culture now, for instance Canterbury, the Crusaders, the All Blacks, we have protocols and a team culture that we set out. The whole team and the management sit down in a room together. And we decide what we want to achieve, how we intend to achieve those goals, what are the things that are going to help us achieve those goals, what's going to drive us, and what are the rules or guidelines we operate by as a team. And one of those things we have to agree to nowadays is to fulfil our responsibilities to the team, to do the commercials and the media interviews. We are contractually bound to do promotional work. So we don't go out and say, 'Mr Weet-Bix, I want to be in your TV ad,' and Weet-Bix pays you for it. We don't get any money for going on TV. We have to do it. That's part of being in the All Blacks.

Now I've got a lot of respect for Colin Meads and I get on with him really well and I've got a lot of time for him. But I think he's out of place in the comments he makes every now and then about professional rugby nowadays because the game's moved on from where he was.

It's all very well to come out and say, 'Well, we never used to do this in our day,' but it's not his day any more. And with great respect he needs to — and it may not happen — spend some time in a professional environment and see the development the game's made because it has evolved, it has moved. And the days when you were only committed to playing six months or so of rugby a year are well and truly gone.

I think it would be a real eye opener for Colin Meads if he spent a week with the All Blacks or one of the other top professional teams today. The first thing he would notice, I'm sure, would be the body weights of the players. Most of the modern backs would probably be as heavy as the old All Black forwards. Our backs range from 90 to 110 kilograms. I think most of the forwards back in that day were in the mid-90s. Hey, I'm 94 kilograms and I'm the halfback!

I hate to say it, but today's player is stronger and faster. And when you've got a stronger and faster player, the game's different.

It irks me and irritates me that whenever there's ever any questions about issues in the modern-day era, they always go back to Pinetree and people like that who always say, 'We never used to do that in our day.' And yet you see Pinetree on TV now making more money than he ever did when he was an amateur player. I mean, you probably never used to make much money through endorsements or speaking engagements in your day either, Pinetree. So there are some benefits to the modern game and even Pinetree can't argue about that because he enjoys them as much as anyone else, if not more.

Test selection

Anyway, back to that tour of Italy and France in 1995. We midweekers won our next three games quite comfortably. I scored tries in the second and third games. The result of the third was 55–17 over a French Selection in Nancy, and it helped lift spirits in the camp after the first test loss. The team played well and I was really happy with my own game too.

I thought, 'This is great. Got through that. Played well. And no more games. I can relax now.'

We were all sitting in the bus, planning our night and what we were going to get up to. Someone had organised us a trip through Moët & Chandon. We had plans to drink bubbly there for a few hours. There were a few other outings planned in the lead-up to the second test too.

So we were all getting off the bus, heading back into the hotel to get changed for the night ahead. Tabs Matson and Taine were ahead of me. I was one of the last to get off. And Laurie gave me the old tap on the shoulder and said, 'Best you don't have very many beers at all tonight.'

I looked at him and I thought, 'Should I say, "Come on, mate, this is the end of the tour for me."' But something in his eyes made me hold my tongue. I was thinking, 'Shit, what's he up to?' So I very quietly, with my bottom lip dragging on the bus aisle, said, 'Sure, Laurie, whatever you say.' But I was thinking, 'Why's he singled me out? I haven't been too bad, not since he had a go at us anyway.'

I just wandered off the bus and said to the boys, 'Look, I've been given the word not to drink too much.'

They were all like, 'Oh, well, bad luck. Obviously, he knows what you're like when you have a few under your belt. Anyway, we'll enjoy ourselves.'

I said, 'Look, I don't even think it's worth me coming out for one or two because you guys are gonna be into it and having heaps of fun and I won't be able to.'

So I ended up having a really quiet night back at the hotel.

The next morning I found out why Laurie had called me aside.

Nowadays they come and see you before you're selected and they go and tell the player who's going to be dropped and all that sort of carry-on. But I just went to the meeting. I looked around the room and saw all the midweek boys. Most of them looked really hung over, like they'd had a good night, so I was annoyed.

I can honestly say I wasn't even thinking about what Laurie was up to. I couldn't see any possible way that he could contemplate naming me in the test side. So when he read my name out I just about fell off my chair.

All the boys came up and said, 'Maybe it was a good thing he told you to stay off the plonk.'

After one of the games you told Justin to concentrate on his main functions as a halfback. Did his response to your talk with him have anything to do with his test selection?
Laurie Mains: His response to my talk with him had a lot to do with his test selection. Absolutely . . . no question. If he hadn't been able to respond to that then he probably wouldn't have been selected. But he did.

Justin: So I had about three days to prepare to play my first test for my country. Suddenly I was training with a completely different team, all the All Black legends, and I felt really out of place. Plus I was right in the midst of it, being the halfback and having to call all the lineouts and call moves. I felt really intimidated in that environment. I was sure they were all looking at me thinking, 'What the hell . . .'

Having said that, I also felt that I was around an extremely determined group of men. They just had this way about them throughout the week. There wasn't a hell of a lot of talking and there wasn't a lot of fooling around. They were just focused. And everything seemed to come together. I was very mindful that it was Laurie Mains' last test as All Black coach. Pinetree ripping them apart about being soft — that was still ringing in their ears. And they still felt all the hurt of the first-test loss. I just knew they were a lot more focused for this test. And because of that I knew it was going to be a good performance.

Part Two:
The first half

My first test

Paris, 18 November 1995: I was feeling a bit nervy the day I played my first test for the All Blacks. Walking out into the Parc de Princes was an experience in itself. What a wicked stadium! I wandered out there and sat by myself for about 10 minutes just looking around, taking in the moment. Every other guy was walking around or in the changing room warming up. But I was thinking about everyone at home and what I was about to do. I was putting all of my energy into playing the best game I could muster. I was making sure that my mind was really clear. I don't think I've done it ever since. But it seemed like the right thing to do on that particular day.

I have a really strong self-belief. And I called on that. I knew that the players around me were the best players in the world and that I wouldn't want to be in any other team. That knowledge also gave me strength.

I went into the changing room. My jersey was hanging from a hook on the wall. I stood there and I stared at it for a while. 'Jees,' I thought, 'am I man enough to pull this thing on? Can I produce a game that will do this justice? Can I wear it with the pride it deserves?' It was just hanging there next to me, the black jersey. And it seemed to be listening quietly, listening as it had done through the generations of hopeful young All Blacks, and patiently asking back, 'Are you?' Challenging me almost. 'Can you?' I picked up the jersey and as I slid my head and each arm in and pulled it over my body, I got a sense of something special, almost sacred. I don't think you have to be a rugby nut to know what I'm talking about, but being a New

Zealander might help. I was pulling on the All Black jersey before my first test and I felt a little overawed at what was happening to me.

That done, I looked at my wrist. It was injured. It's still injured, actually. I'll probably end up with arthritis in it. Anyway, I taped up the wrist with white tape. Then, for some reason, I taped up the other wrist too. I didn't need to, and I'm not sure why I did it. Maybe to give myself a distinct look. Maybe subconsciously it was my modest Kiwi version of Zorro and his 'mark of the Z' or the Lone Ranger and his mask (although 'The Bloke with Two Wrists Taped Up' doesn't have the same ring to it). Whatever the reason, it was the start of a ritual. Every game I've played since, I've had white tape on both wrists.

If you ask most All Blacks about their test debut they'll tell you they were proud as punch to be standing there listening to and singing the national anthem and soaking up the atmosphere and focusing on what they're about to do. And when it comes to the haka, they just don't want to blow it. If you're lucky, you can hover around the back somewhere where you won't be seen. I just wanted to get it over and done with and not do it wrong. I wanted to get the words and actions right and I wasn't thinking anything else about the haka at that stage, although it was awesome to be involved in it.

I remember getting the ball in the first 10 minutes and their second five came at me and I just bumped him off and carried on. I thought, 'Hell, that was easy.'

I must have thought I was indestructible because about five minutes later I got the ball again and I did the same thing. The problem was the player I tried to bump off was Olivier Merle, the huge French lock, and he hit me with all his power, holding nothing back. I ran straight into him, thinking I was going to bowl him over. And he picked me up, lifted me right up high off the ground and cartwheeled me backwards. My arms were flailing everywhere. But I was still trying to hold on to the ball. Of course, the guys paid me out big time after the game because of that effort.

But we won the game quite comfortably. The other memorable incident in the game was a Jonah Lomu try that only Jonah could have scored. He carried about five French players over the line under the posts.

The All Blacks played brilliantly that day and really responded to their critics in the best way possible. The other satisfying aspect was that I was playing with my old Southland team-mate Simon Culhane at first five and we knew each other's games really well.

I couldn't have asked for a better test debut really.

The NZPA match report on the 37–12 win said Marshall had proved himself to be a realistic option as a test halfback for future All Black selectors.

The report said, 'He ran strongly, cleared the ball effectively and visibly grew in confidence as the game went on.'

Laurie Mains gave him rave reviews. 'Justin Marshall, I think, solved one of the real problem areas today,' he said. 'I was extremely satisfied with the way he played. When you lose players of the calibre of Graeme Bachop and Ant Strachan they are not always easy to replace. I was really concerned about that area. But Justin showed there's hope there.'

Laurie Mains, 2005: Now, we had a good reason why we selected him, as a bit of a novice really, for the second test. The French were really aggressive in the rucks and mauls in the first test and in the provincial games. And it was Justin's ruggedness as well as the other things that he'd displayed. We said, 'Right, we need him for that second test.' And it was probably the best selection we made during that tour because he just really stepped up.

And I'll tell you what impressed me most. Here he was, a country kid, and he had players like Zinzan Brooke and Robin Brooke and Fitzpatrick and Brown in front of him with all this experience and he wasn't shy at all to do his job and do his communication as a halfback. It was incredibly impressive.

I just knew when we came home from this tour that that kid had that jersey for a long time.

Show me the money

Around the time of the 1995 Bledisloe Cup series and before the end-of-year tour to Italy and France, an interesting scenario developed, a stand-off between the NZRU and a company called World Rugby Corporation.

The WRC had their own ideas of taking rugby into the professional era and the competitions that could be run.

Both parties approached the players. And I remember at the time being really in the dark as to what was going to happen.

The good thing for me was that I had been recognised as a player with a future. Both parties wanted my services so that meant I was going to get a contract one way or the other, whereas a lot of players weren't contracted.

I remember us having a Canterbury team meeting about the entire process. Richard Loe and Mike Brewer were acting on the players' behalf and they kept us up to date with everything from the WRC. We also had the current NZRU chairman Jock Hobbs, funnily enough, come and see us. He represented the New Zealand Rugby Union.

Aussie businessman Kerry Packer was putting up the money for the WRC. He said he was going to take the game global. He was going to have teams from all over the world, Japan, Argentina, Canada, the United States, as well as the traditional strongholds.

I remember as a 22 year old thinking that his concept seemed incredibly exciting. There was plenty of travel to exotic locations and a lot more money for the players. The WRC offered me a contract of about $US180,000 over five years, which I thought was just fantastic.

On the other hand, the Rugby Union had the Super 12 idea and the current NPC structure. The Super 12 was quite exciting as well. But they weren't really talking about money at that stage.

There was an awful lot of conjecture and speculation about who was going to get the players, whether the players were being greedy, which way it was all going to go. The newspapers and bulletins were full of it.

The next step was that Otago players Jeff Wilson and then Josh Kronfeld showed their allegiance to the NZRU by being the first players to sign with them.

So the Canterbury players went into a team meeting and we decided that this is all getting terribly messy, the best thing for us to do is to stick together as a team. That way nobody would be left out on their own. We made it quite clear that everybody should stick together because we were more powerful as a group.

We knew they couldn't leave us all out, particularly as we had a few All Blacks in our side. So everybody felt reasonably secure. We decided as a team that nobody was going to go out and sign their own contract and look after themselves.

We were either going to go with the WRC, which we were very much in favour of at that stage, or stick with the New Zealand Rugby Union. But whichever way we went, we were going to do it together.

I remember that was quite comforting for me because as a young player I just didn't know what to do, to be honest. Knowing that the decision would basically be made for me was very reassuring.

So we read and heard and listened and talked about what was going to happen. And then the thing with Jeff and Josh came to light and our advice was not to worry. Jeff and Josh had done their personal deals and that was okay. No one had said the New Zealand Rugby Union was going to get it. So we decided to stick with our policy of all staying together.

It got to the point where the WRC was looking like the very likely option. I even remember signing a contract with the WRC. That might seem strange now but the whole Canterbury squad signed contracts with the WRC.

So we had all basically jumped ship. And we were all very happy about that.

But everything turned to shit. The WRC started to lose some backing and lose some ground. And the Rugby Union put the pressure on players and started to sign a few. It actually swung in their favour and they managed to secure most of the players in New Zealand. Not all of them, though. A few All Blacks and the whole Canterbury team had signed with the WRC.

In the end Jock Hobbs and the other people representing the NZRU came to us with an ultimatum. They said, yes, they wanted our signatures. But they didn't really need them because they had almost everyone else and they were going to set up their competitions anyway.

They said, 'Here are your contracts. You either sign them or you don't.' And they offered us the worst contracts they could think of.

My contract comprised the standard $60,000 for a Super 12 and NPC player and another $20,000 for being an All Black. So I signed a three-year contract with the Rugby Union for $NZ80,000.

I had no bargaining power and no leg to stand on. That was really disappointing because I thought what we'd done was a smart thing to do.

But we paid the penalty for turning our backs on the Rugby Union. I remember being stuck with that contract while other guys were just creaming it.

So through the 1996 and '97 seasons when we had such unbelievable success with the All Blacks, I was on a really shitty contract. I received some slight increases. But nothing like what some of the other players were on because they were on such good base contracts for playing in the Super 12 and the NPC.

And other players at Canterbury were in the same position for the first few years of professional rugby.

Summer holiday

The first full year of professionalism was 1996. That year, the Crusaders went on a pre-season trip to South Africa of all places. Why we did that, I don't know. It still eludes me. Vance Stewart was the coach. I guess he thought we'd get a jump on everybody by heading over there and getting a feel for the conditions.

We finished last in the Super 12, so the trip to South Africa obviously did us no good. Why? We spent our whole pre-season trip out drinking and enjoying South Africa for the first time. We drank at night and went to the beach during the day.

At every opportunity the boys had their shirts off in the sun, we played cricket on the beach, swam in the surf, lay around, enjoyed ourselves, drank and ate. We went to Sun City and played golf. We went to water parks. In hindsight, we did everything possible in that little trip to help us prepare poorly for the Super 12.

There's one particular session that the boys still laugh about. We ended up going down to a place called Waterfront in Johannesburg. Now there aren't a lot of places to go in Johannesburg but the Waterfront's all right. It's a whole group of bars and restaurants built around this marina. And you can have quite a good time there.

Anyway, the bus took us to the marina and dropped us off. The management said, 'Right, there are going to be two buses going back to the hotel. We're going for a meal first so one's leaving at 10 and the other's leaving at 12. If you're not getting on the first bus we want you on the second one because we've got this game against the Cats at Ellis Park in two days' time.'

The boys went, 'Yeah, yeah, okay.'

We were all done up to the nines ready to go out. We went and had our meal and then the boys thought, 'Oh, we'll go to a couple of bars before the bus is due.'

So anyway the bus driver turns up at 10 o'clock and no one's there. So he goes away and we're busy doing the pubs and started getting right into it and really enjoying it.

The bus driver comes back at 12 and there were two people there: the coaches, I think. Actually, I'm not even sure if the coaches or management were there to be honest. So the bus came back at 12 and left and nobody was on it. And we had a pretty wild sort of a night. In fact we all got absolutely annihilated.

The game against the Cats was an absolute debacle. We lost, of course. And it was still in those days when, if things didn't go too well in the game, we'd be made to do a few 100-metre sprints. There was no time for recovery. It was just straight into physical exercise. And I remember Simon Forrest having a good spew because we were made to do the sprints. Those were the days.

Batman and Wyatt Earp

That pre-season trip at the beginning of the professional era was just an old-fashioned larrikins' trip. But bizarrely enough, now that the game's truly professional, it's those times back in 1996 and '97 and the sort of antics we used to get up to that I miss most.

Luckily, the Crusaders are still a reasonably fun-loving outfit. We still get together and have a few beers every now and then, usually on bus trips. But you have to be so careful these days. You don't want to bring the game into disrepute. And sometimes you can be creating an incident without even knowing it. I was caught up in a situation like that with Mark Robinson, the former Canterbury and All Black centre, on one of our end-of-season trips.

We travelled over to Akaroa and stayed in a pub there. But we were already well on our way by the time we arrived. We were all dressed up. Some of the guys were superheroes. Mark had a proper Batman suit on, while I was dressed as a cowboy.

We were teasing each other and carrying on. And I ended up chasing him around a car until I eventually caught him and we had a bit of a play-fight.

It was nothing. But about three days later, Darren Shand, our manager, who went on to become the All Black manager under Graham Henry, received a letter from a lady over in Akaroa.

So I get this call. 'Marshy, Shandy here. How are you doing?'

'Not bad, mate. Not bad.'

'I've got a bit of a serious issue, mate. We've received a letter of complaint from the end-of-season trip. Do you want me to read it to you?'

'Oh, yeah.' Well, I was racking my brain, as you do when you've done something wrong that you can't remember.

I was thinking, 'Hell, what have I done? What have I done?'

Anyway, the lady complained that there had been excessive noise and a lot of bad language, which was not appropriate. She said, 'At about midnight I looked out my window, beside the pub, and saw Justin Marshall running around and around my car in my drive. And he was chasing Batman.'

I said, 'Can you read that again to me, Shandy.'

He said, 'I saw Justin Marshall, running around and around my car. He was chasing Batman. And they were making a lot of noise and climbing all over my car. And they were yelling and laughing at each other. And they ended up banging into my door. And I'm not sure who Batman was, if his mask had come off I would have been able to recognise him. But I clearly saw Justin Marshall for who he was. And he looked to be intoxicated at the time.'

And that was the extent of the letter.

I said to Shandy, 'You're fuckin' having a laugh, aren't you? For God's sake, we were just having a bit of fun. It was me chasing Robbo. Yeah, we made a bit too much noise and we shouldn't have been running around the car. But there's no damage done or anything like that.'

Anyway, we apologised to the lady. You have to these days. You have to take every precaution. Players are in the public eye and are expected to be role models. A small story like that — Justin Marshall chasing Batman — being a bit drunk and noisy, that's a great story for a newspaper like the *Sunday News*. And it would be jumped on — loutish, rude, obscene behaviour from All Black halfback. You've just got to be so careful.

One thing I've noticed with professional rugby in New Zealand is that the more successful you are the less chance you have to actually celebrate your victories.

The Crusaders have been victims of their own success, particularly the All Black Crusaders. They go straight from the Super 12 final to All Black assembly three days later. You don't get a chance to celebrate. And it sucks. And it annoys me every year that the people who do well . . .

You'll have to start losing. That'd solve things.

Yeah, I know. But the schedule doesn't reward success. The teams that do well, their players just get thrashed. What irritates me and I think is wrong about it is that you don't get the opportunity to reflect on and rate what you've achieved, particularly when you've just won a Super 12. It's hard to win. In the first nine years, only three teams won it: the Blues, the Brumbies and us.

The Merry Pranksters

The Crusaders could quite easily be called The Pranksters. I don't know why we attract them but we seem to have an endless stream of practical jokers come through this team.

And now that I've left New Zealand, I can confess to being one of those pranksters, as much as I've denied it to my team-mates over the years.

I know that they've suspected me on occasion. But when I do something and the eyes start turning my way, I never admit to anything.

Quite a lot of my best work has involved destroying people's clothing. But I believe they deserved it. Scott Robertson certainly did. Why? He is a relentless singlet-wearer, particularly in hot weather.

His singlet-wearing obsession is so advanced that he even has singlets for going out in. He goes out in his singlet. He's got dress singlets that he likes to wear to nightclubs and bars. These are fashion singlets. And that amuses me.

So I rifled through his drawers one time when he wasn't there and grabbed a couple of his singlets. And I cut through the strap that goes over the shoulder with scissors right through to the point that it was almost ready to break and the shoulder would snap off.

And I tell you what, if you're an avid singlet-wearer and you really pride yourself on your singlet collection, when you pull one on and it snaps, you're not too pleased about it.

I know he suspected me. But I never owned up to it. Never do. I learnt that lesson the hard way, early on in my career.

Scott Robertson: It gutted me when he started cutting my singlets. It was bloody hot in South Africa so we were having a Skins versus Shirts match at training one day. I took off my singlet because I was on the Skins team. When I went to put it back on after the game, he'd sliced off a whole shoulder. So the singlet just had one shoulder strap while the other side hung down on my chest like a girl's top.

I was going, 'Marshall!'

He was going, 'What?' He denied it, and denied it and denied it.

'I'm going to get you back, mate.'

'For what?'

But he stung me again before I even came close to getting him back.

Within two days someone started going into my room, somehow they'd got my room key, and they went into my suitcase and cut all my training Speedos. I say someone. But it was obviously Justin. He cut the sides of them along the seam so they split every time I pulled them on. I had to train Commando-style until I could get to a shop that sold undies.

Justin: Have you ever heard of an honesty call? It's like an amnesty during which people can admit their bad deeds or mistakes and get away with them so that a problem can be solved and everyone can move on. We have them occasionally in the Crusaders. It's just about being honest. You may have been wrong, you shouldn't have done it but if you give the honesty call and say it was you it's all fine. Robbie Deans or one of the other officials will stand up, usually in a court session, and say, 'We need to sort this problem out honestly. Now who did it?'

Guys will usually stand up and say, 'Yeah, it was me.'

But I get a bit of a thrill out of saying nothing, just leaving the whole thing unresolved. I decided that was the best thing to do during that trip to South Africa in 1996.

Now, when I'm in a hotel I'm a big robe wearer. And I decide this robe in the Holiday Inn is primo. It's one of those big white ones that you see on the movies. You tie it up around the middle and it's got that little monogram on it.

I decide to steal it. I put it in my suitcase and away we go. We leave the hotel for the next place we're staying in South Africa. (I've still got that robe, actually.)

But unbeknown to me the boys had set up our physio, Steve Cope. He was the brunt of quite a few jokes. We always loved setting him up. So they grabbed a robe and put it in one of his physio bags and just left it in there and packed it up for him.

I wasn't involved in the prank. So I didn't know they'd done this.

Anyway we get to the new hotel. Cope's in his room and he unpacks everything and obviously this robe is in there. Then the boys start filtering in. 'Oh, where's that robe from?' They start teasing him about it and carrying on. 'Oh, you stole it. Yes you did. You stole it. We're going to ring the hotel.'

And he's going, 'No I didn't. I don't know how it got in there.' They teased him mercilessly about it.

After the game we had a court session and they thought, 'Right, we're going to have to make him drink for this. We'll make him drink for stealing the robe.'

I still didn't know that any of this was going on because I hadn't been in the physio's room. It was just the pranksters who were doing it. Matt Sexton was definitely involved and I think Stu Lowe and probably Aaron Flynn.

So we get to this court session. They're going to make him drink a jug. And they say, 'Righty-oh, we want an honesty call. Anybody who's stolen a robe from another hotel stand up now. We've had a ring from the hotel. It needs to be returned. And you need to stand up.'

So everyone's looking at Cope, for him to stand up, because everyone's in on it. And I stand up. And everyone sort of looks at me and the guys who set up the prank are going, 'What the . . . ?'

See, they'd been saying, 'We need an honesty call. We've got a thief in our team. The hotel has rung.'

I'd been sitting there thinking, 'Oh no, oh no, oh no. I've got to stand up here. I've stolen it. The hotel's ringing. We don't want . . . ' And I stood up. And it took the pranksters by total and utter surprise.

Cope hadn't stood up yet. He was obviously just waiting for his moment. But when I stood up all the eyes shifted because they were all looking at Cope, waiting for him to stand and they were going to go, 'Ha-ha-ha, drink a jug.' But I stood up. And they said, 'What are you doing, Marshy?'

I said, 'It was me. I stole the robe.'

Suddenly, everyone was just pissing themselves laughing.

I said, 'What? What?'

They said, 'Where did you get that from?'

'I got it from our last hotel. I didn't think anyone would notice.'

Everyone was just crying with laughter and I couldn't understand why.

I got punished for that. And that was the last time I ever admitted anything in an honesty call. So, yeah, I've never been caught out again.

Up until these words are read, no one has known about my pranks. A lot of people would assume that a prank would be funnier if you had someone to share it with. But I don't agree. I've kept mine secret and I've derived great satisfaction from them and had a lot of laughs too. I love it. I only record them now as a little gift to the reader . . . and because my playing days in New Zealand are over.

My feeling about pranks is that you don't want other people in on it, because then you've got someone else to worry about. I've worked with other people before, but you never know how they're going to react under pressure or whom they're going to tell.

We were heading away to South Africa with the Crusaders one year. Daryl Gibson bought a brand new pair of jandals for the trip, to wear over there. They were like a $15 pair, knowing him, because he's such a miser. He was always looking for the best buy of the tour whenever we were away anywhere. Now, he's a really good mate of mine, Gibbo, and we're actually related too. But I have to say that he is one of the laziest walkers of all time.

He's got big pumpers — big legs — and he drags his feet around. He scuffs them so you can hear him coming down the corridor. If you're sleeping, he's like an alarm clock. And when he had on these jandals, they made double the click sound when he was walking. Because he's so slow and laboured, they simply pounded between the floor and his flat Maori feet.

Gibbo was as proud as punch of these jandals and everywhere you went he would be wearing them — to training, down by the pool. Slap, scuff, slap, scuff. Until I'd just had a gutsful of it.

So I sneak into his room with a scalpel. I cut into his jandals so that they're all just about cut right through.

I scalpel through the bit that goes between your toes, a real thin line you can hardly see. Then it's just a matter of waiting. Sure enough, he comes in and the first thing he does is put on his jandals to wear them wherever he's going. And, click, away they go. They break on him. He goes to take a stride and snap. And he is furious about it. He's not happy. He knows that he's been sabotaged and he goes about trying to find out who it is.

Obviously, I'm one of the main suspects because I was the one who kept going on, 'Oh, are you wearing those things again?'

Now I'm going, 'Where are your jandals, mate?'

He gives me the old smile, not saying anything, just shaking his head.

But the boys cottoned on to the whole thing and started treating the jandals like some kind of mascot for the trip. The next minute, we'd be down in the team room about to watch a bit of footage and one of the jandals would be tied to the light.

Everybody's sitting there looking at Gibbo's jandal and wondering who put that there, when we were supposed to be looking at the game footage.

Gibbo's jandals started popping up everywhere. So it became an ongoing prank for that trip.

But the Crusaders were pretty good like that. We were always pulling pranks on each other.

I've quite often cut the toes out of people's dress socks after games so they can't put on their number one's because there are no toes in their dress socks.

I'm always on the alert for the right moment. With rugby teams there are always scissors sitting around for people to cut tape with. Usually I try to get them at the hotel before they head down to the stadium because they don't wear the socks until after the game.

Because of my self-imposed code of silence, I occasionally get accused of things

I didn't do. The boys think that I was involved in a shirt-painting exercise, but it wasn't me actually.

I'd been playing some pranks that had set off a little chain of them in the Crusaders team. And during that process, a new prankster emerged, not someone who was working with me, someone working alone.

Anyway, we played the game and afterwards a couple of the boys went to put their shirts on. They discovered the shirts had been dyed fluorescent yellow, red and all different colours. These are their dress shirts, which are plain white.

They put the shirts on and people are just absolutely cracking up. Everyone's saying, 'Ah, the Prankster strikes.' That prankster actually did a bit of that and a couple of other things too. And I'm still not too sure who that was. So that sort of thing was pretty rife in the Crusaders team.

Robbie Deans didn't mind too much. Our routines carried on as normal, no matter what the prank. Those guys just had to wear their fluorescent dyed shirts to the after-match function. The guys had nothing else to wear.

Robbie Deans enjoys a good prank.

A game called Killer

Have you ever heard of the game Killer?

Okay, say there are 30 people. You put 30 pieces of paper into a hat. One of the pieces of paper has got an X on it. Then everybody dips in. If you get a blank piece of paper you're fine. If the piece of paper has an X on it, you're the killer.

What the killer has to do is kill everyone else without getting caught. No one knows you have the X because everyone just screws up his paper and throws it away.

So how do you kill people? What happens is the killer will walk along and if he winks at you, you've been killed. As a victim you must then pretend to die on the spot. You have to be killed properly, in other words, go ahhhhh, and fall over.

Some people go over the top and do it like in the movies. They'll yell out and stumble then fall against something and they'll stagger and then they'll just lie on the floor. And it could happen in a public place, anywhere.

People go, 'What's going on?' People panic. Members of the public go, 'What's happening to this guy?'

What the killer has to do is make sure that he doesn't let anybody see him winking because if they catch the killer out then the game's finished.

There's a time limit too. You usually give the killer a full day or a couple of days to try to kill as many members of the team as he can. And that's really amusing, particularly as you get down to the last few people.

Now I could be passing you in the corridor and you give me the old wink. I've got to die in the corridor. But, because you're the killer, you'll keep going because you don't want anyone to come out of his room and spot you. As for me, I've got to roll around the floor and be killed. And obviously I'm not allowed to tell anybody who killed me. If you did tell other people or you pretended to be the killer when you weren't, you'd get hammered in the court session.

Another thing we do at the Crusaders is nominate a prankster. We have all the names in the hat and a piece of paper comes out with a P, so he's the prankster.

The game works differently to Killer. The prankster can make people do things that he wants them to do. So if he manages to catch you, then he can get you to do something. But he's got to get his victims individually otherwise somebody else will know he's the prankster.

Say you and I are in one of the bedrooms just hanging out. If I'm the prankster, I could say to you, out of the blue, 'I want you to take off your jeans. Go, run out there, grab me a cup of coffee, come back and then put your jeans on, take your shirt off and get me a couple of sugars.'

You're going to say, 'Oh no, you're the prankster, aren't you?'

So you have to do what I tell you. After that you're out of the game.

So instead of killing people, the prankster makes them do things. And if he catches you one on one, you're stuffed.

Reuben Thorne was the best prankster we ever had. He did it in about 2002. He made Scott Robertson wear his Speedos on the outside of his pants for a whole morning . . . and to lunch. So everybody was down having lunch and here's this guy walking around with his Speedos on the outside of his shorts pulled right up.

Reuben got me too. I had to wear all my clothes backwards for a day. And that was the worst day, our day off. I had to go play golf. And it was one of those exclusive country clubs. You can imagine trying to wear stuff backwards out there.

Reuben got people for all sorts of things and he kept going for about three days.

At the end of each day three or four people were allowed to guess who the prankster was. But if you were wrong, you had to pay $100. So, if you were guessing, you had to be sure of who you thought the prankster was. The people that guessed wrong were automatically out of the game, so he's already basically got them pranked.

But what Reuben was doing, and the reason he got me, which was really annoying, was he got innovative.

I was sitting in my room watching TV and the next minute my phone rings. I go, 'Hello?'

'Yeah, Marshy, I would like to see you wearing all your gear backwards for the rest of the day.' And that was that.

A lot of the boys were locking their rooms so that he wouldn't come in, so he started phoning them one by one.

In the end it got down to where he was chasing three guys to prank. And the competition got ridiculous. We were staying at a hotel, the Beverley Hills, in Durban, South Africa. We're up on about the eighth floor.

Everyone's going, 'Is he going to get them?'

And these guys weren't answering their phones. If anyone knocked on their door, they weren't in. They were going to training. But they were living this really bizarre life because they didn't want to get pranked.

Someone would knock on the door. And a couple of the guys actually went out on to their balcony, because the balconies were linked, and climbed over the balcony into somebody else's room. And they went through the other person's room to get down to training, because they were afraid the prankster was waiting at the door.

Now this is high-risk stuff. I am talking about eight storeys up.

So this is pretty desperate. We all knew who the prankster was by this stage. So it was interesting to watch him in action and at the same time watch these players try to avoid an unknown danger. They were running everywhere, so they couldn't be caught. And they were avoiding everybody in the team like a rash.

In the end I think Reuben got everyone except one guy, which is quite amazing. I can't remember who that last guy was now. But he was lucky because Reuben had made the rest of us do the most funny, weird, unusual things.

The funniest was probably what he did to Sam Broomhall. He said to Sam, 'I want you to have a fake heart attack at training.'

Now obviously no one knows what's going on and anyway we're in the middle of stretches so everybody is in a circle and the management are standing around like the doctor and the physio and that sort of carry-on. Robbie's saying something and the boys are stretching before training starts, doing a few back stretches and that sort of thing. The next minute Sam Broomhall starts having this fit, this heart attack fit and going 'agh agh agh' and then rolling around on the ground and then convulsing on the ground.

Half the boys start laughing and the other half are like, 'Oh, what's going on here!' A few of the guys are crowding around, pointing. The team doctor, Deb Robinson, doesn't know what's going on.

Deb comes rushing over and says, 'Get out of the way, get out of the way.' She pushes the boys aside and she's going, 'What's wrong? What's wrong? What's going on?' She's getting really serious.

Everybody's going, 'Oh shit, what's going on here?'

Deb's real panicky and you can tell she actually thinks something really serious is happening, because she doesn't know about the prankster.

People are sniggering, and she's saying, 'Don't be so bloody stupid!'

Then it ended up with Sam saying, 'No, it's all right. I'm just pranking.'

It was absolutely brilliant. Perfect timing too, because you don't really see the prankster do it at training too much.

Spitting the dummy

The John Hart era was at its peak in 1996 and '97. The All Blacks lost only one game in those two years, 32–22 away to South Africa in August 1996.

But it wasn't all fun and games. Even when they were nigh unbeatable, Marshall still found ways to get himself in trouble. The worst incident was during New Zealand's 36–24 win over Australia at Carisbrook in 1997.

The Wallabies were going through a transitional phase. They'd lost a few big-name players and they had others who were new to the international scene. The All Blacks had won every game that year. So they were expected to give the Aussies a good working over.

We started that game absolutely on fire and we scored some brilliant tries. I even scored one myself. By halftime we had the game pretty much in the bag. We'd put them in a situation where they were going to have to do something extraordinary to win the game.

At halftime Harty's speech was all about making sure we continued keeping the pressure on and doing the little things well: the normal things that are said when you're winning a game quite comfortably.

But in the second half the Wallabies started to come back at us. I'm not sure whether it was because of their good work or because we'd come out slightly more relaxed. But as much as we tried, we couldn't pull away from them and they kept dragging themselves back into the game.

It got to a point where there were about 20-odd minutes to go and Australia were suddenly in with a chance. Despite the team hiccup at the start of the second half, I was actually having a pretty good game that day. And I was pretty happy with the way things were going. But I'd taken a knock and that had shaken me for a wee while and even though I'd recovered, John Hart decided, with us under pressure all of a sudden, that he needed to make changes.

The message came out to me that I was going to be subbed. I was pretty angry about that because the test had turned into a real dog fight and I wanted to be part of it. Sure enough, at the next stoppage in play my number was held up and I had to leave the field.

I was right into the game at that point. I felt I was still contributing. And I just wanted to be out there and be involved in the game. There was probably a bit of selfishness on my part and also that competitiveness that has been both my saving grace and my undoing in different circumstances.

I threw a real wobbly. I wasn't happy and I let the physios and the medical staff know all about it.

Unfortunately, as I was coming off, I wasn't thinking about the rest of the sideline. Even more unfortunately, there was a camera focused right on me. But I didn't notice it. And to be honest, if I had noticed it I probably wouldn't have cared. I was busy looking up into the stand, looking at the coaching staff because I was so angry that they'd pulled me off. It felt as though they were blaming me for the Wallabies fighting their way back into the game. And I didn't think I was the reason that had happened. So I'm walking past this camera, looking up at the stands, shaking my fist and cursing, as clear as day, 'This is fuckin' bullshit!'

Of course, it looked terrible. But in the heat of a test match the last thing you're thinking about is where the cameras are and who's on the sideline and how the people sitting on the couch at home will feel about the way you express yourself.

So anyway, I'm swearing and muttering away to myself. I kick a couple of things on the sideline then wander into the toilet and the shower-room and punch the door. I pretty much break my hand but, small consolation, still manage to put a dint in the door. I'm in a really bad, angry mood and it takes me a long time to cool down.

Then the team comes in at the end of the game. They've held on to win. But no one's that happy about how we let the Aussies back into the game, and John Hart isn't either. And I'm sure he must be fuming about the way I acted.

He's across the other side of the changing room. I'm still disappointed with the decision to bring me off so my body language and mood are quite hostile.

After he's been around a few of the guys he eventually turns his attention to me. He catches my eye and I must have had a real grumpy look on my face. So he lets me have it in front of everybody, both barrels.

'And you, Marshall,' he says, 'who do you think you are? The way that you behaved is inappropriate for any All Black. And that reaction to being substituted won't be tolerated in any team I coach.'

I just sat there and shook my head, muttering, 'For fuck's sake . . . ' I guess I was being stubborn and pig-headed about it really.

Deep down I knew I was in the wrong. I knew my reaction undermined his authority to make and enforce decisions he believed would help us win the game. I knew the last thing he needed was players throwing wobblies every time he made a decision. And I knew that in front of the whole world was an inappropriate place to have a tantrum aimed at the coach.

But I also believe it was inappropriate for him to bawl me out in the dressing room in front of the whole team. We both had opinions about what had happened. He obviously felt he needed to replace me. And I was annoyed because I felt I had a lot left to offer. I'd informed the medical staff I was okay. So it was obviously a tactical rather than an injury-motivated substitution. We should have sorted it out between ourselves away from the other players.

Obviously, everyone in the dressing room's heads went down after that and it was really uncomfortable for a few minutes.

I made an effort to have a proper talk to Harty about it later, underneath Carisbrook on the way to the after-match function. I tried to explain how I'd been feeling at that point in the game and why I'd reacted the way I had. And I apologised and he accepted my apology, which was good because I was in the wrong.

And that was the end of that. Yeah, right.

John Hart: I rest my case. He was injured. He slowed up. The medical view was he was struggling. So we took him off.

There's no doubt I probably said something to him in front of the team because he had done what he did in front of the team and it was a team issue. If you let it go and say to a guy like Justin Marshall that it's okay to do that, where does that put the team? Team discipline comes first. And I thought he'd let the team down as much as anyone else because substitutions by then were part of the game and we had to get used to that. So I was surprised at his reaction. I was disappointed. But I also accepted his apology and moved on.

Justin: The next day the newspapers were full of it. And it looked even worse on the TV news. You didn't have to be an expert lip-reader to figure out what I'd said on the sideline.

And the media wasn't just reporting that it had happened. Some people expressed outrage and others questioned whether I was a good role model for kids.

In the end, the New Zealand Rugby Union decided I had to go on the *Holmes* TV show, which most people seemed to watch in those days, and make an apology to the country.

So I went on *Holmes*.

Canterbury had a midweek match so TVNZ sent a camera along. I wasn't playing so the plan was that during the halftime break I'd go down to the sideline and talk to Paul Holmes and try to get an apology across and do the PR thing.

But it was a disaster. The worst thing was I went down there and put in the earpiece and I could hardly hear a thing. The noise at the stadium was so loud that I couldn't hear what they were saying. I said as much but they assured me, 'Oh, it'll be all right when you go live.'

So Paul Holmes came on and I was asked all these questions. But I couldn't hear what he was saying. I was only picking up little bits here and there. But this was live TV so I had to guess what he was saying from these little snippets and then respond the best I could. And you know what he's like; every time I tried to answer a question he cut me off anyway. I knew the Rugby Union wanted me to make an apology. So I just tried to wind that into what I was saying. 'I would just like to apologise to all the young kids out there. It's not the way a role model should act.' Or something like that.

Eventually, I got the apology across but with me unable to hear any of the questions, and Holmes cutting me off all through the interview anyway, the whole thing was an absolute mess.

Wayne's world

Wayne Smith and Justin Marshall first worked together in 1997 when Smith was appointed Crusaders coach. Under his guidance, the Crusaders won the Super 12 in 1998 and '99. In those two years, Smith was also an assistant coach to John Hart with the All Blacks. He took over as chief coach in 2000. But late in the 2001 season, after a narrow Bledisloe Cup loss to the Wallabies, Smith publicly questioned whether he was the right man for the job. His brutally honest reaction to a moment of self-doubt ultimately cost him that job. And he was replaced by John Mitchell.

But Smith and Marshall's paths crossed again when Graham Henry took over the All Blacks in 2004 and named Smith and Steve Hansen his assistant coaches.

Originally from Putaruru in the Waikato, Smith, like Marshall, had to move to Canterbury to kick-start his career and his name is now synonymous with his adopted province.

He was a star of the great Canterbury Ranfurly Shield era from 1982 to '85 and played 17 tests for the All Blacks. But even in those days of lightweight backs, the first five was something of a fragile genius and was prone to injury.

His tactical vision and genius have been the hallmarks of his coaching, though it's fair to say there have been times when his players, including Justin Marshall, have been left wondering what the hell he's talking about.

When Wayne Smith arrived at the Crusaders I hadn't been in Christchurch long enough to know a lot about him. And when he'd played for Canterbury I'd never really watched him that much. So when I heard he was in contention for the Crusaders job I had no preconceived ideas, although I wondered what he'd think of the way I play, as you do.

The thing that struck me straight away about Smithy was just how passionate he was, particularly when it came to his two favourite teams, Canterbury and the All

Blacks. He wears his heart on his sleeve when it comes to them.

He would easily be the most technical coach that I've had in the time that I've been involved in rugby. He's very analytical, very much into statistics and video analysis.

He's the master at spotting tiny details in an individual's play that can be either improved (if it's one of us) or exploited (if it's one of the opposition).

A few of us call him Techno and in 2004 he introduced the All Blacks to a state of the art coaching tool called the Smart Board.

It's something they use in England that he picked up on while he was coaching Northampton. The Smart Board takes video and television imagery to a new level. It monitors and tracks individual players throughout the whole course of a game.

It can tell the coach how many kilometres that Justin Marshall has run in a game. It can follow players and tell you everything that they've done on the field. All you have to do is punch in their code and their name on the board.

You can use it to replicate moves using video footage. Little dots with numbers inside them run around all over the board, doing stuff. They can actually program in a whole game. I've watched a whole game on the Smart Board with the players replaced by little numbered dots. And you can actually write on the screen. So the coach can pause the game or a particular move at any time and draw an arrow or a circle or whatever he needs to make his point.

The nearest thing I've seen to the Smart Board is that screen Tom Cruise uses in the futuristic sci-fi movie *Minority Report*. And I wouldn't be surprised if Wayne Smith's looking into getting the All Blacks one just the same.

But the Smart Board's only one aspect of the technical side of Smithy. He's also into computer analysis of players and teams and into cutting video clips to pinpoint deficiencies and weaknesses in the opposition.

And he's a very well-read person. He's right into books about coaching. He'll read about gridiron coaches, NBA basketball coaches, any coaches who can offer new insights into building a successful team. So he's full of famous quotes too, like 'The only time reward comes before work is in the dictionary'.

Then he takes that all out on to the field and says, 'Okay, if their winger's standing here, and we've got the ball over here, which move should we call? Remember, I showed it to you on the Smart Board last night.' And that's how he does it.

But Wayne Smith and Justin Marshall have very different approaches to the game. Wayne Smith is the rugby version of a computer geek. Heaven for him is being locked up with a video of a match and being left in peace to analyse it. In contrast, Justin Marshall often refuses to watch game videos, unless of course he wants to for nostalgic reasons. And

this can get him offside with coaches, who see his stance as irksome, confrontational, contrary and a bad example. But Marshall makes a strong case for resisting the onslaught of digital rugby.

I just feel that Wayne Smith took the Techno thing to the extreme. He took it to a level that was acceptable. And then he took it too far.

For some players it's fine because they're right into that. But other players start to switch off. Well you can't afford to have half the team switching off.

And I know that at the Crusaders in particular, as time went on, a few of the senior players had to get together and say, 'Hold on, Smithy. We just need to peg back a little bit on some of the video analysis and some of the briefs and debriefs that we're having.'

Smithy trained as a teacher and I guess he liked to impart his knowledge to the class. He's an obsessive genius when it comes to rugby. And when visionaries come along it's only natural they'll leave the rest of us mere mortals scratching our heads occasionally.

And Smithy's excellent with feedback. He accepts it and he's very much a listener because in the final analysis he only wants what's best for his players.

For us at the Crusaders in 1997, he was the man who really turned the game professional for us. He pretty much turned us amateurs into professionals by taking the game up to that level. He made the players realise that this was actually more than just a game now.

All Black captain

John Hart showed incredible faith in Justin Marshall during the Northern Hemisphere tour in 1997 when he named him All Black captain for the game against Llanelli on 8 November. Picking someone to replace the great Sean Fitzpatrick was one of the biggest decisions Hart would make during his four years in charge. And picking a player so young — he had just turned 24 — was a brave call.

Fitzpatrick had led his country like a colossus since the beginning of 1992. For the next five years the captaincy had never been an issue. And there was even talk he might go through to the next World Cup in 1999. But his knee packed it in towards the end of the Tri-series. And although surgery enabled him to return to action in October, it had swelled up again in the UK and it quickly became clear that Fitzy's brilliant international career could be at an end.

At the time, Hart said the decision to make Marshall captain after 19 tests was easy. 'Justin is one of the form players,' he said. 'As halfback he has a prominent decision-making role. And he was one of the few players we brought into the set-up when we were going through the planning process of this tour.'

For many, Marshall seemed a surprise choice; but not to veteran rugby writer Bob Howitt. This was his take on the reasoning behind Marshall's appointment.

Bob Howitt: The natural successor should have been Zinzan Brooke, but his illustrious All Black career had only a few weeks to run.

Taine Randell, long spoken of as an All Black captain, had just turned 23 and only this year secured a regular place in the test line-up.

Ian Jones hadn't enjoyed success as a leader with North Harbour while Craig Dowd was lacking in captaincy experience. Others like Todd Blackadder and Bull Allen weren't in the test 15.

So the All Black selectors settled on Justin Marshall. He was light on leadership experience, but had impressively dealt with every assignment thus far handed to him. And he had Zinzan Brooke to help him through his challenging early All Black assignments.

Marshall's greatest quality, besides his outstanding skill as a halfback, is his ability to take everything in his stride. Shouldering the captaincy didn't faze him, as it might have several others.

Justin: My selection as captain was a real bolt from the blue. I was summoned to a meeting in the team room with John Hart.

To be honest I thought I was in trouble. I'd been out the night before with a couple of the other guys and we'd had a few midweek beers and some pizza. It was nothing too serious. We were back by midnight. But when we came back into the hotel Gordon Hunter saw me. So next morning when they asked to see me, I thought I was going to get told off.

I was sweating and racking my brains as I took the lift down to the ground floor of the Marriott Hotel in Swansea. 'What the hell is it?' I wondered.

As I walked into the room I was pretty nervous about what sort of information Harty had on me. I looked up and realised there was a bit of a delegation. The other two All Black selectors, Ross Cooper and the late Gordon Hunter were there, and so was Fitzy. I was thinking, 'There's something really dodgy going on here. And whatever it is, it must be serious.'

'Hi, Justin,' said Harty, 'you must be wondering why we asked you to come down here.'

'Yes I am, actually. What's up?'

He told me that Fitzy was injured. He said I'd been playing really well and that they wanted me to be captain. I was caught completely off guard. I think I probably just looked at them in shock with my mouth wide open for a couple of seconds.

If playing test rugby for the All Blacks was my life's dream, being captain was something I'd never even dared to dream.

Marshall had come a long way from playing junior rugby at Tulloch Park in Mataura. Apart from two games for the Crusaders at the start of the 1996 Super 12, when Richard Loe was out injured, his previous captaincy experience was in the standard one and two teams at primary school. And those stints hadn't quite prepared him for John Hart's announcement. He was in shock.

Typically, the first question Marshall asked was how the senior players like Zinzan Brooke, Frank Bunce and Ian Jones would react. Hart said the decision had been run past them and that they were happy with his appointment.

Once the selectors told me that, I was fine. I believed I was in a good position at halfback to lead the side tactically and thought that, with the right support, I could do the job.

The tour opener against Llanelli was hardly a test of Marshall's leadership skills, though. The All Blacks hammered them 81–3.

Despite the score, it was a big thrill. To run out there and lead my country and have all those experienced players behind me, helping me out, was just a great feeling.

To be given the captaincy was a real honour and something I'll always cherish. I was a little more nervous than I usually am before a match. But I got some good advice about going out and playing my own game and the team would look after itself.

I just had to go out and toss the coin. I didn't even have to choose what direction we played because I lost the toss.

The only other thing I had to worry about was whether we took a lineout or a kick at goal.

Test captain

Hart and the selectors stuck with Marshall as captain for the test against Ireland in Dublin on 15 November. He became Canterbury's ninth test captain and the first since flanker Jock Hobbs 11 years before.

As always, Marshall was unfazed. 'I hadn't even thought about the test captaincy,' he told reporters. 'I honestly didn't even think I was in the frame. It has all taken me a bit by surprise. But, yes, if the opportunity comes up for me to lead the side again, I'll take it and at the end of the tour re-evaluate things. It's something that's not too daunting for me.'

John Hart was very strong on the philosophy of shared responsibility and that included having leadership all over the park, because the captain can't look after everybody all the time.

So before test matches and tours he'd call 'tactical meetings' in Auckland and all the senior players would be invited to attend. I'd been included in these virtual All Black cabinet meetings along with the likes of Fitzy, Zinzan, Ian Jones, Buncey, Taine, Jeff Wilson and Mehrts.

Harty brought along all the guys he saw as leaders on the field because he wanted to make sure the responsibility wasn't left to one player, Sean Fitzpatrick. I suppose Harty must have seen some leadership qualities in me. The captaincy still took me by surprise, though.

The test against Ireland would have been Fitzpatrick's fifty-first as captain. It was the first he'd missed through injury in 11 years. But he was still a huge influence on the team and particularly on Marshall. The pair roomed together leading up to the test.

'We've just talked generally about what he's doing,' Fitzpatrick explained at the time, 'how things might change a little bit from what they've been. And I've told him to just relax and enjoy it. The last thing the team wants is for him to get uptight and not play his natural game.'

I hung on every word Fitzy uttered in the lead-up to that match. He calmed me down and advised me to let the captaincy take care of itself. The boys really appreciated that Fitzy had done the best thing for the team by pulling out. So we were keen to put in a big performance for him.

I didn't have the perfect start to my test captaincy. I remember getting really confused as to who was the Irish captain, the prop Nick Popplewell or the hooker Keith Wood. I wasn't that confident who was who at that stage. I didn't really know either of them that well. I know now that Wood was the captain. But I shook hands with him before the match and said, 'Good luck, Nick.'

That mightn't have been a wise move. Twice in the first half the shaven-headed Wood, nicknamed 'the mad potato', scored to give the Irish the lead.

But injury forced him off at halftime and a Kiwi, former Auckland player Ross Nesdale, replaced him.

The All Blacks ran away with the match in the second half to win 63–15. Andrew Mehrtens racked up 33 points and Marshall also scored a try.

My first after-match speech as test captain was a bit hairy. Even though Wood had lifted the rafters at the old Lansdowne Road Stadium with his two tries, I still mixed up my Nicks and my Keiths again. But I didn't stay up there too long. When you have a win like that the host team doesn't want to watch a visiting captain rubbing it in. So you just keep it short, thank a few people and get off.

Former All Black first five Grant Fox was one commentator who was impressed with what he saw and said so in his newspaper column:

Marshall is young, his form over the past two seasons has been outstanding, and the halfback position appears to be his as long as he wants it and remains injury free.

You could argue that there are others experienced as provincial captains, but someone of Marshall's youth and ability would offer a chance to appoint a leader to take the team to the World Cup, to 2000 and beyond.

King hit by Martin Johnson

Marshall's next two tests as captain were a 42–7 win over Wales at Wembley, in which he scored a try, and a 25–8 win over England at Old Trafford. England made their intentions clear early on. First of all they encroached rudely on the All Blacks' haka, forcing John Hart to insist on a set protocol for the second test, and then, six minutes into the game, English lock Martin Johnson punched Justin Marshall.

I'd just cleared the ball from a ruck and was ready to follow the pass and he just king hit me. I was in a bit of trouble there for a while it would be fair to say. He's a big guy and he's got a powerful punch, especially when you don't see it coming. I had a bloody sore head actually and a bit of blurred vision. I remember saying to the medical staff when they came on that I couldn't see that well. And my hearing was impaired, so I wasn't able to communicate properly, particularly in the first half.

But I gutsed it out until halftime and then managed to make it through the match. It certainly wasn't one of my better performances. My passing was off and I was indecisive. I was in la-la land most of the time. But we won. And that's the main thing.

Kiwi rugby writer Peter Lampp's follow-up story backs up Marshall's claim that Johnson's punch was a cheap shot:

England lock Martin Johnson got off lightly after punching All Black captain Justin Marshall from behind during Sunday's rugby test at Manchester.

The All Blacks threatened to cite Johnson but eventually were happy for England management to enact what was essentially an out-of-court settlement.

However, it is understood England's citing commissioner was ready to throw the book at Johnson. The usual penalty in Britain for punching is a 30-day suspension

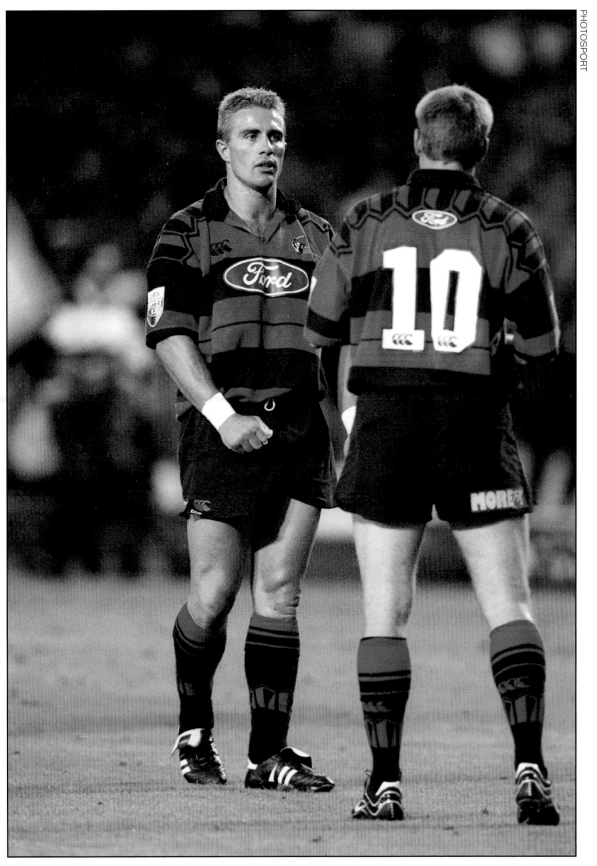

Me listening, Mehrts talking . . . both of us with vintage 1999 haircuts.

Uh-oh! Reaching out for a try in the 1999 Super 12 final against the Highlanders. I ended up short of the line. But we still won 24–19 at the House of Pain.

That winning feeling. Todd Blackadder and I enjoy the spoils of victory after the 1999 Super 12 final.

'Told you that move would work, Razor.' Paddy O'Brien signals my match-winning try against Auckland at Eden Park in 2000. Scott Robertson is on hand to help celebrate.

Come all ye faithful! The fans turn out at Christchurch Airport for the Crusaders' arrival home from Canberra with their third straight Super 12 title in the bag. The final was a 20–19 heart-stopper against our arch rivals, the Brumbies.

I remember saying to one reporter, 'The only reason I grew my hair long was so that people would stop talking about my pass.' This shot was taken during our 34–27 win over the Chiefs in Hamilton in 2002.

Drunk and reasonably orderly. We were having a pre-season game in Greymouth so, after a big night out, I lined up for the start of the Coast to Coast race. Legendary organiser Robin Judkins is on the left. And, no, I didn't try to take part.

My other childhood passion . . . playing cricket with the Crusaders at Hagley Oval in Christchurch in 2003.

Kicking the Crusaders out of trouble during the 37–21 win over the Hurricanes in February 2003.

Who's going to let go of the ball first? Tackled by the Stormers' Cobus Visagie during our 51–13 win in Cape Town in 2003.

Defeat always tastes a little more sour when it's at the hands of Auckland. Daniel Carter and Caleb Ralph know what I'm talking about. The Blues have just beaten us 21–17 in the 2003 Super 12 final at Eden Park.

Rivalry alive and well. Here I get a pass away ahead of Byron Kelleher in the Crusaders' 36–15 Super 12 win over the Chiefs in Hamilton in 2004.

Checks and balances. If the ball was round, this shot could pass as a photograph of a soccer striker about to volley at goal. Instead, I'm looking for touch against the Chiefs.

Reuben Thorne knows it. I know it. And once I put this ball down and start skipping about behind the try-line, the crowd is going to know that we've beaten the Stormers and are into the final of the 2004 Super 12.

and that would have ruled Johnson out of the second test against the All Blacks at Twickenham.

Hart spotted the incident from his low vantage point at Old Trafford, had it confirmed by video after the test and called it 'an act of thuggery'.

England coach Clive Woodward and manager Roger Uttley agreed the allegations were founded and they suspended Johnson for one game, the next weekend's test against South Africa.

Woodward said he had spoken to Johnson about the incident: 'He has accepted responsibility for the incident and he will be making a full apology to Justin Marshall.'

Justin: Because of what he did that day and me being a grudge-holder, I'm not a big fan of the guy. So when people start going on about Martin Johnson being one of the greatest players of all time, I'm like, 'Whatever.'

I've played against him a few times but I've never really respected him, mainly because I believe it was a cheap shot. I'd rather he said something to me or we pushed and shoved each other face to face and then we just had a scrap. Now I'm probably not going to come out on top. But at least I'm able to stand up for myself.

In my opinion, his hit was just filth and a real coward's cheap shot . . . similar to the one I gave Ginge Henderson that time probably.

Remember? That upper cut in the Metropolitan versus Eastern trial match back in Southland. Yeah, that wasn't much different when I come to think about it. But at least Ginge was running towards me and he could see what I was up to.

Marched 20 metres

As captain, I was never too concerned about being the person who had to do the after-match interviews. I've never been too fazed by the media. Even since I was young, I've always taken the approach that you should be honest and straight up and not stick to any criteria or any set lines that people try to give you.

I was more concerned about talking at the after-match functions to be honest. I had a bit of a public-speaking phobia.

And that was the one side of the captaincy that I didn't enjoy very much. I wasn't a big fan of all the stuff you have to do off the field. The public thinks that your job is just leading the team on the field. But that's only part of it. When you're All Black captain everyone wants a piece of you.

In the build-up to a test match you're required to go to all sorts of press conferences and dinners and functions. But when you're a player you just have to train. You might have to do a bit of media after training, but that's it.

I didn't really like being over-exposed and having to front all the time. I don't mind fronting. But when you're captain, you have to front so often you run out of things to say.

The hardest after-match speech I ever made for the All Blacks was the last one I ever made as captain, which was after the 26–all draw with England at Twickenham. It's well known I had issues with referee Jim Fleming that day. So you can imagine how I was feeling after the match.

The All Blacks of that era were widely regarded as one of the greatest teams of all time. The second test against England was their last of the year, and they'd won the other 11. Most experts believed the All Blacks would want to atone for their 'poor display' in the 25–8 win over England in the first test.

On the other hand, England had followed up their loss to the All Blacks with a 29–11 loss to the Springboks.

So what happened in the second test?

England defied all expectations to score three tries in the first 18 minutes, of course. That's how it works in sport. That's why we keep watching.

The All Blacks fought back but, by Marshall's own admission, were lucky to escape defeat.

His after-match quotes, as always, were refreshingly honest and candid.

'We were very lucky to manage a draw,' he said. 'You can't give international teams like England a 23-point start. Our ball retention was shocking for an All Black side.'

But Marshall also believes the All Blacks didn't get a fair go from the Scottish referee.

Jim Fleming let England get away with murder at the breakdown and they slowed our ball down all day. We were playing an expansive game at that stage. But they contained us really well because they were allowed to be so negative at the breakdown.

I went up to Jim as a captain during the first half, while we were really under the gun, and said, 'Look, my players are getting really frustrated. If you're not going to stop their players from lying all over the ball, we'll do it ourselves.'

He said, 'Oh, you can't speak to me like that.'

I said, 'I'm the captain.'

And that's when he walked me back 10 metres.

I went back to him and said, 'Look, I'm the captain. They're being negative. It's affecting the way we play.'

And he marched me another 10 metres.

Now that incident has become part of All Black folklore and people cite it as an example of how I lost my cool and why I didn't have the right temperament to captain the All Blacks.

And to a certain extent, I concede it might have been more diplomatic to give up. But I wanted to get my point across to him and I wasn't doing it in an aggressive way. And I actually was wanting to point something out that was causing us concern.

But Fleming was in that referee's mood that sometimes you see with the likes of André Watson or Steve Walsh when George Gregan's talking to them and they just brush him away. As a captain, that's a little frustrating. And in the case of England, what they were doing was well and truly illegal and affecting the game and how we wanted to play it.

I was bitterly disappointed with the way Fleming reffed that day and particularly the way that he wouldn't listen to any genuine feedback that we wanted to give him. The refs have to control the game but at the same time they've got to be open to a little bit of feedback from the players via the two captains. My forwards were saying to me, 'They're lying all over the place. Get him to sort it out or we will.' But I couldn't communicate with him all day.

So when it came to the after-match speech I couldn't help myself. It all just came out. 'Look,' I said, 'I'd just like to thank England for the game. It was probably a fair result. A draw is sometimes frustrating but there's no loser today. So thanks very much, England. It's been a great series. To our guys, it's been a fantastic tour. Congratulations, Zinny, on your fiftieth test. It was a bit frustrating out there for us today. I don't think the referee helped us very much. He didn't let us play the game we wanted to. There were a lot of penalties. And I actually think he spoiled what could have been a pretty free-flowing test.'

A few of the old-school English rugby types were squirming in their seats and clearing their throats nervously as I made my speech. I guess it's an unwritten rule of rugby that the captain doesn't bag the referee in his speech at the after-match function, especially if it's after a test match. Even if a referee totally ruins a game and single-handedly decides the result, you never see too many captains get up and bag him for it.

It's an etiquette thing, really. It's like in golf; you don't stand in another golfer's line while he's putting for the hole. Or in surfing, you don't drop in on someone else's wave. It's not written down anywhere, but everyone knows you don't do it.

But I did. And it was pretty much the last thing I did as All Black captain.

Undefeated

Back in New Zealand, the attitude after that second test in England was that I didn't have the temperament to be an All Black captain because I got marched 20 metres in one hit.

I was really disappointed with that attitude from people and with John Hart's lack of support for me. He didn't really back me up. He just said, 'Yes, Justin's got to watch his temper sometimes.'

People really climbed into me over that one incident and I'm not the only captain to question the referee and be marched 10 metres. It does happen. Okay, I did it twice in quick succession. But nobody ever asked me about it. They just assumed that I was back-chatting. But I wasn't.

John Hart: I don't think anyone would have been worried about him being marched for talking to the referee. If that was the case, Sean Fitzpatrick would have never captained the All Blacks because he used to get marched early on in his captaincy. I think it was the *way* he spoke to Fleming that concerned people not the fact that he *spoke* to Fleming.
Do you remember if you came out and said he was a bad captain?
No, I certainly do not.

Justin: I'd been talked about as a possible captain for 1998. I'd captained the side pretty well in the previous three tests. Then suddenly, in one two-minute spell with a whistle-happy referee, I'd become a bad captain. It really knocked me around. And I remember thinking, 'I can't be bothered putting up with this, if this is the way that people are going to react. And if this is the way a captain gets dragged through the mud after three wins and a draw against some pretty good sides in Europe, I'd hate to see what the future holds.'

When I look at the year we had in 1998, I was probably lucky I had the captaincy taken off me. They appointed Taine Randell instead. And Taine got absolutely caned. When you think about it Todd Blackadder and Reuben Thorne were hammered when they were All Black captains too. So maybe it's just the job.

John Hart: That's another point he should remember. It was me who gave him the opportunity to be captain in 1997. I had the option of Zinzan Brooke. But I knew Zinzan was retiring. So we decided, of the various people available, that we would give Justin the opportunity. In hindsight it was a mistake because he probably lacks the control and the composure to be captain. He likes to express himself, he gets very involved, he's a very physical player. I'm not criticising him. It's just a fact that maybe he wasn't suited to captaincy. But we gave him the opportunity and we don't regret that because we didn't have many options available to us. With his experience, we thought he might be someone who would lead us into the future. But that was something, if I look back, that was probably a mistake. And if he looks at his career, he'd probably say, well, maybe I wasn't cut out for captaincy because the captaincy also involved a lot of things off the field like media and things like that, which he didn't necessarily enjoy or handle. On-field he could handle some of the aspects but even then he could get a bit flustered, as he did in that last game against England.

Taine Randell: I think Justin got a pretty rough ride over the captaincy. People got stuck into him after the draw to England. But I think they were more upset at us not beating England than they were over Justin's captaincy. He was unlucky that the image of him getting marched 20 metres was quite memorable.

I took over as captain from Marshy, but I think he could easily have carried on or returned to the job at some stage. He commands the respect and he holds his position and everyone knows what a determined fighter and committed leader he is.

Andrew Mehrtens: His personality lends itself to being captain and his style of play does too. I've always thought he was a fantastic captain and particularly when he captained the All Blacks in 1997.

He did bloody well. He led the team. He led by example. Your captain's not necessarily your tactician, ever. Your captain's there to liaise between the decision-making and the grunt, but also obviously to inspire with what they do and what they say. And he's got that perfectly.

He spat the dummy once, when Martin Johnson hit him from behind. But the same things that made him angry about that and made him fire up then also make him into a great leader. He's competitive and he wouldn't ask guys to do what he wouldn't do. He'll get in and lead from the front.

I thought he was a wonderful captain. But he copped a fair bagging from the media, the public and from the coach after that tour. And to have not fired up in the media and fired shots back to defend himself, I thought, showed a lot of character. And I don't think he's spoken to anyone openly about how much that hurt him, being accused of being a poor captain.

In the absence of a giant of the game like Fitzy, Justin stepped into his shoes remarkably well. And he's never had the credit for it that he deserves.

Justin might have been a bit rough and ready from a PR perspective. But on the field, we couldn't fault him as a captain. I'll guarantee that.

John Hart: Justin injured his Achilles tendon early in 1998, so wasn't an option for the two early tests. By that stage the All Blacks were already moving ahead with Taine Randell after two big wins at home over England.

But we supported him as a player in terms of his recovery from his Achilles injury. We certainly went down to see him during his rehab and tried to get him back from his injury as quickly as we could.

I do not understand Andrew Mehrtens saying I bagged Justin as a captain. But regardless I don't think captaincy of the All Blacks was actually the right thing for Justin Marshall. Subsequent All Black coaches have clearly agreed.

But at no stage should anyone doubt his commitment and energy to contribute on the field as a player.

We decided he shouldn't carry on as captain during our review of the 1997 year. While he lost his cool on a couple of occasions, I don't think he really wanted the off-field responsibility. In hindsight we might have been better to go with Zinzan Brooke. But that wouldn't have taken us anywhere in the future.

Justin: In the end, I wasn't gutted that I lost the captaincy. But I was gutted about the way I lost it. I was disappointed and annoyed at the lack of support from within the 1997 All Black management and senior players. Nobody really came out and said, 'Justin did a great job and it's not his fault we drew that test match.' It didn't give me a lot of confidence that the captaincy was a really good thing to have, going into the better half of my career. I just don't think it was handled very well.

Nicolle

Aussie McLean: Nicolle's helped Justin make some huge shifts. She's a lovely lady and he's bloody lucky to have her.

Robbie Deans, Crusaders coach: Obviously, Nicolle's made a big difference. That's my observation anyway. He's become a very well-rounded person. And she's obviously been very influential in that. She's provided a bit of stability in his life.

Ask anyone who knows Justin Marshall, even remotely, what the hell happened to that guy, the answer is always, Nicolle. She didn't tame the wild man or extinguish the inferno. She loved them too much to do that. But she did help keep them both at a manageable level. The result is a more mature and mellow person . . . and a better rugby player.

Nicolle: Justin and I are two people from different backgrounds who have come together and our differences complement each other.

I tend to like to play life safe whereas Justin likes to play life on the edge a little. So I temper him in some ways whereas he forces me to take risks that I wouldn't normally take.

We are so different that at times it's incredible that we're together. Then in other ways we're so alike.

He is such a combustible personality, like an inflammable liquid. He's so passionate about life. And two things I admire about Justin are his integrity and his honesty.

With other people I might hedge around an issue. But with Justin I don't. I know he won't and I feel safe responding in kind. For that reason, our communication is awesome — we don't always agree but we always find common ground eventually.

As a person, he is in the belly, not in the back. He'll actually say to me, or his friends or his colleagues, I don't believe in this, you guys need to work on this, and this is an issue we need to address now.

And he's not a person who talks about people behind their back. I think that's a really rare human trait because it's so easy to sit at home and discuss stuff and then, when you see the person, not front up about it.

It's something I've really learned from him to try and be more like him in that way.

Justin: When I first moved to Christchurch, I was flatting with Canterbury player Simon Forrest and Tabai Matson's girlfriend Nadia, who later became his wife.

Nicolle Burgess was a friend of Nadia's and she would sometimes come round to see her.

I'd say, 'Gidday, how're you going?' and it was just a friendship. We'd also bump into each other in town quite a bit.

Nicolle: Nadia told me the rugby union had set them up with a new flatmate, this guy who'd come up from Southland.

Funnily enough, I was single at the time. I didn't give it too many second thoughts, but my ears did prick up. 'Getting a new male flatmate, that'll be interesting.'

And I went round to the flat and I met him. He was lying on the couch watching *Oprah*. He had a blond mullet and I didn't think much of him to be honest.

I met him a few times after that and he was always lying on the couch. I said to Nadia, and I remember my exact words: 'You could have got someone decent.'

I remember thinking: 'He's a lazy bum. He doesn't do anything. He just lies on the couch.'

What I didn't realise was that he was actually recovering from that major groin operation he had.

I went round there one time and he was on his back, sliding around on the floor, squeezing a huge spaghetti can with his thighs. I was a bit embarrassed and said, 'What are you doing?'

He explained that he was doing rehab exercises and told me why. Well, my attitude towards him obviously softened. After that we'd always have a chat and we got on well. But we were really just acquaintances in the same social group.

It's kind of funny, though, like fate in some way. I'd always be out and I'd just be leaving a bar about 3 or 4 in the morning. I'd be leaving town. I'd have had enough and I'd be waiting at the taxi stand. And the taxi would pull up, the door would open and it would be Justin. He'd get out of the taxi and go, 'Gidday.' We'd have a bit of a chat. 'Do you want my taxi?'

'Yeah, that's great.' I'd get into the taxi and leave. He'd go into the bar.

Our paths crossed a lot like that. We weren't best friends. But we kept bumping into each other.

Justin: In 1997, when I was touring England, she gave me a call and said, 'Hi, it's Nicolle here. I've been living over here for a while.'

I said, 'Yeah, I knew you were over here. Nards gave me your number before we left. But I didn't know whether or not I should give you a call. But, yeah, we should catch up for a coffee.'

So we did that. Then I caught up with her one time when we were in Manchester. She came to the game and I caught up with her afterwards. She had a boyfriend at the time and I had a girlfriend. But we were just hanging out as mates.

I will say, though, that I felt very relaxed around Nicolle. And I think probably around that stage, in 1997, I began to look at her in a different way. I thought, 'It's a shame we didn't make an effort with each other when we were younger because we've got a lot in common and I haven't met anybody like you before.'

I remember thinking that after we'd met for a couple of chats and then that was pretty much it.

Nicolle: It was quite strange because even though we weren't close friends we could sit down and have dinner and discuss quite personal stuff quite openly. We were both seeing other people at the time. But after the tour ended and he'd gone back to New Zealand I thought, 'I hadn't realised what great company he is.'

Justin: Then she came back to New Zealand and we finally managed to get together. She split up with her boyfriend. I split up with my girlfriend. Nicolle was hanging out in the same circle again with Tabai Matson and Nards. And we began to see a bit of each other again.

Nicolle: When I came back to New Zealand, we were both in the wedding party of Nadia and Tabai Matson. Justin was a groomsman and I was a bridesmaid. And it kind of went from there really. He phoned me up a couple of times. I was only in Christchurch for six weeks and then I was returning to London. He asked me out and we went for pizza with Mark Morton.

Justin: The first time we ever went on a date I took Mental with us. I don't know what I was thinking. We went out to Sumner, to Club Bizarre, and Mental was sitting there with us.

Nicolle: They were flatting together at that stage and we just went to a local restaurant, so Mark came along. I'm sure we didn't think much of it at first because Justin and I had been friends for quite a long time. Then all of a sudden we were both aware that the situation had changed. And it seemed a little odd having Mark sitting there. He wasn't just a mate; he was a gooseberry.

I remember very distinctly going out that night and all of a sudden I couldn't talk to Justin. I felt very nervous and I spent the whole night talking to Mark.

From then on, whenever Justin rang I'd be like, 'Oh no, it's him. What'll I say?'

We started doing stuff every day. It was very platonic. But it was going somewhere. We both knew it was.

But we both obviously had to get our houses in order. Once we'd both done that, we really put the brakes on and asked ourselves, 'Where is this going?'

I remember we were out one night and there was innuendo from a few people that they knew Justin had a partner. They *thought* they knew Justin had a partner. He'd ended his relationship by then.

I sat down with him and I said, 'Look, you're so well known in public. I'm not well known. But I do have friends and family. And it is important to me that people know I'm not just someone you hang around with when you're not with a certain other person. We've got to stop where this is going. Maybe in six months' time if we're both still single and we think that it's going to work out we can hang out again.'

His life had changed dramatically since I'd met him. He hadn't changed. But we couldn't go to a restaurant without people staring at him and approaching him. I really wanted the relationship to continue. But the outside pressures were something I hadn't encountered before. And I wasn't sure how I felt about it all.

But he sat me down and he talked me through it. And I distinctly remember him saying, 'I don't think I've handled it very well. I think I need to make an announcement to the Canterbury team that I have a new partner.'

It was really bizarre because I can remember the date and everything that he went to the team and he made this big announcement that he had this new partner, Nicolle with two l's.

After that every time I went to a Canterbury rugby function, people would come up to me and say, 'Hello, Nicolle with two l's.'

It was all because he'd stood up so seriously at training and made this big announcement. But I suppose it stopped a lot of speculation. He'd had a fairly high-profile relationship. I think he just wanted to let people know that they were going to see him out with a different person and that's how it was.

The date he asked me to be his girlfriend was 17 January 1998.

Achilles heel

Justin Marshall's career came to a shocking, albeit temporary, halt on Friday 6 March 1998, when he ruptured an Achilles tendon in the last minutes of the Crusaders' clash with the Waratahs.

To that point he had appeared in 23 consecutive tests since his debut against France in November 1995. Suddenly he was out for the international season, opening the All Black door for Junior Tonu'u.

Medical opinion indicated Marshall would be sidelined for about six months, which would have him back in time for Canterbury's defence of the NPC first-division title. Marshall's own opinion was more optimistic.

I remember before the game my other Achilles was a bit sore, so I had it strapped up. It was a little bit tight, so I put a heel rack in both boots, just as a precaution.

We were beating the Waratahs quite comfortably when I snapped my Achilles tendon. It was about 10 minutes out from the end of the game. Daryl Gibson made a break and he was headed for the try-line. But David Campese came across and was beginning to mow him down.

Now, we call Daryl Gibson the Black Widow because if you're around him or near him for a certain period of time, someone always gets injured. He's always the guy throwing the last pass before an injury or having a bit of fun that ends in somebody snapping a ligament. People would get injured at training and we'd all go, 'Uh-oh, the Black Widow struck again.'

So anyway the Black Widow's heading for the try-line. And I can see he's about to get tackled by Campo. So I'm coming up behind him screaming for the ball. But the Black Widow holds on to it too long. He's got it tucked under his arm as Campo tackles him and clings on. In desperation Daryl pops out this rough pass that I have to jump for. So I leap up for the ball. I've got an open try-line in front of me. And I'm thinking, 'Yeah! This is too easy.' I come down and I feel what I can only describe as a small explosion in the back of my foot. My first thought is that somebody's ankle-tapped me. But no one's going to stop me with an open try-line ahead of me. I go to step on the foot. But there's nothing there. My foot has no push and no resistance. It's just flopping at the end of my ankle. So I pull my foot up and hop over the line to score the try.

I knew straight away that I'd torn my Achilles or a calf muscle or something like that. Steve Cope, the physio, came on and started pushing and prodding about at my ankle. I actually swore at him because it hurt so much. I knew straight away that I was in big trouble. I was taken into the changing rooms and they took off my boot. It was obvious something major was wrong. So I'm lying there in agony. I've just snapped my Achilles tendon, which is a rare injury in rugby and bloody serious. And the St Johns man asks me if he can have my boot. Yeah, he wanted my boot. And he wanted me to sign it!

I was pissed off for a second or two. Then I thought, 'Aw well. I won't be using it for a while.' So I signed it and handed it over. You should have seen his face.

Nicolle: No one welcomes tough times. But they often have a positive spin-off that isn't noticed until later.

When Justin's Achilles tendon tore apart, our relationship pulled together. It changed quickly and forever . . . I could feel it happening and noticed I felt remarkably comfortable with that. I had to be there for Justin and I was ready.

The injury was devastating for him and horrible for me to watch. I knew it was bad just by the way Justin was reacting on the field. Everyone in the stand was discussing it and saying it looked like an ankle. I was certain it was his Achilles as he'd mentioned a sore Achilles during the week.

Errol Collins, the Canterbury masseur, came and told me that Justin's leg was bad. They wanted to get him out of the stadium really quick. 'Go and get Justin's car from the car park,' he said. 'Bring it around under the stand to collect him and you'd better get him straight home.'

It was so surreal. I drove the car into the restricted area under the stands and was taken towards the changing room. That's where I encountered my first taste of rugby red tape. The doorman wouldn't let me into the changing room with men in there showering and I didn't have the correct pass.

Everyone else was saying, 'It's Justin's partner. We need her to go in to see the doctor.' But the doorman wouldn't budge. It was ridiculous really. If it had been a neck or spinal injury I might have had a strong word to the doorman myself to gain entry. And I wouldn't have given the least bit of thought to the men showering.

Anyway, they carried Justin out into the hall and he was in agony. It was awful.

The doctor told me all I needed to know about Justin's admission to hospital and explained how I could best help him over the next 12 hours.

From that moment on I was more deeply involved in Justin's life than ever before. Because he was being operated on in the morning, he wasn't allowed any painkillers that night. I did everything, from getting him up the stairs into his house, to helping him shower, to sorting out the ice packs throughout the night, to dealing with the flood of phone calls. Even while he was still being operated on, there were calls requesting media interviews at the hospital. I had to call his mum

Lois and tell her how he was. And I helped arrange her travel to Christchurch. Yet we hadn't even met in person! We had only talked on the phone. It must have been so strange for her having to meet me for the first time at the airport.

This was only two months after Justin had asked me to be his girlfriend. After a long time looking, I'd just found myself a nice flat and I was actually at the game that night with my new male flatmate. But Justin said he was going to need my help and asked if I would move in with him. I said yes, and we've been together ever since.

It was a really tough time for Justin. But this injury that had the potential to end his career actually brought us closer together. We crossed a lot of bridges in the following months dealing with it. And a lot of the discussion held during that time mapped out our future together with or without rugby.

Errol Collins, Canterbury masseur: You know why the boys often call him LJ, don't you? It was when he was hurt. We were away and we had a big game coming up. And he sent the boys a fax wishing them all the best. And on the bottom he put, 'Love, Justin.' You can imagine the boys' reaction. That's why they call him LJ.

While Marshall was injured, the Crusaders went on to win their first Super 12 title, beating Auckland at Eden Park in the final. Marshall went to the game, but later dubbed himself the 'world's worst spectator'.

It was an emotional time for Marshall. He bypassed the victory parade down Colombo Street in Christchurch, saying he felt he didn't deserve any pats on the back.

Robbie Deans: Justin's a guy who takes huge pride in the team performance. I think that's one area where he has matured enormously. Now, even when his personal ambitions aren't being fulfilled, he will still offer the group a lot.

But if you look back to 1998 when the Crusaders won the Super 12 for the first time, Justin was injured and he distanced himself from the celebrations. He felt like he wasn't really part of it because he hadn't played in the final. But no one else felt like that.

These days I'm sure he would take part and would recognise that he had contributed significantly even though it might not be on the field on that particular day.

'Miracle' recovery

The Achilles tendon injury kept me out for only three months and two weeks. That was incredibly quick. It was considered a medical miracle. Nowadays I get asked about that more than practically anything else that's happened in my career. Even now I get about a dozen letters a year from rugby players or athletes who've ruptured their Achilles, asking me how I came back so quickly.

A lot of people I've spoken to since reckon I should have been out for a minimum of six months. Very few people have come back as quickly as I did. I don't know why I got back that quickly. But I did.

I can say I was really aggressive with my rehab work, though, to the point that it made a lot of people feel a bit queasy and uncomfortable. I started stretching it really early. I was constantly testing it. They strapped a rubber band over the bridge of my foot to a boot underneath. I would just lift the rubber band up and down with my foot.

As soon as I could I was walking up and down stairs.

I was doing strengthening work on it early too, walking on it, running on it, pushing it to the max. There was a certain element of risk in there, which I didn't care about at that stage. I just wanted to get back on the field and play rugby. I was young and keen. With a tendon like the Achilles they can sew it back together but if you start pushing it too soon, it can stretch and heal longer and you lose all your power.

But the surgeon who did the operation said, 'Look, they repair, they're not pleasant but they repair and they repair stronger than what they ever were.' So that's all I needed him to tell me.

The thing is you need mental strength too. You can't be squeamish because when you snap an Achilles you're just waiting for it to go again. I had a real scare over in Hong Kong.

I was commentating for TV3 at the sevens about three weeks after my injury. I was still on crutches and had a special boot on.

At a live commentary spot there's thick, black, sticky gaffer tape everywhere. Cables are all taped to the floor with it and bits of it come loose and it'll stick to anything.

I was trying to climb over something on my way out of the commentary box when my crutches slipped on a piece of gaffer tape. They just went *phomp* and I slipped. And what's your first reaction when you're off-balance and something slips? I put my foot down.

For a second I thought I'd ruptured it again. Nicolle was there with me and she remembers seeing my face. I think it's the closest I've ever come to crying in public. I thought I'd done all sorts of damage to it.

My point in that story is that when you've snapped your Achilles, it's such a strange feeling, such an awful feeling, that when you're rehabbing it and you're pushing it you're just waiting for something to happen, you're waiting for it to snap again. And that's the thing: you've got to get through that. You've got to get to the other side and just say, 'I'm going to push it,' because a lot of people will just decide very early on, 'I don't dare push it, I'm not going to go through that ever again.'

But they risk allowing scar tissue to build up, which isn't good for the healing process. The other thing I believe is that if they take a passive attitude and don't push the rehab along, whether it heals or not, the injury will always have a psychological hold over them.

When you rupture your Achilles, you feel helpless. You can't wiggle your toes or even put your foot down and just stand still. Your flaming foot is flapping about. And you know that somehow you've done a lot of damage.

Your foot's just dangling there because the tendon is like the string in a pulley. And if the string snaps, the pulley's rendered useless. You don't realise how lucky you are when your body's functioning normally until one of its crucial parts is injured or taken out of commission.

Suddenly every waking second is dedicated to protecting that injury, compensating for it by developing new ways to perform simple tasks, and coping with the pain and discomfort the injury causes. You inevitably start thinking about how much you take for granted in your day-to-day life. But, of course, you forget all that as soon as the injury heals.

George Gregan: The two years after the 1995 World Cup the All Blacks were the best team in the world by a country mile. I didn't have too much to do with Justin during that time because we were always on the receiving end.

I think where the friendship really started was during the rehab for his Achilles injury in 1998. I rang him up and wished him all the best and told him I hoped he recovered okay and would be fine for the Bledisloe Cup.

Since then we've both made an effort to keep in contact with each other and it just grew from there.

Nicolle: People have been debating the merits of Justin's pass on and off for as long as I've known him.

I remember one time the All Black selectors, John Hart, Ross Cooper and the late Gordon Hunter, had come to Christchurch to meet with Justin. They wanted to see how his recovery from the Achilles injury was going.

The relationship between the selectors and Justin was very good at that time, and I got on particularly well with John Hart. They were keen to see Justin back in action as soon as possible.

We were driving them to the airport and the selectors were obviously trying to include me in the conversation. 'So Nicolle, have you been helping Justin with his rehabilitation?'

And without even thinking about it, I said, 'Yeah, actually we've been down at the park and I've been catching his passes. But I get sore hands so I have to wear gloves.' It was true. The passes hurt my hands so much and made them so red, I'd started wearing these woolly gloves.

Well, before I'd realised what I'd said, everyone in the car literally erupted into laughter, even Justin.

Then all of a sudden it dawned on me that I must have sounded like the protective girlfriend putting in an unconvincing plug for Justin's pass. The selectors thought it was hilarious. They were saying, 'Sounds like a rocket, this pass. Oh, you'll have to keep her on, Justin.'

I was feeling rather silly and uncomfortable. Afterwards when we were alone in the car, I said, 'Oh, no, that sounded dreadful.'

Just 16 weeks after snapping his Achilles, Marshall was fit again and back in the No. 9 jersey at international level, playing for New Zealand A against Tonga in Wanganui.

He was given the go-ahead from All Black doctor John Mayhew and coach John Hart after a fitness test in Dunedin the previous weekend.

His test results were close to his personal bests. At the All Black training camp in Taupo in March, just before the injury, he did 11.42 seconds for the 3 kilometre run. At the Dunedin fitness test he did 12.07 seconds.

But his most important result was in the 10-metre sprint, because he needed that explosive speed. He did 1.76 seconds in Taupo and 1.77 seconds in Dunedin.

New Zealand A won the match 60–7. *Manawatu Evening Standard* sports editor Peter Lampp wrote that Marshall had 'displayed his full repertoire'. Lampp predicted that Junior Tonu'u would be watching from the bench when the first Bledisloe Cup test was played in Melbourne 12 days later. Lampp was right.

Reality check

While Marshall's rehabilitation was nothing short of phenomenal, he was able to keep the injury in perspective thanks to a special friend. He met seven-year-old Beaumont Armstrong in March when they were both in Christchurch Hospital. Justin was recovering from his Achilles injury. Beaumont was having radiotherapy for leukaemia.

The pair became great mates when Beaumont invited Justin to his ward to play on his video game machine.

Beaumont was way too good for me. I let him celebrate his victory by allowing him to sign my plaster cast. I wanted him to feel special so he was the only person I allowed to sign it.

I admired Beaumont's positive attitude. He was really smiley, great company, and we got on really well. In a way, this young boy was a mentor to a grown man: his bravery changed my life.

Here I was thinking my world had come to an end because my rugby season looked like it was gone. Then you see a kid like that who's battling for his life. It makes you realise how lucky you are.

We kept in contact after we left hospital and I visited Beaumont several times at home to see how he was getting on. Every time he looked more ill, but just as happy to see me.

Beaumont liked his rugby so Marshall arranged for him to be taken to some of Canterbury's NPC matches. He also gave him his All Blacks 1998 Tri-series jersey with the inscription: 'To Beaumont, my very best friend.' The last time they met was at Beaumont's seventh birthday party.

It was tough. I could see things weren't good. Beaumont didn't have too long to live. He was very quiet and hardly spoke. It makes you feel awful but he was still being very brave. He was struggling but trying very hard.

Beaumont died of cancer on 15 November 1998.

Excess baggage

If 1996 and '97 had been glorious years for the All Blacks, then 1998 was a dog. The All Blacks had their usual four Tri-Nations tests plus an extra Bledisloe Cup match against Australia, and lost them all. They started off with a 24–16 loss to the Wallabies in Melbourne and followed that with a 13–3 loss to the Springboks in Wellington.

The next match was against the Wallabies again in Christchurch and Justin Marshall was starting to feel the heat.

It was a tough time. I'd lost the captaincy and I'd just recovered from my Achilles injury, so I was feeling my way back into test rugby. And after two losses there was intense pressure on us to turn things around.

Leading into the test, Harty called me up to his room and said he felt I was carrying around too much baggage. 'You're listening to every opinion out there,' he said. 'You're reading all the newspapers, you're listening to talk-back radio and you're taking it all on board. I think it's starting to affect your game.'

He had probably seen the comments I was making in the newspapers and magazines to defend myself. So I guess he would have figured I'd bought into the whole debate.

And, to be perfectly honest, the criticism was affecting me. I hadn't really encountered a wave of media criticism before that. From 1995 to the end of '97 I'd had a real dream run. I'd been in great form so I'd had no criticism of my game or questions over whether I was the right guy to wear the jersey.

So this was the first time I'd been heavily criticised in my career. And I didn't handle it very well. I was listening to every little bit of criticism out there. And, because of that, I did have a lot of baggage on board. Harty was right about that.

All of a sudden my pass had become an issue. And as anyone with a vague interest in rugby knows, it's an issue that's followed me ever since.

Previous All Black forward packs I'd played behind were pretty much the best packs in world rugby. But our new forwards were stuttering along, I wasn't getting good front-foot ball, I was having to dig in and get it, and we weren't playing free-flowing rugby. And all of a sudden my service was the problem. That's when commentators like Chris Laidlaw, the former All Black halfback, started to criticise me.

The week before we'd played the Springboks in a howling gale at Athletic Park in Wellington. I tried to throw a cut-out pass with one of my first touches of the day. It got caught by the wind and blew forward about 10 metres. It was weak and it looked really poor. I only lasted about 20 minutes before taking a heavy knock on the hip bone that forced me off. So that day's work did little to enhance my All Black career.

I probably should have hidden myself away from the criticism that followed. But that's not the way I am. When someone attacks me, I defend myself.

So Harty said he was considering leaving me out of the test match that weekend because he felt I wasn't in the right frame of mind. Now this was a shock for me because up until then there hadn't been any question marks over me starting test matches.

So I just had to swallow it and take it all on board. I couldn't really disagree with him because he was right.

That was back when the All Blacks first started allowing the players to go home during the week leading up to a test. So Monday, Tuesday, Wednesday, you were allowed to go home, when you were in your home town. And Thursday, Friday you had to stay with the team.

So I went home after this. I think it was on a Tuesday after training. I talked about it with Nicolle. I said, 'I don't know what to do about this. I think he's right in what he's saying. And I don't think he's going to pick me and I really want to play. If there's a turnaround I want to be part of it. Otherwise who knows what might happen.

'He reckons I've got all this baggage. Maybe I can do something with that.'

The next morning I went up to Harty's room and I was carrying this rickety old bag. He invited me in and I said, 'Look, Harty, I know what you're saying. I understand it. I'm really keen to play this weekend. The decision's yours. But I just wanted to let you know that the baggage I am carrying I'm keen to put behind me. This is it all in here. Look.' I started pulling stuff out of the bag. 'Here you go, a transistor radio, the sports section of the newspaper, a couple of rugby magazines and a rugby ball.'

Harty laughed. 'What's the ball for?' he asked.

'The ball represents all the debate over my pass. I'm leaving that behind with everything else.'

I guess the only thing I left out was a TV. But I didn't have a big enough bag. Anyway, I put everything back in the bag and left it on the floor behind me.

John Hart: He blew up in the meeting with us on the first day. And we told him to go away and think about it. At that stage, I've got to say, we were seriously considering not playing him because he was in such a bad state of mind and the way he reacted was so bad.

In fairness to him, he came in the next day and did exactly as he said and I thought it was quite a nice way of dealing with it and I admired him for it actually.

Justin: From my perspective, it was a real plea to be allowed to keep my jersey and to be given a second chance.

Harty picked me for the test. I played better, but I couldn't do anything to turn things around.

The All Blacks lost to Australia 27–23. But it wasn't a wholly surprising result considering the All Blacks were rebuilding and the Wallabies were still chock-full of legendary players such as John Eales, Tim Horan and Jason Little.

The next match was even closer, going down 24–23 to the Springboks in Durban. The All Blacks led in the latter stages of the match, but went down to a controversial try, believing they'd held up the try-scorer.

The international season was put to rest with a 19–14 loss to Australia in Sydney.

It was a season that saw Marshall's old mate Andrew Mehrtens feel the All Black selectors' axe for the first time. And as the song says, the first cut is the deepest.

Andrew Mehrtens: Justin was really good to me in 1998 when I first got dropped for Carlos Spencer in the All Blacks. It doesn't take much, especially guy to guy. I remember Justin saying to me, 'Look, mate, no matter what happens, I know how good you are.' That made all the difference, especially coming from the closest guy to me, on the field, off the field or whatever, that just meant a huge amount.

And it wasn't an endorsement of me over Carlos because I know he enjoys playing alongside Carlos. It was more like, 'Keep your head up, mate. I believe in you.' And that's all I needed.

Hairdos and don'ts

When I first arrived on the scene in Christchurch I still had The Mataura Kid mullet. There was no design or anything going on. I progressed from there to a very slick style that had short sides and was shaved at the back. It was an army look but spiked up through the middle.

But things got really funky in 1998. It's a bit unfair to say I was pushed into the situation. But I went into the hairdresser and said I wanted something a little different. I said, 'I don't want to be too radical with the style. But maybe we should play around with the colour a little bit.' And we decided that blond was the way we wanted to go.

So we agreed to blond but the result was a bit more extreme than I envisaged. I ended up bleached blond. When I went out of there I felt like a bit of a lightbulb-head actually. I stood out and everybody was looking at me.

The worst thing was going to training. No one had seen me. And then I turned up and, oh, you should have seen the looks on the boys' faces. The mouths dropped and the eyes popped and there was plenty of laughter and teasing.

It was one of those ones where people saw me completely different to what I'd been before. And it was pretty full on because I'm quite dark featured anyway with dark eyebrows and my facial hair's dark as well. So platinum blond is going to stand out.

So I played one game and the media had a field day. They dubbed me Billy Idol in the papers. There was nothing much about the game that weekend. It was just all about my hair. People were making comments and there was a readers' poll about what they thought, all that sort of carry-on.

So I got rid of that in just over a week. I went back and got it re-dyed and toned down. I succumbed to peer pressure and media attention, unfortunately. I wasn't strong-willed enough to stick to my guns and I wish I had now.

There were a few racy haircuts doing the rounds in '98. You might remember Carlos Spencer sported a similar bleached blond lightbulb-do for a while and Jonah Lomu dyed his Tintin tuft a striking red. So I wasn't alone.

This was all before David Beckham started getting adventurous with his hairstyles, so we weren't influenced by him. Personally, I just wanted to try something different and take a bit of a risk. It was as simple as that.

It must have been amusing for people to see me pretty much return to normal just over a week later. They would have been thinking, 'Hell, that didn't last long.'

In the end I decided that my rugby game was under so much scrutiny that the last thing I needed was extra attention. So I steered away from it.

After that I went through a stage of just growing my hair long. I thought I'd go through that stage again but try to do it a bit better than when I had the mullet. I let it go a bit messy.

I like to go through different phases with my hair and try different styles. I suppose it's a bit womanish really, wanting to try all these new things.

There was one stage where everyone thought I looked like Meg Ryan. People would yell out, 'How are you, Meg?' The papers would describe me as 'Meg Ryan look-alike Justin Marshall'. Once again there were surveys about my hairdo. This was in about 2002 and by that stage it was amusing me. It became a focal point and everyone kept asking me about it. I remember saying to one reporter, 'The only reason I grew my hair long and styled it like Meg Ryan was so that people would stop talking about my pass.'

Get Harty

Justin Marshall's opinions about John Hart are often strong, and obviously coloured by strong and raw emotions. After writing some of them up I decided to approach Hart for a response.

I went over to his apartment in Remuera to discuss the issue.

Hart wasn't happy. Marshall had expressed his opinions and versions of events once before, in a rugby magazine, and, Hart said, he'd been factually wrong. At the time, Hart had said nothing. But he didn't intend to let Marshall get away with it again. He had to decide whether to let me interview him (he was reluctant to help Marshall sell books and make money) or just wait for it all to come out and then set the record straight himself.

As we were chatting away, Jeff Wilson walked into the room. He'd been staying with Hart. Wilson's wife Adine had been playing for the Silver Ferns netball team against England in Auckland that weekend. He was just about to jump in a taxi to the airport.

It seemed like a strange coincidence that Wilson would be staying there the day I was talking to Hart about Marshall. It was like life had handed me a little symbol. I might not understand it, but I could write it up with everything else.

I thought about it.

Justin Marshall and Jeff Wilson both made their debuts for Southland on 19 July 1992, losing to Canterbury 20–17.

One was called Goldie, the other Blondie (but not by his mates, who knew better).

They both went on to play for the All Blacks, and both earned their place among the greats of that team.

They both spent much of their international careers in the same All Black team coached by John Hart.

And yet Wilson's a big fan of Hart. And a close friend. And Marshall isn't.

It's strange how two people can look at the same thing (in this case another person) and see something completely different.

I voiced my concerns about John Hart to a couple of Rugby Union board members at the end of 1998. People wanted John Hart replaced. And after all those losses, the New Zealand Rugby Union wanted to know how we were going to win the World Cup. Mike Banks and Bill Wallace made separate trips around the provinces and talked to the players to get their thoughts. The main topic of discussion was John Hart and whether he was good enough to coach the All Blacks. And when they came to Christchurch I told them, and particularly Bill Wallace, what I thought.

Now at that stage I had no personal issues with John Hart whatsoever. He'd picked me right through from 1996 until the end of 1998 and the first two years had been pretty good for the All Blacks.

But I didn't think John Hart was the man to bring back the World Cup. I said there was an uneasy feeling in the team about him. There was a lack of confidence in his coaching. There were a lot of players who had real issues with him. And they couldn't be resolved in the short amount of time we had.

The reason John Hart was so successful and was such a good coach in 1996 and '97 was because he inherited a great team from Laurie Mains. Harty's very good at team management and if he has good-quality resources, he knows how to get the best out of them. Now in his first two years he had excellent resources. He had a lot of the great All Blacks that he'd already coached with Auckland. He knew these guys well and he knew how to motivate them and keep them motivated. But then in '97 and '98 all those guys like Fitzy, Zinzan Brooke, Olo Brown, Michael Jones and Frank Bunce retired. Anyone would struggle trying to replace such strong All Blacks. And Harty certainly did.

Those guys left a huge hole. They were the guys he used to fall back on and confide in and who he would use as a coaching tool: to talk to, to get their advice, to see how the boys were feeling and all that carry-on.

But then he had to move on from that and take a bunch of fresh-faced kids and mould a totally new All Black side to take into the future. And it just wasn't his style. The players just didn't get enough good coaching from him basically. I could tell there were going to be problems heading into the World Cup. But the Rugby Union stuck with him.

Mike Banks, All Blacks manager 1996–99: I went to Dunedin and Christchurch and we got the Wellington guys up to Auckland for a meeting with the players here. I took my findings to the board and members agonised over a very lengthy board meeting to decide the coach for the 1999 World Cup, which culminated in John's reappointment.

It would be fair to say that Justin did have some issues with John's coaching. But I certainly came away from the Canterbury contingent with the consensus there was nothing to say John shouldn't be reappointed.

There was a feeling that he was stronger on the management and PR issues than the coaching. That was mirrored in what came out of the board meeting, with Peter Sloane and Wayne Smith taking a more hands-on role with the coaching and John concentrating on more of a management role, while using their expertise.

John Hart: To say that I didn't have the ability to work with new players, well, I'd suggest he looks at the history books. In 1982 I picked a new Auckland side and developed it with no All Blacks. In '86 when we finished I had 14 or 15 in the '87 World Cup squad. So I have no doubt that my record shows that I have the ability to move and develop players and develop a team.

In '98, sadly, we lost the nucleus of the team. We lost five tests that year, but we lost them all by about four or five points and we should have won three. All I can say is that I worked with the technical director Wayne Smith, the assistant coach Peter Sloane and the management team to do the best we could and we turned it around substantially in '99.

Don't laugh

None of the new players really knew John Hart very well. And he could be a hard coach to warm to.

All of the other All Black coaches I've had — Wayne Smith, John Mitchell, Robbie Deans, Graham Henry and even Laurie Mains — you could take the piss out of them a bit and it wasn't a big deal. Each one had authority and respect as the coach, but they also had their little idiosyncrasies that everyone in the team picked up on and punished them for. Everyone's aware of these little quirks of character, ribs them about it in front of their face and everyone has a laugh at their expense. But it never happened with John Hart the whole time I was involved with him.

We used to mimic and joke about his idiosyncrasies behind his back because he wouldn't have been okay about us winding him up to his face. He just wasn't that personality type.

I remember in early 1999, he had the whole squad at some flash hotel on the North

Shore. He was standing in front of all the players telling us what he hoped to achieve with the team and what he had planned for us. This included an SAS-style army camp which, in my opinion, turned out to be a complete waste of time.

As he talked he moved back and forth and from side to side. Harty was always on the move while he talked. He was standing in front of a trestle-style table and every now and then he'd sit on it, clap his hands, get up and begin pacing again. The funny thing was that every time he clapped his hands the strap on his wristwatch would snap open and hang loose on his wrist. Without missing a beat, Harty would snap it shut again and carry on with the speech as if nothing had happened and we could stop biting our tongues until he did it again. I was keeping an eye on guys like Robin Brooke, older guys from Auckland who knew Harty from way back. I noticed that every time Harty clapped his hands, they'd take it as a cue to look at the ground. And they'd look up again once the watch strap was sorted out. One thing was for sure — no one was laughing, not even an involuntary snigger, and this seemed a little odd to me.

Anyway, after this had happened a few times my mind began to wander to other things: like the trestle-style table. 'Whoa,' I thought, 'that table doesn't look too stable. If he sits down on that thing, it could quite easily buckle under his weight and collapse.' Automatically, I glanced over at Andrew Mehrtens. He didn't know I was looking at him. And to his credit his face gave very little away. But underneath the mask of composure I could see his playful side peeping out. I knew the guy well enough to recognise hints of fear, hope and fascination and the traces of a little smirk. He was thinking the same thing as me.

Sure enough Harty sat down on the table, clapped his hands, popped open his watch strap and, as the table gave way, collapsed in a heap on the floor.

It was the most hilarious thing I've ever seen. And if it had happened to any other coach the whole place would have exploded into laughter. But everyone just put their heads down, bit their tongues and waited for Harty to get up, dust himself off, do his watch strap back up and continue with his talk.

The SAS camp

We were put through a two-and-a-half-day SAS camp at Whenuapai in West Auckland in January 1999. It was part of the process of building towards the World Cup that year. Personally, I've never been a fan of those types of team-bonding exercises. At the Crusaders we used to do things like that all the time. We'd go away to Burnham Army Camp and pitch tents and do all that sort of stuff. I'm one of those guys who feels your time's much better spent on the field doing proper rugby drills and then going to the pub and having a few beers. I much prefer everyone getting to know each other that way.

They say these team-building sessions help show your true character. So there's my true character: I don't like it, and I don't feel it makes any difference to what you do on the field, and I don't think it gets you any closer as a group. It just takes you out of your comfort zone and puts you in positions that you're not used to. I don't see the point in it. The seasons are long enough as they are.

Guys like Norm Maxwell came out of that SAS camp in Auckland losing between five and 10 kilograms for God's sake, because they hardly fed us.

This is where Andrew Martin, who would later become All Black manager, first came into the whole scene. He was the colonel on the camp.

We arrived at the base camp and they took us into a big hangar where we put down all our stuff and they gave us overalls to put on. After that they gave us something to eat. I picked at the food, not realising it was the most I was going to eat for the next three days.

After that we were taken out to the courtyard. We're all standing there in our overalls, while they told us what would be happening on the camp. Then we were put into two teams. Each team was given a massive log, like a telephone pole. We were told we had to take this thing with us wherever we went. It had a name. I can't remember what the name of our log was, Bertha or Betty or something. Anyway, that was our team log. We also had team captains. Ours was Norm Hewitt.

So everyone was standing next to their logs and we all got blindfolded, except the team captains.

Norm directed us so that we were organised on either side of the log and when he said, 'One, two, three,' we could lift the log up on to our shoulders and off we'd go.

Now along with our logs we were also given jerry cans filled with water and, because I was up near the front, Norm put me in charge of our team's jerry can. So I knelt down beside the container. So here I was with my blindfold on, waiting for the next instruction. And in the meantime, he's going to the boys, 'Okay, one, two, three and lift.' And as they lift the log it cracks me just above the eye and splits my eyebrow. I didn't need stitches. But it just bled enough that I could feel the blood running down the side of my face and that sort of carry-on. So that was my start to the SAS camp.

It unsettled me, but I didn't want to say anything about it because you know what those army people are like. Imagine it: 'Hey, excuse me, I've got a cut above my eye.' 'Get down and give me 50 press-ups, Marshall! And stop moaning!' So I just thought I'll keep my mouth shut and put up with it.

We went through a series of exercises. We did endurance swimming. We had boxing. We boxed each other with two guys on to one guy for two or three minutes and you just had to try to fend them off. We wore boxing gloves but it was full-on punching. We did lots of walking. Abseiling blindfolded: I hated it. You just had to trust the rope and feel your way down the wall. It was horrible, but never mind. And you never knew the results of any of the tests they gave you, whether you'd done well or failed. We did another test where they put you into a dark room and you were blindfolded. Then they gave you some sort of a gun. You went in as a team but they only tested you one at a time. And they'd go, 'Right, you've got three bullets, now you're gonna come out of this dark room and there'll be three targets in front of you. I want you to shoot them.'

They whipped off my blindfold and said, 'Okay, go,' so off I went through the door and there were three targets there. I shot all three targets. There were two targets that were villains or whatever and the other was a woman with a handbag. Now that was some sort of a test that they recorded. But there was no feedback, so to this day I have no idea whether what I did was right or wrong in the context of that test. It all seemed a bit pointless, really.

We did a whole series of other similar exercises and a couple of those team-building crap things that I hate where you're not allowed to touch the ground here and you've got to put a plank there and walk across here. You know, 'There are alligators in this pond,' and all that sort of rubbish. You've got to get the whole team across to the other side and stuff like that.

We got taken back to the hangar and given water and something else to eat. Then we got taken out to the forest. We were given a leader cum guide. He said nothing. He was the old army, 'I'm not gonna say anything,' guy. If you asked him questions he wouldn't answer you. He just made us march and march and march.

Then there was a series of exercises, really physical things to do. We had to get these ammo canisters, which were full of sand. And they were heavy. It took two guys to lift one of them. We had to carry them to the top of sand dunes, and when you got them all up there, they'd go, 'Okay, you can take them back down now.' And we'd move on to the next thing.

Another one was we had to carry stuff through a swamp. That was followed by more endless, mindless walking. Suddenly you'd be told, 'Right, stop. You'll find some biscuits and a bit of rice in your bag. Eat that and we'll be away again at 5 in the morning.' And we just slept in the open bush.

The next morning we were off again. It's the hardest thing I've ever done. Everyone got blisters, sores, rashes, was sleep deprived and suffered weight loss. Everyone was a physical mess when we came out of it. And just to reinforce it at the end, while we were all suffering with the blisters and sore feet and all the rest of it, they made us do training in grids with the rugby ball, just to see if we could still cope with it. Then we got a really good feed given to us and we went home.

And everyone went out of there feeling absolutely shagged and no better for it. It wasn't even the World Cup squad. There were about 40 players there. So you're not really doing team building. They were trying to test us for mental toughness and all that carry-on, I suppose. But really, *really*, what was the point? I might have done terribly on that camp, but what happens if I was *the man* in the Super 12? Do you think they're not going to pick me because I didn't do very well at the SAS camp? I don't think so.

I came out of there all disillusioned and I just don't believe in those camps to be honest. I think they're of no benefit to creating a better team or a better environment.

Maybe something like Outward Bound might work. That way you'd have a good feed and a good night's sleep and you'd wake up looking forward to taking on the challenges and overcoming the obstacles put in front of you the next day. But when you're deprived of sleep and pushed ridiculously hard, it's just over the top.

John Hart: We went into that camp because after 1998 there were a number of concerns about our leadership. It was suggested to us that we should talk to the SAS. Andrew Martin was, in fact, in charge of the SAS. And we left it entirely to them in terms of the nature of the programme. We said we wanted to test individual decision-making under pressure, we wanted to test leadership and we wanted to test mental toughness because those were some of the issues that had been our biggest concerns in '98.

I think, yes, it was gruelling. And it may have been harder than what we would have liked. But it was not about team building. It was just to get to grips with some of these issues and questions we needed answers to. We got individual reports on all players as a result of that course. I don't think a lot came out that we didn't expect to come out, to be honest.

How I teased Bobby Skinstad into crashing his car . . . yeah, right!

The worst rugby injury I've ever been accused of inflicting on another player didn't even happen on the rugby field. The Springbok flanker Bobby Skinstad claimed I was responsible for the terrible knee injury that kept him out of the game for about five months in 1999. I can understand Bobby being upset about the injury. It put him out when he was at the height of his powers. The South Africans loved him and many experts believed he was one of the best players in the world. But the claim that I was responsible is one I refute totally, although I was with Bobby the night it happened.

The Crusaders had been in Cape Town playing the Stormers at Newlands. It was a tough match and we ended up losing. A few of us in the team were quite keen to relax and get over the loss with a few beers. But it was a Sunday, so there weren't too many bars open.

Bobby mentioned to some of the boys at the after-match that he knew of a nice place, the Green Man pub, where if we mentioned his name we'd be able to go in and have a drink. So I went along with our trainer Mike Anthony.

Motsy and I were having a quiet chat when we saw Bobby at the bar with his girlfriend. We decided to go up and say hello.

Bobby started to give us a bit of cheek, telling us the only reason we were allowed into the bar was because of him.

Motsy decided to give him a bit of cheek back. There's a huge culture of banter at the Crusaders so it's just natural to us. If someone starts getting a bit big for their boots or attracting a lot of media attention the boys usually give them heaps. So anyway, Motsy says, 'It must be good being rated one of the best forwards in the world. Personally, I can't wait to see you hit your first ruck.'

Unfortunately, Bobby didn't get the joke. And he certainly didn't think Motsy's comment was as funny as we did.

He started to get a bit toey, reminding us of the result that day and adding he thought we'd played like rubbish.

We conceded that the Stormers' forwards had had a brilliant game and that he'd done quite well out in the backs as well.

This was all getting too much for the South African superstar. And he left in a bad mood. A couple of the other Crusaders arrived and asked us what the hell was up with Bobby Skinstad.

'Why?'

'We just passed him on the stairs and he was muttering about Justin Marshall and that bloody trainer.'

The next thing we hear about Bobby is from one of our players, Matt Sexton. He was down at a service station buying a pie. Why he wanted to eat anything from a petrol station in Cape Town I'll never know. He's a braver man than me. But he said he'd been standing outside munching away when he saw this car swerving like mad. And it came off the road and crashed into the barrier on a bridge wall. Matt went over and had a look and saw Bobby Skinstad inside. And he was in a real state. Anyway, people started to arrive at the scene and Matt drifted off.

Well, Bobby always blamed me for that accident. And in South Africa I'm pretty much blamed for the accident that literally brought his career to a crashing, if temporary, halt. Sure, the conversation went too far at the bar and that is a shame. But we weren't in the car with him when he had the accident. So how can it be my problem?

I suppose he thinks that if he hadn't met me that night he would have been fine.

Mike Anthony, former Crusaders and All Blacks flanker Scott Robertson and Crusaders coach Robbie Deans, who were all at the bar, tell identical stories, right down to the words used to tease the angry Skinstad.

Robbie Deans: The most public issue I had to deal with involving Marshy was the Bobby Skinstad injury. That was back when I was the Crusaders' manager. I got a call from a South African newspaper the night before the Super 12 final against the Highlanders in 1999. They told me they were going to run an article that suggested that Justin Marshall was responsible for Bobby Skinstad's injury, which was absolute nonsense.

The fact that I was there at the pub the night Skinstad had his crash was an advantage. I said to them, 'You do what you've got to do. But I was there and I know what happened. And you weren't.'

So I think they watered it right down in the end.

Skinstad was just having a discussion with Justin at the bar. Mike Anthony was probably more of a nuisance than anyone. He was buzzing around offering his 10 cents' worth. He probably aggravated Bobby more than Justin did.

Bobby left, went to refuel at a petrol station, where one of our other players was getting some good nutrition, and then drove into the end of a bridge. Our player saw him do it.

But the South African media had a different, almost unbelievable, way of telling the story. There was often no mention of the fact that Skinstad had been at a bar let alone a suggestion that alcohol may have contributed to the crash.

A Reuters story explains in the eighth of 10 paragraphs, 'He was injured after his car went out of control in wet conditions.'

According to a Sapa report: 'The accident occurred . . . due to slippery road conditions, caused by excessive rain. It was not serious and no other person or car was involved.'

Mike Anthony, former Canterbury and All Black trainer: Well he'd had quite a few. And the next thing we knew Matt Sexton saw him at a garage. Skinstad was driving and he pranged his car. There was a bit of a cover-up, I think.

There was a story came out before we even got back to New Zealand that he'd had the crash because he was upset. He'd got us into this bar but we hadn't shown him any thanks. Apparently, we'd abused people and there'd been fights and all this carry-on. There hadn't been any of that. It was just a cover-up of him and his accident. Well, when I say a cover-up, I mean that the story was turned around so that we were suddenly at fault for his car crash.

Janet Heard, *The Sunday Times* (South Africa), 25 April 1999: Bobby tells of pub clash: Tension between the Canterbury Crusaders and the Stormers spilled over from the rugby field into the pub last Sunday shortly before rugby hero Bobby Skinstad crashed his car.

Hours after the final whistle of the crunch game against the New Zealand team at Newlands, Skinstad, 22, crashed his car into the barrier on a bridge wall after skidding in Cape Town's first winter downpour . . .

Yesterday Skinstad confirmed certain events that evening — after a week of rumours about how he had diplomatically stepped in to defuse tension between a drunk Crusaders player and a patron at the Green Man pub, one of Skinstad's favourite watering holes.

However, Skinstad said he had arrived at the Green Man pub in Claremont only after the incident. He said he got there at about midnight after spending the evening with friends at a private party at another pub.

Skinstad said he arranged with the owner of the Green Man to keep it open late as a courtesy to the Crusaders.

Skinstad confirmed he decided to leave after the Crusaders player 'threw phrases at me. I left because the last thing I wanted was a confrontation.'

Skinstad said he was sober when he climbed into his car.

He said he had not spoken out about the incident earlier because he 'did not want to get any rugby player into trouble. Now that I've been directly asked about the incident, I have to comment.'

Justin: The knee injury ruined Skinstad's World Cup build-up. And the incident has come up a few times when I've been in South Africa since then. But I've seen Bobby only once. It was after the World Cup final between France and Australia in Cardiff later that year. For some reason John Hart wanted us to go to the game. He thought it would look like sour grapes if we didn't turn up.

At any rate, after showing our faces for the TV cameras, a few of us left at halftime to go and have a few drinks. And we ended up at a bar where some of the Springboks and people involved with them were.

Bobby was there with Robbie Fleck. I had a chat with Fleck but Bobby didn't say a word to me and I didn't approach him either. He didn't seem to mind me being there. He didn't leave. But he obviously didn't want to share a drink for old times' sake.

Nice one, Stu

One of the nicest touches for me heading into the 1999 international season was that Daryl Gibson and I were both selected for the All Blacks squad.

We'd played together for Canterbury and the Crusaders. So a lot of people knew we were team-mates and good buddies too. What many people didn't know is that we're also related. We have common great-grandparents, Tony and Rose Marshall.

My grandfather Les and Gibbo's grandmother Doris were brother and sister, which makes us second cousins.

There were plenty of nice touches on the field too, as the All Blacks returned to their winning ways. They thumped France 54–7 at Wellington in late June and followed that with a comfortable 28–0 win over the Springboks at Carisbrook two weeks later.

Christian Cullen scored his eighth try in four tests, while Marshall also scored two in Dunedin. One of them was particularly special. He dashed from behind a maul to split the defence and sprint 30 metres to the try-line.

In his match report in the *Sunday News*, Campbell Mitchell noted: 'Justin Marshall silenced his critics with an impressive defensive effort. He's looking sharper with every match.'

The good vibes flowed into the next game two weeks later. Marshall eclipsed Graeme Bachop's record of most capped All Black halfback when he ran out against Australia at Eden Park in his 32nd test. And there were two more reasons for Marshall to celebrate afterwards. The All Blacks won 34–15 and he scored another try.

The victory ended the Wallabies 10-match winning streak. Campbell Mitchell declared in the *Sunday News* that the win erased the nightmare of three straight losses against Australia in 1998.

But that was a big call because there was still one more match against Australia to play. Maybe they were just setting us up for an even bigger nightmare, a loss to the old enemy in our last game before the World Cup?

The New Zealand public had to wait more than a month to find out. In the meantime the All Blacks went to Pretoria and beat the Springboks 34–18, with Marshall picking up another try.

As for erasing that nightmare . . . in typical fashion the Wallabies managed to un-erase it, beating the All Blacks 28–7 in Sydney.

It was time for former All Black captain Stu Wilson to throw an almighty tantrum in *The Truth*. His column was headlined 'Gutless Wonders', with the sub-heading 'Players shame the black shirt'.

Stu Wilson: It's tough when the All Blacks lose. And it's a fact of rugby life that we will lose from time to time. But what I can't tolerate is when we lose without putting up a fight — and that's exactly what happened last Saturday night . . .

We could have gone to the World Cup as the undisputed heavyweight champion-in-waiting but now we've been relegated to the rank of mere contender . . .

(After bagging various people) . . . Justin Marshall, too, must be on very thin ice.

Once again his efforts behind a beaten pack were awful and he returned to his laboured, rambling style of game.

He simply cannot reproduce the gutsy aggressive game we've seen from him in the past and John Hart must now be tempted to start with Byron Kelleher, whose passing is superior to that of the pedestrian Cantabrian's.

Ouch. Nice one, Stu.

Once again the passing issue was out in the public arena. It was also being talked about in private by the All Black management team of John Hart, Gordon Hunter, Peter Sloane and Wayne Smith. Marshall had played under Sloane and Smith at the Crusaders. But they weren't playing favourites where Marshall was concerned. Marshall was subbed off for Kelleher during the loss to Australia. Kelleher was in top form. He was the New Zealand Super 12 player of the year in 1999. The management team were looking at both players, weighing up the pros and cons of each and preparing themselves for a very tough decision.

1999 World Cup

The All Blacks started the World Cup with a 45–9 win over Tonga and a 30–16 win over England. On both occasions Marshall was subbed off so the selectors could watch more of Kelleher.

I think I'd been playing pretty well. The thing was when Byron was coming on as an impact player he was making an impact. He scored a try against Tonga. And when he came on with 20 minutes to go against England, he scored a try in that game as well. But that's not to say I wasn't doing my job . . . because we were winning and things were already going well whenever he came on. That gave him the freedom to try things and do things and express himself. That was because of what had been done before he even got on the field.

If Marshall was starting to worry, and you can be certain he was, Andrew Blowers gave him even more to think about. The pair collided at training and Marshall suffered a nasty cut that needed 10 stitches under one eye and down the side of his nose.

He wasn't picked for the win over Italy as the selectors played all of the remainder of the squad in this match, giving Kelleher a start and Rhys Duggan some game time.

Marshall was given the full 80 minutes in the 30–18 quarterfinal win over Scotland.

But when the team to play France in the semifinal was released, Kelleher was in the starting line-up, Marshall was on the bench.

Jim Kayes, *The Dominion*: Kelleher's selection is a surprise not because he does not deserve it, but because coach John Hart has steadfastly indicated throughout the tournament that Marshall was the out-and-out No. 1 halfback.

As recently as four days ago Hart reiterated Marshall's superiority in many aspects, but justified the apparent change of heart by saying Kelleher's selection was specifically for the French test.

'His selection is an assessment of the game and the opposition,' Hart said. 'He is a player we have seen developing all year and we have picked this game as the game for him.

'He has come on in three games so he has been exposed to the World Cup and the attributes he is showing are what we need against France.'

Those attributes include strong running around the fringes and a quick and accurate pass. Marshall's passing has been criticised constantly this year but Hart said the former All Black skipper, who has played 37 tests, is still in the picture.

'We're looking at each game as it comes and the final, if we get there, may be a totally different scenario.'

When you took his place at the 1999 World Cup was there any noticeable change in the way Justin acted towards you?

Byron Kelleher: I don't think he spoke to me for the rest of the year. But, sure, that would have been something that would have been highly disappointing for him. So communication wasn't great at that time.

Down and out

John Hart handed me one of the biggest disappointments of my career when he dropped me for the 1999 World Cup semifinal against France. And I wasn't satisfied with the reason he gave me either.

He called me up to his room. And his explanation to me was that I'd been copping criticism back home in New Zealand and that he and the management team had been defending me. It had been all over radio and TV and in the newspapers the past couple of days. People reckoned my pass was too slow and that it was disrupting the backline. So they were going to play Byron.

Black magic. Making a run during my New Zealand debut in the All Blacks' 51–21 win over Italy A in Catania in 1995.

Surrounded by legends. Sean Fitzpatrick (No. 2) lays down the law to the All Blacks before my test debut against France in Paris, 1995. We won 37–12.

Flying high. Diving in for a try during our 43–6 demolition of the Wallabies in Wellington in 1996.

FOTOPRESS

Phase one of the 1996 tour of South Africa is accomplished. Zinzan Brooke and I shake hands on a job well done, after beating South Africa in the first test, 29–18, in Cape Town. But Fitzy knows there's a long way to go.

PHOTOSPORT

'Best I hold on to it, boys.' I get swamped by Springboks during the 1996 tour of South Africa.

A taste of things to come. The All Blacks with the Tri-Nations' spoils after the first test win in Cape Town in 1996.

'At last!' We secure the All Blacks' first ever series win in South Africa, beating the Springboks 33–26 in the third test in Pretoria in 1996. The faces, on both teams, say it all.

All Blacks captain Justin Marshall. I always thought the title had a nice ring to it. But it only lasted for one tour match and four tests, including this one against Wales, which we won 42–7 in 1997.

'Has anyone seen my head? Martin Johnson seems to have misplaced it.' I've just been king hit from behind but no one seems to have noticed (during our 25–8 first test win over England at Old Trafford in 1997).

Out with the old and in with the new. Christian Cullen and I (right) sport the Canterbury All Black shirts for the last time, before the 54–7 win over France in Wellington, 1999. And, below, at Eden Park a month later, Taine, Mehrts, Kees Meeuws, Norm Maxwell and I wear the new adidas strip, before our 34–15 win over Australia.

A great rival. Joost van der Westhuizen shows the fighting spirit that helped make him such a brilliant halfback for South Africa. On this occasion, in 1999 in Pretoria, we beat them 34–18.

'Don't think I'm going to pass this one!' George Gregan knows it's too late to stop me charging through this gap in Tri-Nations action in 1999.

Under pressure. John Hart and I, above, are on a collision course but we're not quite aware of it yet. This photograph was taken heading into the 1999 World Cup quarterfinal against Scotland. I played and we won 30–18. Right: Gutted . . . Tony Brown and me on the bench during the semifinal against France. We lost 43–31.

I guess what I would have liked is for them to have sat me down and told me you've got deficiencies here, here and here and this is the reason that we're not going to play you. I could have dealt with that. But don't tell me that you've been listening to criticism back home that I'm not playing very well and you're going to base your decision on that.

I was stunned. We'd won every World Cup game I'd been involved with comfortably up until that time. So I must have been doing something right. For him to say *that*, and not actually give me a decent reason for leaving me out. . . I was just in a state of shock.

I tried to reason with them. I understood what they were saying but I didn't feel that media pressure was a reason for me to be left out of the side. I felt the team was doing fine. I agreed that Byron was playing well when he came on. So maybe they should do the same thing. Maybe give me the first half and him the second. Did they really need to make a drastic decision like this?

John Hart: Byron Kelleher played very well in that game against Italy and reinforced some of the views we had.

We were disappointed with Justin's game against Scotland. We decided to leave him out there for the full 80 minutes to see how he handled it. At the end of that game we certainly had a meeting as a selection panel. The selectors were the late Gordon Hunter, Peter Sloane and me. Wayne Smith was not a selector. But he was involved in all the discussions on selection. And in fact my recollection is that it was actually Wayne Smith who first raised the idea that we should drop Marshall.

We discussed that. We all believed that Kelleher's game at that stage was sharper, that we needed his clearance and that was the reason that we made the decision.

In the communication of that the normal process would be for the coaches, Peter and me, to meet with the player, which we did. We told him that we had dropped him because we didn't think his game was up to par, that we were concerned about his form and concerned about his pass.

To say that we dropped him because of media pressure is quite laughable. Maybe it was easier to believe that than the truth.

Taine Randell, All Black captain at the 1999 World Cup: They did explain to me why they were dropping him. Basically it was about his pass. They believed they needed a crisper pass against the French. There were a few other reasons as well but basically that's what it came down to, the sharper pass from Byron.

Justin: I didn't feel I'd been playing poorly enough for John Hart to leave me — somebody he'd had as a starting halfback for three years — out of the most important game in his coaching career or in my playing career. Did he not think that I was going to be able to produce the goods for him in the most important game the All Blacks had played since he'd been coaching?

It just really shocked me. And I took it badly.

And the worst thing — and it's something I feel bad about to this day — was that Peter Sloane was with him. The fact that he was in the meeting and that he was just nodding his head in agreement really irked me because Peter had coached me at the Crusaders. He's a guy who'd played a big part in my career. He must have known that if he said something, I'd listen to what he had to say. I respected him. Instead he retreated into his shell and went along with what Harty was saying, which, in my opinion, was a load of rubbish. I guess Peter Sloane probably agreed with the decision.

Sloane says he did agree with the decision to drop Marshall in favour of Kelleher. And he agrees with Hart and Randell that Marshall was dropped because his form hadn't been crash hot and there were concerns about his pass. He says that while the media pressure was discussed it wasn't offered to Marshall as the reason why they were dropping him.

Sloane says that he may have been sitting there saying nothing in the meeting with Marshall, but the real meeting had taken place between the selectors after the Scotland game. He'd had his say at that meeting and agreed Marshall should be dropped.

Sloane says that Justin Marshall aired his views on what happened at the World Cup once before in an article. Sloane personally found Marshall's comments hurtful and thought his attack on Hart in the article was nasty. He agrees with Marshall that their friendship has fallen away, but adds he still has huge respect for him as an All Black and a halfback.

Sloane concedes that dropping Marshall might have been the wrong decision.

Taine Randell: Firstly, I was astounded by the decision to drop him. But I felt that even though we were really good friends, because I was captain, I had to support the coach . . . and Byron. But now I'm ashamed of that.

I didn't go and chat to Justin straight after he was dropped. I left it for a few days. And that's the biggest regret of my career. It's a massive regret for me, more than anything else.

If I'd been a stronger captain at the time I would have stuck up for Justin. I definitely didn't think Harty was making the right decision, having played with Byron at Otago and having played with Justin a lot longer.

And, also, to take someone who'd been playing through the tournament, through the year, through the last four years and drop him at semifinal time seemed a bit strange.

I couldn't believe what they were doing, but I just said, 'Oh yeah, okay, righty-ho.' And it's annoyed me ever since that I didn't stick up for Justin and actually try to convince them otherwise and also that I didn't go and give him some support immediately after.

I was very mindful that Byron had come into the team and I didn't want to be seen to favour Justin. But at the very minimum I should have immediately gone and had a quiet word to him about the whole thing.

Flashpoint

Looking back, how would I describe the way I reacted to Harty's decision? Well, in a word, poorly. I've always been a bit of a sulker. So I sulked. I just couldn't get my head around it. And because the reasons he'd given angered me, I couldn't swallow the decision.

I couldn't stand being around Harty from then on. I avoided him and didn't communicate with him or talk to him for the rest of the trip pretty much. It was probably the classic example of someone who doesn't get their own way throwing their toys, I suppose.

Harty was on my case again throughout the week. He was obviously annoyed by my reaction, the way I'd been around the team, and the way I was treating him, which was basically not recognising the fact that he was there.

It came to a head at one of the training runs when, in front of the whole team, he said something like, 'There's a test match to play. Lift yourself up. Lift your feet or I'll take you off the bench and Rhys Duggan can have your place.'

I can't remember his exact words because I wasn't really interested in his voice at that stage.

I snapped back, 'We haven't even fuckin' *started* training yet.' That was about the last thing I said to him on tour.

He saw my body language, saw the way I'd reacted to the whole thing and he just took it upon himself to personally jump on me in front of the team. The boys knew how I felt. The whole thing was a bit of a shock to them. A lot of them were saying, 'What's going on? What did he say?'

I told them, and they couldn't believe it either.

Daryl Gibson: We were doing laps of the field and Harty had a go at him because he'd dropped his lip and got all shitty. And basically Justin told him to get fucked.

I thought it was a pretty harsh decision by Harty. And in hindsight it was probably the wrong decision. But, then again, we know the result now.

John Hart: I don't think it was the wrong decision. The decision was right. But the way he handled it wasn't great and I think he impacted quite negatively on the team during that time in terms of his reaction and the way he carried on at training, which made it very difficult.

My recollection of the incident at training is not as he alludes to it at all, other than the fact that I did say to him at some stage you'd better sharpen up because in terms of a team's preparation, he was doing nothing for us by sulking. Maybe they're the reasons he's not an All Black captain.

Taine Randell: There was a training session afterwards and Justin was just jogging around and Harty gave him an absolute rip about his body language. And that was unfair because everyone was just jogging around and he picked on Justin. Well, for whatever reason, you can't do that. You can't expect a guy who's been dropped from the semifinal to be overly cheery about it. I thought it was pretty harsh at the time.

Was he petulant? I don't remember Justin being destructive. In fact, no, it's not true at all.

I talked to him a few days after the decision had been made. It was before the game. He said, 'Why didn't you come and talk to me about it?'

I just admitted to him that I'd buggered it up.

Justin: And then we lost the bloody semifinal! Byron was injured so I came on for the last 10 minutes.

But the game was lost by then. It's a match that will live in the memories of all New Zealand rugby fans. The All Blacks led 24–10, only to lose 43–31 following an awesome second-half onslaught from the French. Afterwards, the All Blacks accused their opponents of testicle pulling and eye gouging. The All Blacks had no answers to the French dirt and no answers to the French flair. Some would say the man with the experience and personality to combat both those issues was sitting on the sideline.

Byron Kelleher: That loss in the semifinal had nothing to do with individuals. That was a team situation. We just didn't respond to the challenge in that second half as a team.

Taine Randell: It would have been interesting if he'd played, to see how things might have turned out.

Byron at that time was a lot younger. Physically, he was a fantastic athlete. But in terms of a rugby player, there was no comparison.

Justin also provided a lot of leadership. And the team we were, we didn't have a great deal of experience and leadership.

John Hart: In retrospect you'd probably say it might not have been the right decision because Byron got injured early in the game so we didn't actually get the advantage of Byron. But I don't think it was the wrong decision to pick him when you consider what we were trying to do and the form Byron was in. Unfortunately, our forwards didn't play well that day. So that didn't help, whoever was the halfback.

Justin: Byron's injury meant that I also had to play the match against South Africa to decide third and fourth. But I'd lost a lot of confidence because of what had happened to me as a player. I didn't play well in that game, at all. It would be one of the worst games I've ever played as an All Black.

John Hart: The other thing is Justin was still in the frame for the final against Australia, if we'd made it. Maybe against them Justin's set of skills might have been more what we wanted. We would have had Byron's game against France to weigh up as well. So we hadn't made that judgement. I think he made it for us himself, however, with his reaction.

We gave him another chance in the play-off for third and fourth. I see he takes it the other way. If he was a broken man by then, as he says, we should have played Rhys Duggan. But it doesn't matter.

Justin: John Hart was gone after that. He resigned as All Black coach. Wayne Smith was selected. And I was back in as All Black halfback.

Part Three:
The second half

Marriage

I came home from the World Cup depressed. But I had my wedding to look forward to.

All the boys were saying, 'Is your eye going to be all right? Nicolle's not going to be happy.' I was desperately rubbing vitamin E into the cut I received when I clashed heads with Andrew Blowers.

Nicolle had done all the planning while I was away. It was a huge undertaking because we had 200 guests. But it was a beautiful wedding and the guests still talk about it.

So the wedding and the honeymoon were a great change from rugby. And after the World Cup I really needed it.

Going into 2000 with this new direction in my life I made a conscious decision. I'm just going to go out and play my own game. If I don't get picked for the All Blacks, well I've had a good run. I've been to a World Cup and I've won a lot of test matches and I've really enjoyed it.

The result of that decision is that I've been an All Black ever since. From that point, being an All Black hasn't been a must for me, it's just happened. And I believe that has everything to do with the balance I've got in my life since being married.

Nicolle: Justin is very committed to his rugby. He'll freely admit that he hasn't got where he has purely by natural talent. It's also taken sheer hard work and his willingness to work harder than anyone else.

He's so incredibly disciplined. He went running in the snow on our honeymoon. We went to Hawaii and then we went skiing in Banff, Canada. He found a gymnasium wherever we went and he'd take off in the morning to train.

I was like, 'Give it a rest. Don't worry about it. Just sleep in and then we'll go and get some lunch. You can fit the training in later.'

But Justin said, 'No, no. If I do it now then it's out of the way for the day and then I can relax.' That's just how he is.

Justin: My life is different to a lot of other people's. Being a professional rugby player and a long-standing All Black puts its own strains on a relationship. We travel a lot. We're high profile. There are a lot of rumours about what we do. When we're away we have a lot of time on our hands and that can be difficult because you have all that talk about, 'When the boys are away, what goes on tour stays on tour.' That sort of crap can be a little unsettling, particularly when you're first starting to go out.

The good thing about Nicolle and me was that we never had a problem with that. Nicolle's not the sort of person that needs reassurance all the time. She doesn't need me to be ringing twice a day every day. I see some guys on tour and their phone bills must be horrendous.

But it's just something they need to do. They need to comfort their partners.

So that was quite good that I never had that added stress of a woman at home constantly needing that reassurance. I didn't need to ring back every day saying, 'I went here, I went there, and the team did this.' Too much of that gets uncomfortable. It gets to a point where you don't want to say what you're doing because it sounds like you're having too much of a good time. 'Oh, we went to the Eiffel Tower today. Then we went to the wax museum.'

And she's thinking, 'Well, you're really missing me, aren't you? Here I am at work and driving around in my car every day and sitting at home having dinner by myself. And you're gallivanting around Paris.'

I remember telling Nicolle once, 'We went out to this restaurant. It used to be rated one of the top five in the world and we had 12 courses.'

And she didn't seem very excited about it. That's when I started to click on to it. 'We should go one day, dear, when we come back to France. I'll keep the card.' I've still got the card actually. So maybe we'll go.

But Nicolle's independent attitude was a huge relief. It meant I was able to go away and not have to worry that Nicolle was unable to function on her own. She would just go out with her friends from work. She doesn't wait for me to come home before she goes out and does stuff. She just lives her own life.

It meant that I became a lot more comfortable within myself. That was important because I've got a stressful enough job as it is. I seem to invite a lot of criticism and I often feel under pressure. So I've really appreciated having a smooth home life and an understanding ear.

Jeans genie

Mike Anthony: Marshy and I did a good prank on Todd Blackadder once. Toddy had these jeans and they were bloody horrible. We got them as a team issue from Canterbury International in about 1996. And this was 2000 so he'd been wearing them non-stop for four years.

They were big saggy old things, just horrible, and we used to get into him about them. And one day we'd had enough. So we got into his room and flogged them. And we cut them up into small pieces and started posting them to him, or we'd leave some in his room or on his seat in the bus or in his place in the changing room.

So bit by bit he got his jeans back.

I'd rung Toddy's wife Priscilla and said, 'Look, we're going to do this.' So she went out and got him a new pair of jeans. Of course, he didn't like them. He preferred the old ones. And eventually he got them back.

There was a similar prank they were running in the Canterbury NPC team at one stage. They were cutting legs off guys' track pants and arms off guys' jackets.

But Marshy loves any of that carry-on.

Paddy O'Brien, New Zealand referee: Justin's biggest quality in my view was his insatiable desire to be a winner. He would give his all for his team and could be quite dour on the field. He wasn't a big sledger. But he was a player who would question a call and then appear to sulk if things didn't go his way.

As my career went on I gathered a huge amount of respect for Justin simply because of the completely professional way he approached games and his ability to shrug off a lot of negative feedback he used to get from the public.

Being a fellow Southlander I always admired his straightforwardness and the fact he was prepared to just be himself. His longevity at the top level speaks for itself and I would rank him right up there with George Gregan as the best halfback I refereed throughout my 10 years at the top level.

I only really saw him lose it completely once. That was the day he clashed with André Watson in a round-robin game and started walking from the field even though he hadn't been sin-binned.

Oops, I did it again

The Crusaders versus the Brumbies is always a grudge match because the two franchises have been so dominant in the Super 12. It's usually pretty close between us and this one in May 2000 is no different.

We're at Jade Stadium. There's 11 minutes left and they're up 17–12. But we're on attack. We've set a maul and the plan is to drive the ball over for a try. So I'm pushing the forwards along and step by step we're making ground.

André Watson, the South African, is refereeing. 'That maul's stopped,' he says, 'you'd better get it moving again.'

'Come on, guys!' I yell. 'Keep going forward!'

The maul rumbles on slowly. 'Yeah, yeah,' I say, glancing at André, 'we are still going forward, sir.'

'Clear the ball, halfback,' he says. 'Clear the ball. You must clear the ball.'

'But we are still moving forward, sir. We are still going forward.'

He blows his whistle and awards a turnover to the Brumbies. I mean, this is a crucial stage of the game. There's very little time left on the clock. And this is possibly our last opportunity to score a try and win the match. I'm furious. The maul was clearly still moving forward so there was no reason for us to have to clear that ball, and they were struggling to contain us. And suddenly, thanks to André, they've got the advantage.

I can't help myself. 'Shit, André! What are you doing? There was nothing wrong with that maul!' I'm just fuming by now and I pretty much give it to him. His face sets in that 'don't you start that with me, young fellow' sort of look. He pulls back a step and reaches with his hand towards his pocket.

I'm watching him closely and I'm thinking, 'That's it. He's going to yellow card me or red card me. Either way, I'm gone. Hell, I don't want to be here anyway. This is ridiculous!'

So I start walking toward the players' tunnel.

You might have seen the TV footage. André Watson looks like the disgruntled boss and Marshall the defiant office worker. Suddenly, Marshall throws his hands up and storms out of the office, muttering, 'Take this job and shove it!' Except Marshall isn't in an office. He's in a rugby match. And time's running out.

So I'm storming off the field and eventually, as I'm jogging along, I notice the noise in the stadium drops down a notch. It's quieter. I glance up at a couple of the players. And they're just staring at me. I slow down to a walk. I look around at a few more faces. And they're all staring at me. Suddenly, I realise the whole bloody stadium's staring at me and I stop. I turn around and look at André Watson. He's staring at me too, and his face says, 'What the . . . ?'

Then it hits me. He hasn't given me a card at all. And everyone's wondering where the hell I'm going.

For a split second my anger evaporates and everything is clear. I can see that I must look a bit foolish running away from the ref. The other thing is I've moved away from the spot where my immediate responsibilities lie, back where play's stopped, and I need to get back there, preferably without making an even bigger tit of myself. I'm going to have to make it seem that what I just did was a perfectly normal mistake.

Anyway, I sheepishly yet grumpily head back to where André's waiting and get back into position for play to restart.

We lose the game. And afterwards there's a huge reaction to my behaviour in the media. I also end up getting cited for it by the citing commissioner. I didn't get a yellow card on the field, but I got the equivalent of one at a judicial hearing the next day.

The judiciary panel gave me a real working over. They told me I was lucky I hadn't got more of a punishment because it was my second such incident, the first being when I cursed and shook my fist at John Hart for subbing me against Australia.

Once again my status as a role model had been called into question. The panel was well aware there was a swarm of media waiting for me outside. So they told me: 'When you go out we want you to apologise for your behaviour and make sure that your message comes across. Do it right so that people recognise you can't carry on that way and react to referees that way.'

So I went out and faced the media. They were waiting in a room called the Principal's Office, which was quite appropriate because I felt I was being treated like a naughty schoolboy. And I didn't like it. I knew I was right and that André Watson had made a wrong decision that probably cost us the game. Sure I had overreacted to his mistake but he was probably lucky that my overreaction had overshadowed his mistake.

I was still pretty wild when they told me to go and apologise. So I just went out there and went through the motions. I put no heart into it at all. I skirted around the issue. I eventually got the words out: 'I'd just like to apologise for the way I reacted.' But I did it in a really sombre voice and didn't put any effort into it whatsoever, so it looked like I was just reading off a sheet of paper.

The Crusaders went on to win their third Super 12 title in a row, when they famously pipped the highly favoured Brumbies 20–19 at Canberra. It was a fitting way to mark Robbie Deans' first year as coach.

Robbie — 'It's simple'

Robbie Deans is, arguably, New Zealand's most successful rugby coach. In his first season in charge of Canterbury in 1997 they won the NPC. After managing the triumphant

Crusaders in 1998 and '99, he coached the team to the three-peat, in 2000, to a fourth title in 2002, and to the runners-up spot in 2003 and '04.

Deans joined John Mitchell as assistant coach of the All Blacks in late 2001 and the team had a brilliant run until the semifinal loss to Australia at the World Cup, after which they both lost their jobs.

Robbie and I have had a lot of success in the time we've been together. But I think a lot of that has to do with the way we relate to each other. Robbie knows that I can be volatile and I know he can be a bit like that too.

I feel that when I speak to him and I question some of the things that he's trying to achieve, it actually is helping him. And he is doing the same thing for me. So we actually work together quite well.

We've had our run-ins. I remember I've had times when he's sat me on the bench for a game or two or he's questioned aspects of my game. And I've spent nights in the kitchen complaining about him to Nicolle and nights when I couldn't get to sleep because I'm stewing about something Robbie's said or done.

But Nicolle advised me that I just had to go and tell him how I felt. He's the type of guy who senses when I'm not happy. And if I don't get things off my chest I'm a real sulker and things tend to eat me up.

So what I've done in the last few years of our relationship is that if he does something that annoys me I'll just front him about it. He either gives me a lame explanation of his reasoning or he'll give me an explanation that I can understand. But either way I'll accept it. And if it's one of those answers where I feel I need to prove him wrong, you should see the determination in my eyes to do that. The best part is always proving him wrong.

But we've come a long way in the last three or four years and we've worked really well together both in the Crusaders and the All Blacks.

We've had a couple of run-ins. He left me out one year in a Crusaders game. He had his reasons. I'd played averagely and he wanted to give Aaron Flynn a game. But I wanted to be involved and I wanted to play.

Often if I've had an average game, I find the best way for me to put it right is to go out and play another game. I always say to coaches, 'If you're thinking about giving me some game time but giving the other guy a start, well don't. Start me because I'm used to starting. Bring me off after 40 minutes. What difference does it make? We'll still both be playing 40 minutes.'

I think I start the game better than Aaron Flynn, and I think he's a better impact player than me because I'm not used to adapting to the pace of the game.

Anyway, Robbie decided to leave me out of this game for one reason or another.

And I was down. I sulked. I was depressed. It really got to me. My lip dropped and the boys could see it. They started teasing me.

We got to training and I refused to get off the bus. The team all got out of the bus and grabbed all the bags and started to head out towards training. And there I was, sitting on my own in the back of the bus with my arms folded looking out the window, sulking like a spoilt little child.

It wasn't that long ago. That's the worst thing. I would have been about 28.

So that was a really bad moment for me and my time with Robbie. But I got over it. I got off the bus eventually. He loves teasing me about that.

Deans also had an exceptional playing career as a fullback for Canterbury, scoring 1641 points in 146 appearances, and the All Blacks, playing five tests and 14 games in 1983 and '84.

Robbie Deans and I were helping Daniel Carter with his high kick-offs at training the other day. And Robbie said, 'This reminds me of when I was doing kick-offs with the All Blacks. Andy Haden said to me, "Don't kick them so high." I said, "Why?" And Haden said, "Because I'm getting there too quick and I can't compete for the ball."'

Robbie turned round to him and said, 'It's simple, Andy. Just run a little bit fuckin' slower.'

And that just about sums Robbie up. It does actually make sense. If you run a little bit slower you're actually going to get there at the right time.

But it's a bit like that story with Richard Loe and me at Canterbury scrum practice. Haden was a legend while Robbie hadn't been an All Black all that long. But he didn't give a shit.

Robbie Deans: We had a Crusaders camp at Hanmer at the start of 2002 and we gave them an exercise at the start. They had to do some orienteering that would lead them to the place where we were camping for the night. So first they were given tents and food and other survival equipment. Marshy's group managed to get the biggest and flashest tent. The downside of that was they had to cart it during the orienteering phase through some rough country to get to the campsite. In the meantime the weather started to pack in.

'There's a change of plan,' I said. 'We won't camp out here after all. Make your way with your tents back to the Heritage Hotel. When you get there, you can select your campsite out in front of the hotel.'

When we got back Justin was standing there and his team hadn't selected a campsite. Everyone else had chosen their sites and were putting up their tents and so forth.

So I said to Marshy, 'Are you going to put your tent up?'

'You can't be serious?'

'Yeah, I am.'

'But it's raining. And I've got a sniffle.'

So what came out of that conversation was that Justin's team had cracked. Everyone called them Team Crack after that and the name stuck.

In the end, though, everyone camped outside the doors of the hotel. Actually, I think Norm Maxwell might have snuck back into the hotel at one stage. But the message was to resist temptation, even when it's right at your doorstep. There are no short cuts.

So we pushed that theme throughout the campaign. The upshot of it was that we went through the Super 12 unbeaten that year. We played the Brumbies in the final at Jade and beat them 31–13.

Well, I walk into the dressing room after the win. All the boys are over the moon. And as soon as Justin spots me, he yells out: 'Now tell me this. What good did it do us, camping out at Hanmer?'

That's Justin to a tee. He just wouldn't let it go.

Justin: The one thing that I want to stress about Robbie Deans is that, for my money, he's the best coach I've ever had. While Wayne Smith is the most technical coach I've had, Robbie's the best technically. And there's a difference. In terms of understanding the game and planning and achieving what he wants to do, Robbie's very on to it.

He's not too long out of the game as a player. He knows what sort of environment the players thrive in. He knows when to give them a bit of rope and he knows when to pull the rope back. And that's not something you can teach people, that's something you pick up through experience.

I think what he's done for the Crusaders and Canterbury will be unmatched. He and John Mitchell had the All Blacks playing the best rugby I've been involved with. And it's a real shame he was made a scapegoat and never got to show his full expertise. I believe he, even more so than Mitch, could have made a real impact on New Zealand rugby.

And he still could. I'd like to think there are no sulkers up in the Rugby Union. And that if there was an opportunity that they would open the door for him again because that's a door that needs to be opened.

You never know whether our paths will cross again in a working rugby environment. But I certainly hope so.

Robbie Deans: Marshy never likes getting subbed off. He's getting better at masking his body language. But I don't have a problem with that. That's the way he is and that's what drives him. That's why he is who he is. He's got a big flame that burns. There's nothing wrong with that. The only issue is — and we've talked about this — if he allows that to manifest itself in a way that's not constructive to the team.

In the early days he used to take a bit of flak about his bottom lip. But he's moved on from there.

By George!

Sport is full of great rivalries. In boxing, there's Ali and Frazier, in tennis, Borg and McEnroe. And in the era of professional rugby, the most fascinating and fierce rivalry has been between Justin Marshall and George Gregan. And it's been played out in the shadow of two even bigger rivalries, the Crusaders and the Brumbies in the Super 12 and the All Blacks and the Wallabies in the Bledisloe Cup.

The first couple of years I played against George in the Bledisloe Cup were 1996 and '97 and the All Blacks won comfortably.

But in 1998 they cleaned us out 3–0, starting a five-year reign. That was a real frustrating time for the All Blacks and for all of New Zealand because from then on there were only two matches in each series and, as the holders, Aussie had to win only one of them to retain the Bledisloe Cup. They 'won' three of those series 1–1. And they always seemed to win the second test in the final minutes of the game. It was great drama but hell on the nerves.

And of course George Gregan was always in there directing traffic for the Aussies, yapping at the ref, having a go at us and generally buzzing around like a hyperactive bee in a bottle.

Playing against George is like playing against a character from an Energizer battery commercial. He just keeps going and going and going. Some players will have a little lull and then regroup for another burst. But George knows only one speed — flat out.

Of course, that's brilliant for the Wallabies. But it seems to rub a lot of Kiwi fans up the wrong way. And because of that George isn't all that popular over in New Zealand. So people often get a shock before big Super 12 and test matches when they see us out together having a coffee.

When we first started playing together, I'd shake George's hand at the end of the game and that was it. I guess I took my rugby off the field. I wanted to stay aloof and keep that rivalry strong.

But over the years I've loosened up, matured and realised George is a bloody good bloke. We've developed a solid friendship. But we're still staunch rivals on the field.

Those personal battles on the field have been as close and keenly fought as most of the Bledisloe Cup matches they've played.

In 2000, New Zealand won the first test 39–35 in Sydney with a last gasp Jonah Lomu try. The Bledisloe looked set to return to New Zealand in the second test in Wellington until Wallaby captain John Eales kicked a pressure penalty to win the match 24–23 in the fifth minute of injury time!

George Gregan: One of the funniest verbal stoushes we had was in that test in Wellington. The All Blacks were on attack. We turned the ball over and I cleared from our 22 and I kicked the ball out.

He looked at me and said, 'That's really positive, George. Thanks for giving us the ball back.' He had this smile on his face because he thought he had me.

I said, 'It's all right, Marshy. The way your lineout's going we'll just knock it back like we've been doing all day. It's as good as won.'

The competitive bloke he is, he just shook his head and cursed under his breath. He had nothing to come back with. I got him that time.

In Sydney the next year, in John Eales' last game as captain, Toutai Kefu broke New Zealand hearts. With 80 seconds left, he crashed through four tacklers, including Justin Marshall, to plant the ball next to the posts for a 29–26 win.

All Black coach Wayne Smith pretty much walked the plank after that one, and John Mitchell took over with Robbie Deans helping out.

In 2002 we thought we were on our way.

We beat the Aussies 12–6 in freezing conditions in 'the battle of Jade Stadium'. The tackling that had kept the Wallabies at bay all night reached heroic proportions after All Black centre Mark Robinson was sin-binned for an early tackle with seven minutes left.

Afterwards Justin Marshall told reporters that the All Blacks now had the self-belief and resolve to beat the Wallabies in the close ones that counted.

If that was tempting fate the newspapers went a step further. The NZPA match report said the win in Christchurch erased the bad memories of a string of last-minute losses to the Wallabies.

Just like they did in 1999, the newspapers claimed a first-test win would erase the bad memories.

On that occasion, the Aussies un-erased the bad memories by beating us in the second test to retain the Bledisloe Cup and take a huge psychological advantage into the World Cup.

If anything, Kiwis' bad memories of last-minute losses were more vivid than ever. We were all thinking, 'Surely, they can't do that to us again. Can they?'

Meanwhile, Justin Marshall was consorting with the man many Kiwis consider the enemy.

While his team-mates flew back home, Gregan was up in Sumner, having a barbecue at Marshall's house, which the Zambian-born Aussie had dubbed the Taj Mahal.

I'd been talking up my barbie skills for three years and finally George took me up on the offer. I actually think that weekend I was more nervous about the barbecue than I was about the test at Jade Stadium.

The reason I was nervous went back to a small but embarrassing incident during a previous visit by George. Now George holds a coffee franchise in Australia and is an expert on the drink. So when I innocently offered to make him a coffee and pulled out the packet of instant, he was mortified.

He jumped to his feet and magically produced a plunger and his own supply of the real stuff.

I promised I'd buy a plunger and some real coffee before he returned.

And how did we go, erasing those memories of last-minute losses? Well, the All Blacks went over to Sydney and Matthew Burke missed a simple conversion that would have put the Wallabies ahead with six minutes remaining. That was fairly positive. Unfortunately, he showed nerves of steel to kick them to a 16–14 win with another penalty in the last second. So, not that good. Shame, that.

Sometimes it's easier to handle being thrashed than being pipped. Being pipped is the worst feeling, particularly if it's in a test match against one of the old enemies and particularly when you've dominated the game. If you look at the contests George and I have been involved in over the years, he's won more of the tight ones. I don't like that but I do have to concede it to him.

There's also one other area where he beats me hands down. That's yapping at the referee. It actually gets on my wick during a game. And I usually tell him too. Because we're good mates now, he'll sometimes flash me a smile. But if he's really wound up it'll go right over his head and he'll just keep complaining.

In the end John Mitchell's rampant All Blacks of 2003 had to do a smash and grab job on the Wallabies to wrest back the Bledisloe.

So did we have the last laugh? Not at all, because winning the Bledisloe Cup that year was a bit like winning the first of two tests in previous years, not quite half the job. In 2003, George Gregan had the last laugh as he taunted Byron Kelleher, 'Four years, mate, four years,' in the final stages of the All Blacks' 22–10 World Cup semifinal loss.

And in the post-World Cup apocalypse, Graham Henry's team managed to hold on to the Bledisloe Cup in 2004 in the least satisfying way, winning the first test and losing the second.

But only a year after the World Cup loss, most New Zealanders were still shrugging their shoulders, saying, 'Bledisloe, Schmedisloe.'

Match of the century

Like so many before him, Wayne Smith's All Black coaching reign started like one of those dreams where you're flying, but ended like one of those dreams where you're falling.

First up there were big wins over Tonga and Scotland. And then there was the Bledisloe Cup clash they call the match of the century. The test was played in Sydney in July 2000 so it's hard to know which century the experts were talking about. But it could possibly qualify as the best in either century.

Tana Umaga, Pita Alatini and Christian Cullen all scored tries in the first three minutes. Andrew Mehrtens converted them and added a penalty to give the All Blacks a 24–0 lead after nine minutes.

The world record crowd of 109,874 was silent . . . but not for long.

The Wallabies hit back with four tries and two conversions to lock the scores 24–all at the break.

Justin Marshall scored a brilliant try, which boosted the All Blacks' confidence with half an hour remaining.

But the bloody Aussies clawed their way back again when Jeremy Paul — originally a Kiwi! — crashed over out wide to put his side up 35–34 with only three minutes left.

Just enough time for flanker Taine Randell to flick an overhead pass to Jonah Lomu and for the giant winger to tiptoe down the sideline to pinch a 39–35 win.

'I'm just really proud of these guys,' said Wayne Smith at the time.

'Quite often when momentum swings like that, you can't halt it. But these guys were able to halt it and throw it back at them in the second half. It's a pretty proud moment.'

I haven't even sat down and watched the test they call the match of the century. But I don't feel I need to. I've watched hardly any of the great games I've played in.

Dad's taped almost all of my 77 tests and a lot of Crusaders and Canterbury games too. They're all sitting in a big box at home. It's a fantastic resource. But I'll save that pleasure until later. I'm sure that once I've finished playing, I'll get a lot of enjoyment out of watching what I used to do.

At this stage, I prefer to use my own natural video, my mind. It's good for my game. And I don't like to let other images interfere with that process too much.

In their next test, the All Blacks beat the Springboks 25–12 in Christchurch. And Neil Reid of the *Sunday News* singled out Justin Marshall for special praise in one of his reports.

Justin Marshall confirmed his standing as New Zealand's top halfback yesterday.

The Crusaders No. 9 made his presence felt in the first five minutes when he out-sprinted his South African opposite Werner Swanepoel to a loose ball during the Tri-Nations test at Jade Stadium.

Swanepoel looked like he was about to open the scoring when the ball bounced loose behind the All Blacks line but Marshall pounced.

He lunged at Swanepoel and got his fingertips to the ball a fraction of a second before his opposite.

Seven minutes later Marshall ignited an All Blacks attack with a sharp burst into the Springboks' 22-metre area.

When he opted not to run his passing was sharp and accurate.

Marshall has been in sizzling form for the 2000 All Blacks.

But things went downhill from there. Wallaby captain John Eales made sure of that in Wellington with that penalty kick in injury time. Then the Springboks got their revenge, beating the All Blacks 46–40 in Johannesburg.

Video uneasy

As I've said, Wayne Smith is the most technically proficient coach I've worked with. That doesn't make him the best or mean that I agree with all his methods.

For instance, Wayne's a big fan of video analysis. But as I've said, I have huge reservations about it. I think it can sometimes give you a false sense of reality, a false sense of what actually happened out on the field. I believe that by looking at footage players can make excuses for themselves.

And I've always said this to coaches. What players have to recognise is, yes, they can get the feedback and the information off the video screen. But a lot of what they feel and see in real time on the field is what they should go with. In a game if you feel, 'Man, I should have got that guy,' then trust that. You should have got him. And don't let it happen again. If you feel, 'Shit, I made the wrong decision and we missed a try,' then trust that. You mucked up.

If you get that gut feeling and you know within yourself at the time, during the game, what you should have done, then make that your reference point, not what you might see in the video afterwards. The reason for that is you don't play rugby in a video room. You play it out on the field.

I remember talking to Richie McCaw after a close loss for the Crusaders once.

I'd been ill and he asked, 'How'd you feel coming through that, Marshy, after that virus you've had?'

I said, 'I actually felt quite good, Richie. I was pretty much thinking I was going to hit the wall, coming up against the Brumbies. But I felt okay. I really only started to struggle in the last 10 minutes. And to be honest, mate, I could have done more, but I guess I was worried about my fitness and I was trying to pace myself.'

'Funny, you should say that,' he said, 'because I kind of felt the same. There were times when I could have done a bit more. And there were times when I thought I couldn't get somewhere when actually I could have.'

'Yeah, okay,' I said.

And then the next day we were chatting away and he said to me, 'Hey, I had a look at the videotape and I saw that I actually got around the field okay. I got about a lot better than I thought I had.'

And I said to him, 'But mate, you shouldn't trust that because you said that you felt that you could have done more and could have got to different places. But now that you've seen yourself on TV and watched yourself, you've suddenly decided that it was okay.'

But it's not okay.

The TV image that you're watching might be okay. But the TV image is something completely different to the person. One is a video image. If you make excuses for it, it won't change or respond. The other is a human being. If you make excuses for it, it will respond accordingly and quite possibly negatively.

The other thing players need to remember is this: If you're using video to analyse yourself out of trouble before a game, that's useful. But if you're using it to analyse yourself out of trouble after a game, that's too late. The final whistle has blown, my friend.

A player will say straight after the game, 'Sorry, Marshy, I think I went the wrong way there.'

And I'll say, 'Yeah, you did.'

Or they'll say, 'I should have made that tackle.'

And I'll say, 'Yeah, I think he was your man. You should've got him.'

Then they'll come back a couple of days later and say, 'Mate, if you look at the video this guy's coming across here, and we needed to cover this guy over here. And I didn't really have enough time to go there.'

But I believe players can fool themselves because I don't think TV is a great judge of distance and time and the views coming through the camera are different to the ones on the field. I believe a lot of what people see when they're watching a game on TV is different to what the player sees on the rugby field.

And because of this belief, I don't review my games any more. The coaches are always at me about it. But I've always been one of those players who can totally take in my entire game and analyse it in my head.

I can come off the field, sit back for 20 minutes and go through the whole thing. I know what I've done on the field and I know when I should have done things differently. I file it all away in the back of my mind and use it as homework for my next game.

Wayne Smith: Justin's a unique person. He's the kind of player that you model things on to teach others. You use great players to turn other people into good players.

And while you might use Justin as a model, not everything he's able to do can be replicated by the players you're coaching.

He's able to go back and break down every move in a game and he has got great self-awareness. And that's what you want your players to have. Coaching is about ensuring players have self-awareness and encouraging them to take responsibility for improving their performance. Most players need some help with that, particularly early on in their development.

Not every player develops that ability and someone like Justin is very lucky in that regard. Other players rely on assistance to work out what they did well and what they can improve and that's often why video is used.

John Mitchell, All Black coach 2001–03: The guy has such great self-awareness that you don't actually have to sit him down on a computer and have a formal meeting about stats and so forth. He's the type of guy you just go and put your arm around, walk to training with and say, 'Go have a look at this clip on the video. I'm interested to know what you think.' Just leave it with him. If you want to demonstrate something, you just chew the fat with him and move the salt shakers around at the lunch table.

His self-awareness is so good, you just have to let him know what your concern is informally and he'll make all the necessary adjustments. You don't have to put him through total formality to achieve that. When you've got a guy with his knowledge, you have to trust their self-awareness.

Accidents will happen

Scott Robertson: Because Justin and I both lived in Sumner, he always used to pick me up before games or vice versa. So I got to know him quite well.

And I'll tell you what, it didn't matter who we were playing or what the occasion was, his preparation for matches was always the same.

He never liked anyone that we played. Any team that we played, he basically said, 'I hate these bastards.'

And that was it. He'd build himself up into a little storm of anger.

NZPA, 12 May 2001: All Black halfback Justin Marshall has avoided suspension despite being found guilty of stamping rival Byron Kelleher during the Crusaders' final round Super 12 rugby game with the Highlanders in Carisbrook on Saturday.

Marshall received a temporary suspension, the equivalent of a yellow card, for the incident early in the Highlanders 26–21 victory.

Kelleher had to leave the field briefly to receive treatment for a gashed hand.

Byron Kelleher: It was just the cowboy in him coming out. He's definitely a feisty competitor and I suppose that was just a heat of the moment action that happens during a game. But as far as I'm concerned whatever happens on the field stays on the field. I don't judge people on how they behave on the field. I judge them off the field and off the field he's awesome.

In our earlier clashes I think it was definitely a case of the schoolboy bully trying to stamp some authority on the young kid. Every now and then there'd be a few nudges towards one another. He'd be at the bottom of a ruck and I'd accidentally wipe my sprigs across his back. And if Justin saw me at the bottom of a ruck I'm sure he'd give me a nice little jab or an elbow to the face. They're just little reminders to each other.

Justin: The thing I remember most about that game is the refereeing of Steve Walsh. For some reason he penalised me three times in 10 minutes. And they were little things. He marched me for backchatting at one stage. Now if you look at the 'penalties against' column in my stats year in year out you'll find that I get penalised very rarely, maybe three to five times in a season. But this guy found three reasons to penalise me in 10 minutes!

When Steve Walsh and I are on the field, you have two similar egos going at each other. And on this particular day he was pissing me off the way he was carrying on. It was a spiteful game anyway because it was Canterbury-Otago. The crowd at Carisbrook gets into you; that can be annoying. And Byron was pumped up about playing against me. So everything conspired to create a very charged atmosphere.

There was an incident where I ran around the side of the ruck, passed the ball and was about to carry on following it up when he just hit me late. Obviously, he'd been gunning for me. He'd seen me run with the ball and he'd come after me. Fortunately, I saw him out of the corner of my eye. I actually managed to half-pie catch him on the way and I flipped him with a hip-toss. He ended up on the ground. And, because I knew he'd come after me later, I stormed straight over to where he was lying and planted my feet right beside where he was, so I could grab his jersey and, basically, give him what for.

I was in a bad mood as it was, so hitting me late was just asking for trouble. But while I was planting my feet next to him, I must have stood on his hand. Now that was a total fluke; not a bad idea when I think about it, but still a total fluke.

A lot of people, including team-mates and players from other teams, have said to me since then, 'You did that on purpose, didn't you, Marshy? You could see on the TV that you did it on purpose.' But I can tell you now: I didn't. And I've got no reason to lie about it. Why would I lie? If I did it, I'd say, 'Of course I did. I saw it sitting there. If you're going to late tackle me, then don't leave your hand lying around within stomping distance. It might get split open.' But it was actually a fluke. It's just where my foot ended up as I went to grab at his jersey.

Todd Blackadder was there as well and he was grabbing at Byron too, because he saw the whole thing unfold. There was actually a good picture of the incident in one of the papers. Byron's lying on the ground and Toddy and I are standing over him with the angriest faces.

Anyway, the game continued from there. Toddy and I carried on. The next thing I knew Byron was going off the field and I had no idea what for. I didn't know anything about his hand until the end of the game when somebody said I'd stood on it.

There was no malice intended; well, not towards his hand anyway.

The response in the media was mixed. One reporter wrote, 'Justin Marshall was at his petulant best. The Crusaders halfback showed . . . why he cannot be considered for the All Blacks captaincy.

'His spiteful stomp on Byron Kelleher, cheap high shot on Tony Brown and then the abuse he directed at referee Steve Walsh were not what you'd expect from a 48-test veteran.

'And it was a display that should silence the Justin Marshall for All Blacks captain brigade.

'Marshall is New Zealand's best halfback when he plays the game. But last Saturday's display was a shocker. And the slap on the wrist he received from the New Zealand Rugby Union a disgrace.'

Now that's a telling off!

NZ Rugby World started their article saying: 'That bloody Justin Marshall! He shouldn't be an All Black.'

But they began to show their true intentions later in the piece.

'That's the thing about Marshall. He's a scrapper. His game is in your face, abrasive and aggressive.

'His approach is akin to that of a street brawler. He'll improvise, do everything he can

to beat you, won't give up until he's knocked out cold and when he does get one up on you he'll take great joy in letting you know about it'.

And finished up with: 'Yep. I think of all this and say Justin Marshall shouldn't be an All Black. He should be All Black captain.'

Clashing egos!

He says when you're both on the field it's as if two very similar egos are clashing against each other.

Steve Walsh, New Zealand referee: I think that's . . . yeah, that's right. Here's how I feel. At the end of the day I have always, on the field, thought Justin Marshall was a bit of an arsehole.

When things don't go his way, and let's face it, the referee's always going to make decisions that teams aren't happy with, he goes out of his way to let me know he's really unhappy and he throws his toys out of the cot.

When you walk past someone, pre-match or after the match, usually you'd acknowledge them. He'll just keep on walking but give you the impression he knows that you're there.

So he'll kind of walk past and he won't snob you but . . .

No, he does. He definitely snobs you. And he does it in such a way that he lets you know he's doing it deliberately.

But I think he is right. We're probably both pretty similar and we both don't like to be wrong.

Do you remember the game when he stamped on Byron's hand?

In that game he and I and the Crusaders had a real clash. I was penalising them heavily.

I know I allowed a player to get under my skin. And I still remember that day and have learned from it so much. Because he and I clashed, I ended up focusing on Justin as opposed to focusing on the match.

From that moment onwards, whenever I've refereed a team with Marshall in it, before the match, I've had to talk to myself and tell myself that he's got to be totally out of the equation. I tell myself that if he has a crack at me then I'm just not going to respond to it.

Because he had got under your skin that day?

He did, yeah.

You don't remember what he said?

Look, mate, I can tell you now. He had a crack at me a couple of times through the game. And I'd had a gutsful of it, banged him, and then once he just gave me a bad look and I penalised him for a bad look, which is just the worst.

Mate, when he had that lightbulb hairdo or the Meg Ryan one you could've penalised him every game.

And he knew what I did and I knew what I did and it didn't go down too well.

But in saying all of that, the first time I got to speak to him on a social basis was last year (2004) and I liked the guy as a person. Up until then I've always told people I hated him. It's getting to know somebody on a personal level away from the game.

This was after a match. We were out on the jars. I just think he's probably matured a bit. Anyway, he comes up and says, 'I understand you hate me.'

He's a subtle character. And what did you say?

I told him I did. But then we had a chat about the reasons why. I know that he's mates with Gregan. And I told Gregan that I didn't like Marshall and stuff. It all got around. Funnily enough, I've just come home from South Africa on a plane last night with Gregan and he said, 'I understand you and Marshy had a sort-out.' So the word's got around.

Are there any other games where you two have clashed on the field?

Look, to be frank, I think almost every time. But there's been nothing quite as dramatic as what happened down at Dunedin that day.

Other than that, he's been replaced with 10 minutes to go, as I remember, in Christchurch and it's just before a kick-off at halfway and as he's leaving he just says, 'You've had an absolute shocker!' You know? Just as he's running past me. I can hardly stop and penalise him for dissent as he's leaving the field. He just used to say things like that to get under my skin. Or he might have said something like, 'You're a joke,' as he's left the field. It used to really bug me.

So next time you do a Crusaders game do you think he's going to bug you?

I honestly think that we've probably had a sort-out. We probably understand where we both are.

And I'm actually pleased because I spent three days in Nelson with the All Blacks prior to the 2003 World Cup. Before that, look, I always used to think that Justin Marshall was a bit of a slack halfback, you know, slow pass, like everybody. And actually getting in there and seeing him in the team, that was the first time I realised just how important he is to a team. He's such a dominant figure. Look, I mean, I still feel he's the best halfback New Zealand's got, by a long way.

Dog Eat Dog

During the writing of this book, Justin and I tossed around a few possible titles. He suggested *Nine Lives*, which, interestingly, I'd already thought of, because it was a play on his jersey number and reflective of the way he kept making it back into the All Blacks. But we both felt it was a bit soft. And Justin was adamant he didn't want any 'cheesy' plays on his position as halfback.

A friend of mine at TV3, where I'm a producer, suggested *The Better Half*. I tried it out on a few people in the office and noted quite a few women liked this title (you have to consider carefully what appeals to women when you're writing a sports book).

The publishers meanwhile were very keen on *No Half Measures*. Both were clever and relevant. But Justin felt, and I agreed, we should stay away from anything including the word half. And the publishers reluctantly gave in.

In the end Justin suggested *Dog Eat Dog*. I loved it straight away. And both our wives liked it too. They felt it captured Justin's confrontational, combative nature. So, basically, it was settled. Justin and I were happy and we had the women's perspective on board too.

The main reason I liked it, I admit, was because one of my favourite crime writers, Edward Bunker, had written a novel called *Dog Eat Dog*. Having said that, to me, *Dog Eat Dog* sums up Justin's attitude to rugby and, particularly, his battle with arch-rival Byron Kelleher, the former Otago Highlanders and current Waikato Chiefs halfback.

I did notice, however, that the same women at work, who liked *The Better Half*, screwed up their noses and furrowed their brows at *Dog Eat Dog*. And even though they were out-voted on the female front by our wives, it still got me thinking.

I said to Justin: 'I like *Dog Eat Dog*. But it's a very tough title. We're going to have to work very hard to live up to this title. We can't call a book *Dog Eat Dog* and deliver *Cat Laps Milk*. Okay?'

'Of course,' he said.

But there was one other problem.

In the process of writing, the rivalry between Justin and Byron Kelleher kept arising. I'd write it up and email it off to Justin with everything else for him to look over before I added it into the manuscript. But when it arrived back in my inbox, invariably, any reference to Byron Kelleher had mysteriously vanished.

'Hmmm,' I thought. 'This could be a bit tricky.'

I brought it up the next time I met Justin in Christchurch. I'd interview him for a few hours in a spare room at the TV3 office there. It was near the airport and saved travelling time to and from his home in Sumner. 'Look,' I said, 'You're adamant you want the book to be called *Dog Eat Dog*?'

'That's right.'

'But you keep taking any reference to Byron out of the book.'

'*Dog Eat Dog* doesn't refer to Byron. It's about professional rugby and my attitude to the game.'

'And what better way to show the reader your attitude to the game than by sharing with them your attitude towards your biggest rival for the All Black No. 9 jersey.'

'There hasn't been that much rivalry with Byron in my career to be honest. He's been there or thereabouts. But he hasn't really been a rival.'

'What do you mean?'

'He hasn't been around that long. He only really came into the All Black scene in 1999.'

'That's the last six years! That's a long time in the All Blacks. It's been you or him for six years. And it's mostly been you. That's dog eat dog. I understand you're competitive and all that. But if you don't mention Byron, people will find that very odd.'

'Do you reckon?'

'Yes. At the moment you've only got one dog. You've got Dog Eat. You need the other dog.'

'Mmm. I'm still not all that comfortable with it.'

'I'll tell you what, why don't we just write a little section about all your rivalries in New Zealand. We'll start off with the early days and go right through. If Byron comes up, he comes up. We'll just see how it goes.'

'Yeah, okay.'

By the way, the title after all that, if you hadn't noticed: *Justin Marshall*.

All those rivalries

I was quite fortunate because Graeme Bachop and Ant Strachan, the two All Black incumbents, both left for Japan just as I was arriving on the scene with Canterbury in 1995. When they left, the All Black selectors had a clean slate in my position.

And there were a few of us who were all pushing for the spot. Otago's Stu Forster and I went to France. But Jon Preston and Junior Tonu'u were also playing excellent rugby from 1996 through to '98.

Preston was a really gifted player, who could also slot into first five. He was an accurate distributor of the ball, a very intelligent footballer and one of the fittest guys I've ever met.

I had a good healthy rivalry with Jon Preston and I got on really well with him too. He was an excellent player and an excellent team person. I actually played a couple of games for the All Blacks at halfback when he was first five. I remember one particular test against the Springboks in Pretoria in '96 when he came on and slotted home a crucial kick to help us win the series. It was our first series win in South Africa. So that goes to show how good he was.

Tonu'u was the epitome of Polynesian flair. He had all the exciting attributes we associate with Island rugby: incredible strength, a wicked side-step, good skills and a mind-boggling ability to improvise. But what I'll always remember about Junior was his pass. He had that gigantic dive pass that could skip out two or three players every time and give a team an instant overlap. And he worked wonders for the Blues in that period when they were really dominant.

I remember the first time I saw him on the scales. I got quite a surprise. He was quite a bit heavier than me and I'm big for a halfback.

Out of Jon and Junior, I think Junior was my main rival.

And when I got injured with my Achilles heel in 1998, he played two home tests against England. Unfortunately for him, the All Blacks didn't play very well in those games. You couldn't blame him for that. But he was criticised for some of his play. When I was fit again the selectors were looking for ways to change things and picking me was an easy option. They probably thought they weren't going to lose anything, but if they were lucky, they might gain something.

As it turned out, I came back into the side for the Tri-Nations and we went on to lose every game that year.

Junior didn't get selected the following season and that's when Byron Kelleher came along, during 1999, leading up to the World Cup.

Who?

That was the first time that I came into contact with Byron. He was pretty much an unknown. I think he played a little bit for Otago in 1998 and then he was selected for the All Blacks in '99. He virtually came from nowhere. As far as I know, he hadn't really been in any rep teams. He played some good rugby for Otago, got picked as an All Black and in his first year he pushed me out in the World Cup semifinal. When he took my semifinal spot that started a real rivalry between us.

I'd been pretty fortunate that during my run with JP and Junior, while we had rivalry and were competitive, I'd been able to play just about every test match unless I was injured. But when Byron came on to the scene it was like two different political candidates. People preferred Byron or they preferred me. It was one way or the other and that was the simple reality of it.

I think it's just in my blood, part of who I am, that when the rivalry stepped up, the friendship stepped down.

We're mates and we can say gidday and get on and obviously we've got to function in the same team. But I wouldn't say that we're the best of friends. When the team goes out we don't really move in the same circles. And I think that's probably more my fault than his. Well, it is, because he's made more of an effort than I have.

The way I see it, this guy wants my jersey, *my* jersey. Everyone's writing him up as the next All Black No. 9. And whenever he's in the papers or on the TV it's Byron pushing for my spot or Byron's a bubbling can of Coke waiting to explode and things like that. And I read these things and hear these things and he's talking about the jersey that I'm currently occupying and because of that it creates this competitive edge in me. And it also annoys me a little bit. I'm thinking, 'There's no point in talking about it, Byron, you might as well earn it. Outplay me and earn it.'

Every time we play the Highlanders or Otago or more recently the Chiefs, I make sure I, and the team, perform. My attitude towards Byron has always been this: prove your point against me. Don't worry about going out and playing well against George Gregan or somebody else. Play well against me, Byron. Outplay me consistently. Then you'll get the jersey. Don't just talk about it.

So, because of all that, I developed a little bit of annoyance about him making these statements instead of actually backing them up. And he didn't back them up for a long period.

Friendship is a pretty strong word. I guess it's fair to say our bond in the team didn't really develop very far. We sit at the same tables at dinner occasionally and beside each other at times and we've got things in common. But since 1999, he's always been there, snapping at my heels.

He's been my main rival. And there have been times when he's left me sitting on the bench. Everyone in sport has their rivals. But in individual sports it's easier to talk about it and make comments that are more honest. But in a team sport it's not considered the ideal thing to be sending signals out from the team that you probably don't get on that well with this bloke. So you just avoid it or brush over it and pretend everything's fine.

A lot of people say we play different styles of rugby, that I'm more of a runner and he's more of a snappy passer. But I reckon we're quite similar. We're both quite big for halfbacks, we both like to run with the ball and we're both good defensively.

What about the pass, though?

A lot of people would say Byron's got the better pass and that he distributes the ball better. It's been the talking point of my career. And I have my own opinions on the issue.

Byron's got a very fast pass through the air and it looks absolutely brilliant on TV because it's hurtling towards the first five. If you timed from when the ball left his hands until it arrived at the first five, he'd probably be one of the quickest around. But when you time him from when his hands first touch the ball to when the first five receives it, he's no faster than most of the international halfbacks.

That's because of the time he spends going in and getting the ball, picking it up, propping himself and then winding up his pass. A lot of other halfbacks, and I include myself in this, don't move the ball as fast through the air, but clear it a lot quicker from the maul. They just go down, get it and clear it.

I can't prop myself and have the ball speed through the air because the minute I start to come up and prop I lose a lot of my strength.

But tests were done at one stage on six of the best halfbacks in the world. They measured how long it took from when we first touched the ball to when the first five touched it. I was the quickest out of all of those surveyed.

I felt pretty chuffed about that. But nobody seems to take any notice of it, which really pisses me off. People make assumptions because my ball flight looks laboured. And that's true. But it doesn't mean it's getting there slower.

Byron Kelleher: My pass is something I pride myself on. I work very hard on my pass. And I think that part of the basic skills of a halfback is to distribute the ball as quickly as possible. And statistically when you look at the records I have got the fastest pass and have had it for many years.

Internationally?

Yes, internationally.

Is that through the air? Or from when you first lay your hands on the ball until the first five receives it?

From when I first lay my hands on the ball, from the base of the ruck to the first five's hands. They measure all that stuff. But every halfback's going to have different strengths.

No. 1 halfback

With Marshall and Kelleher pushing each other all the time for the All Black No. 9 jersey, the media was always looking for new opinions on the debate. After Canterbury successfully defended the Ranfurly Shield 52–19 in late October 2001, Waikato and New Zealand Maori halfback Rhys Duggan was asked for his opinion.

'I still rate Justin as probably the No. 1 halfback in New Zealand,' he said. 'Every game you play against him you know it's going to be tough — you can't back down or he'll run all over you. But the Canterbury forwards played very well and it's easier when they're going forward.'

Canterbury went on to win the 2001 NPC, beating Otago 30–19 in the final at Jade Stadium and providing the perfect end to Aussie McLean's first year as coach.

Since then, under McLean, the team has continued a remarkable run with the Ranfurly Shield. Canterbury held the Log of Wood from mid-2000 until their last home game of the NPC round robin in 2003, when they lost it to Auckland, 40–31. Auckland defended it twice in 2004 before losing it to Bay of Plenty, who defended it once before losing it to Canterbury, where it stayed for the rest of the season.

During his years with Canterbury, Aussie McLean has forged a strong friendship with Justin Marshall and been well placed to watch the man and his career develop.

Aussie McLean: The mark of him as a player is that so many coaches have picked him. That to me shows how important he is to the teams he's played for.

He's the conductor at Canterbury and the Crusaders and I suspect in the All Blacks as well. If you stand behind a training run for a red-and-black team there's one voice you'll hear above all the others. He's always organising things, particularly on defence. His involvement mentally and as a communicator is at least as important as anything he does with the ball in his hands. And I think that's what the three teams he's involved with miss most, when he's not there.

I try to get other halfbacks I coach in various teams to conduct the defence the way Marshy does, but he's unique. You can coach it to a certain level, but he takes it to a whole new plane. People just don't realise the influence he has out there. He runs everything on defence.

Marshy's a great leader, but there are certain aspects of captaincy he's uncomfortable with. I spoke to him when he came back from that All Black tour where he was captain and I offered him the captaincy one year myself. But he doesn't like a lot of the off-field stuff.

He takes a leadership role within the team and at meetings and at training and on the field anyway. Sometimes he might as well just be the captain.

But the other thing with captains is that they also get involved in selection meetings about who's going to be in the team and why. And he doesn't like talking about his players like that. He's very uncomfortable with that. He doesn't want to sit down and talk about the merits of this guy versus that guy. He'd rather just be another player.

Natural-born winner

That's right. Justin Marshall doesn't mind being just another player . . . as long as he's just another player who wins. And it doesn't matter whether he's playing rugby, golf, pool, squash, whether he's swimming, whether he's dancing or playing Trivial Pursuits. Justin Marshall must win.

John Mitchell: Justin treats a game in training no different to a game he plays on Saturday. He gets just as pissed off when things don't go his way.

I remember one day at Eden Park. It was our second camp leading into the World Cup. I was refereeing one of the games. And he was trying his guts out and his team was trying its guts out. And like any game when you're referee, if you're not strong enough the boys will certainly let you know. So you've got to be pretty assertive. And I made some decisions that Justin didn't like.

Well, I think his team lost and he wouldn't talk to me or the opposing team afterwards. He kept it up for a while. I remember he still wasn't talking to me after lunch. But that's the way he is. And you love him for that really because it's all gone by the time you get back into the next camp.

Aussie McLean: His expectations as to what he should be doing as a golfer far outreach his ability. This is how seriously he takes it. Most rugby guys who play golf will get a couple of lessons. The coach will tell them not to play with their mates while they're getting lessons and they'll say bugger that. They'll just play with their mates anyway. But Justin wouldn't play with anyone for three months while he was getting these lessons. So he took his game from someone who was on about a 20 to about an 11 or 12. And he has stormed off the course a few times too.

Errol Collins: He had the nickname Lemon for a while because he gets sour every now and then when things don't go his way.

He's a shocker on the golf course. He'll just pack up and leave, walk off. He could be on the seventh or eighth hole. If things aren't going well: 'Goodbye!' He throws the toys right out of the cot. The boys love it.

The worst time I've seen his competitive edge come out was when I beat him 5–0 on the pool table up at his house. And he rates himself as a bit of a gun. First time up there I beat him 5–0. He was gutted.

He had me up there three times before he finally got me, 3–2.

But when I beat him 5–0, he was shattered. He just walked away. I don't even play pool. Did I tell you that score? Five–love . . . He didn't like it.

Robbie Deans: We've got a long-running competition on the squash court. He's almost got me nailed. But he hasn't got me nailed yet. And he's running out of time.

Mike Anthony: Marshy's not a horse-racing man or a gambler. But he loves to challenge people and he'll always have a bet on the result.

Justin and Nicolle have a nice pool and he's always talking up the number of lengths he can do underwater. I think four or five was the record.

And he's good mates with Simon and Anna Forrest. And with Anna being the former Olympic swimmer Anna Simcic, she took up Marshy's challenge and doubled his record.

In fact I think everyone who's gone up there has actually beaten his record. So I guess it won't be long before his young fellas are doing the same.

Scott Robertson: In the early days Justin, Tabai Matson, Mike Anthony the trainer

Is it a bird? Is it a plane? No, it's Supermud . . . competing in a mud-diving competition following a wet training session in Marseille, 2000.

'Oh no!' This is the moment when I tear my hamstring with the try-line open against England in Wellington in 2003. Jonny Wilkinson's lying in my dust. We don't score the try, though . . . and we lose the test 15–13.

The All Blacks fired up for the haka against the Springboks at Carisbrook in 2003. We won 19–11.

Psyched up. Richie McCaw, Reuben Thorne and I line up for the national anthem before our 21–17 win over the Wallabies at Eden Park in 2003.

'Catch me if you can.' Richie McCaw has more chance of taking up the challenge than our Italian opponents. I score in our first-up 70–7 win at the 2003 World Cup.

Media scrum. I prefer to be at the back of the scrum, not in the middle of it. But there's huge interest in the All Blacks before our quarterfinal clash with the Springboks in 2003.

Taken out. Physio Steve Muir attends to me after George Smith's late tackle that eventually forced me off with injured ribs in the 2003 World Cup semifinal against the Wallabies.

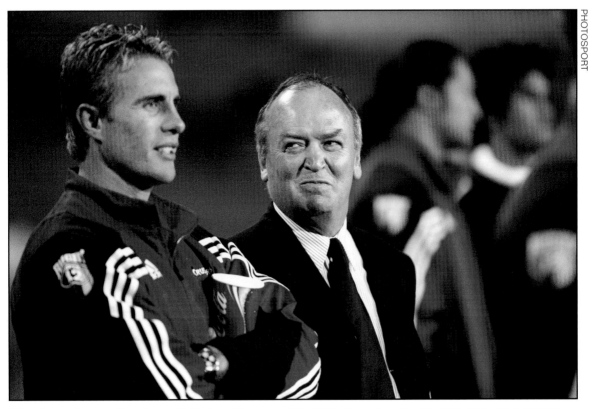

Meet the new boss . . . I catch up with Graham Henry, my fifth All Black coach, before the trial at Eden Park in 2004.

The pass that launched a thousand talkback calls. This time, in 2004, helping us to a 36–3 win over England in the first test in Dunedin.

Cannon fodder. Brendan Cannon is set upon by the All Blacks after king-hitting Keven Mealamu in Wellington, 2004.

'Your place or mine for that barbecue, George?' Tackling George Gregan during our World Cup semifinal loss to the Wallabies at the 2003 World Cup.

Rivals on the field, mates off it. George and I, enjoying a barbecue at his place in Sydney, during the off-season.

and I used to go out to a bar, any old bar, and after a few drinks we'd make a semi-circle and have dance-offs. Basically the song comes up and you go head to head with another player.

Inevitably, you end up dancing against Justin. He's a bloke who hasn't been blessed with rhythm. But, jees, his work rate was unbelievable!

He had all these moves. They were all out of time. But other than that they were impressive.

His go-to was this werewolf move. He'd lean right back, put his hands in the air, start howling like a werewolf and then lean right into your face and growl. He had this Teen Wolf thing happening. I was blown away when I first saw it. But after I watched him do it three weeks in a row, I knew that was it, that was all he had.

Of course, he'd follow it up with a break-dancing backspin or something like that. Then he'd come back up and pull an assortment of moves that no one had ever seen before. But the Werewolf was definitely the go-to move when he was desperate to make an impression.

Some of the other boys would be judging. And Justin would usually win through sheer enthusiasm. It was a sight to behold.

The other patrons never knew what was happening.

It was usually a final between Justin and Tabai. Tabs had the rhythm and Justin had the moves. He was just relentless. Sometimes the music stopped and he'd still keep going for a while just to try and score an extra point with the judges.

Nicolle: I'm competitive. But I'm competitive in a different way. You should see us when we play Trivial Pursuit. We're always on different teams and we get so competitive we're almost at the point where we're ready to fight.

I beat him six out of 10 times. But he stoops to a different level when the chips are down. He'll start getting ridiculous about pronunciations.

I remember one time Errol Collins was over with his wife, Karen. And the question was: Who was the first female politician in Pakistan to actually have a child while in office?

I said, 'Benazin Bhutto.' I pronounced it Benazin but it's actually Benazir.

And they said, 'No, sorry.'

I said, 'Come on.'

Justin said, 'Pronounce it again and spell it.'

I spelt it with an 'n' at the end instead of an 'r'. And they said, 'No, that's not good enough.'

That question was going to win the game. I was disgusted. Those boys dined out on that for weeks.

Mitch — from team-mate to coach

I was quite intrigued when John Mitchell was named coach of the All Blacks. I'd always respected his approach to the game. So I was keen to find out what his plans were.

I'd toured with him when he captained the Development team to Argentina in 1994. We'd had a bit to do with each other because he was No. 8 and I was one of the halfbacks. And having worked with him in both roles, I can now say that John Mitchell the coach is a very similar person to John Mitchell the player. He was very clinical in his approach and the way that he played was uncompromising and totally committed.

He was a typical Waikato forward from that era that produced the likes of Duane Monkley. And that comes through loud and clear in his coaching too.

When Mitch took over as All Black coach in 2001 the first place we assembled was the Poenamo Hotel on Auckland's North Shore. That used to be where all All Black teams assembled. But we hadn't stayed there since Laurie Mains had been in charge. We went away from it with John Hart. He had us in all sorts of new hotels.

I read the return to 'The Poe' as a pointer that John Mitchell wanted the All Blacks to return to some of the old traditions, to connect with the history and have things in common with the teams of the past. So it was nice to go back to The Poe.

That was the first place that I assembled as an All Black in 1995 and I hadn't been back there since. It brought a lot of memories flooding back about my first time there, rooming with Zinzan Brooke. And it made me take stock of how far that fresh-faced kid from the Deep South had come. Sometimes when I looked back, that kid seemed like a different guy. I was now a hardened professional athlete. There were still a lot of similarities I suppose. I was still a bad-tempered bugger if things didn't go my way on the field. The main difference now was that when I threw my toys, the whole country, in fact, the whole rugby-playing *world* knew about it.

Anyway, the first thing we did with Mitch, not long after he addressed us, was to go out and have a game of touch across the road. Mitch and Robbie Deans joined in. And Mitch and I ended up having an altercation because I'm a competitive person and he's just a menace.

He was just annoying. He was exactly as I remember him when he played. Let's face it, the game was as much about fitness work as anything. But Mitch took it to the hilt. When we were playing touch he was running through and running hard and you'd touch him and try to get out of the way and he'd grab your shirt and hold you back. He was like this serious monster running around in the middle of this fun game. He was aggravating me even when I wasn't involved in touching him. He was so aggressive.

Every time he was touched, he was running three or four metres past the mark and playing the ball. And he had that determined John Mitchell look on his face. For a game of touch he was very physical and confrontational. And when he did it to me a couple of times, I ended up giving him a push back and it was pretty tense for a wee while.

Luckily, Mitch has played top-level sport and didn't think of it as anything more than your average on-field altercation. In fact, knowing Mitch, he probably enjoyed the bit of niggle. He just carried on with the game as if nothing had happened. Hell, he probably doesn't even remember it.

But I was thinking, 'Your shaved head's still the same and so's everything else about you. You've just taken those qualities that worked for you as a player and carried them through into your coaching. You haven't changed a bit. You're still just as aggressive as you always were.'

But I was a fan of those qualities he possessed as a player. So I was excited about the future of the All Blacks with Mitch in charge.

Marshall missed the end-of-season tour to Ireland, Scotland and Argentina with a heel muscle injury. Not surprisingly, though, the All Blacks won all their games.

Even without Marshall and the league convert Brad Thorn, who pulled out because he didn't feel ready to wear the black jersey, there were still 14 Canterbury players on that tour. That equalled the record for provincial representation in an All Black squad, established by Auckland, which supplied 14 players to the 1987 and 1991 World Cup squads.

In 2002, Canterbury broke the record, providing 15 members of the squad to play Italy in John Mitchell's first test in charge on home soil. And Canterbury flanker Reuben Thorne was named captain. Canterbury were the undisputed heavyweight champs of New Zealand rugby at that time. The All Black squad was named on 27 May, two days after the Crusaders had won the Super 12. And the newspapers were raving about them.

James Belfield, *Sunday News*: The Crusaders are invincible.

The Robbie Deans-coached side maintained their unbeaten Super 12 campaign when they beat defending champions the Brumbies 31–13 at Jade Stadium.

It was the fourth time in the seven-year history of the Super 12 that the Crusaders have won the title.

The result ended the Brumbies' one-year reign and was a brilliant return to form for the Crusaders who finished 10th last year.

Booed off the Brook

Marshall wasn't picked for the test against Italy. But the All Blacks won comfortably.

He came back into the team for the first test against Ireland in Dunedin. Once again, the team was full of Canterbury players. The media was calling it the Canter-blacks and a lot of New Zealanders didn't like the red-and-black monopoly. The All Blacks won 15–6 but, incredibly, were booed off the pitch.

I couldn't believe it. Our own fans booed us after we won a test match! It makes you wonder what they'd have done to us if we'd lost.

I know there's a school of thought that says the modern-day All Black isn't allowed to complain or get upset about anything because we're well paid. Well, my response to that is: what a load of bollocks! Do you have any idea what it feels like to be in the middle of a packed stadium, wearing an All Black jersey, and all your fellow New Zealanders are booing you — why? — because, although you've beaten the opposition, you haven't done it in emphatic enough fashion. We were supposed to beat them by 50 points, obviously. Do we realise, for a start, how insulting that is to the opposition?

Anyway, I get so sad and so bloody furious when the All Black fans act as if they're our most ruthless enemy. It's like, 'Hello, we're all on the same side here.'

And then all the analysis starts; the media have to find out the real story behind what went wrong in the All Blacks' win. Imagine what the Irish must feel like reading the papers and watching all those talking heads on the news every night. They must think they've landed on another planet.

To me it's like a sideshow. And all those commentators are the open-mouthed clowns with the painted faces, turning from side to side. And I just couldn't let the sideshow leave town before I'd pushed a few ping pong balls into their mouths and down their throats.

Jim Kayes, *The Dominion*, 21 June 2002: Wet weather is unlikely to deter the All Blacks from a game plan they believe will eventually see them win the World Cup.

Halfback Justin Marshall revealed that the All Blacks deliberately persevered with a possession-based game plan in slippery conditions against Ireland last week.

He said the team had agreed that keeping the ball in hand and attacking from anywhere on the field was the best way for the All Blacks to be successful.

That was especially true in what should be hard and fast conditions in Australia for next year's World Cup.

'But we think it would also work against England and in the Tri-Nations,'

Marshall said. 'Last week was a day we could have kicked all day and won the test more comfortably — we've got one of the best first five-eighths (Andrew Mehrtens) in the world for that — but we didn't want to do that.

'We can resort to that game plan, it's there and we know it's there, but we wanted to grind it out. We got what we wanted out of it.'

Anyway, the All Blacks went out and belted Ireland 40–8 in the second test at Eden Park.

While New Zealand's rugby administrators were kicking themselves over losing the sub-hosting rights to the 2003 World Cup, the players were doing the business on the field. Maybe that home semifinal wouldn't be that important after all.

The All Blacks followed the wins over Ireland with a thumping of Fiji, a close win and a close loss to Australia and two wins over the Springboks.

Marshall was rested for the 2002 end-of-year three-match tour, where the All Blacks posted some worrying results: a 31–28 loss to England, a 20–20 draw to France and a win over Wales.

Warning signs? Alarm bells? Who knows?

Fight club

Scott Robertson: I have a story that sums up Justin Marshall to a tee. This happened in about 2002, when Justin had already been an All Black for seven years. He'd left Old Boys and joined my club Sumner.

He'd just finished with the Tri-Nations and had a couple of weeks before the NPC started. Aussie McLean, the Canterbury coach, wanted Justin to have a rest. But Justin wanted to play a game of club rugby. And as Justin does, he eventually got his way.

So he turned out for his one and only club match for Sumner. It was a home game in the second division competition against a traditional Maori club called Otautahi. Word had got around that Justin was playing so about a thousand people turned up, adding a real festival atmosphere to what was otherwise an average club game.

I played too, and it was the first time Sumner had had two All Blacks playing for them.

You could tell that some of these club players were in awe of Justin and they were pretty amped up.

Anyway, during the course of the game Justin started to get a bit frustrated. And when one of the Otautahi players came around the side of the ruck Justin tackled him and dropped his knee on him.

Suddenly there were players from both teams coming from all directions. And the sideline got involved too. It was all on. After about two minutes order was restored and Justin emerged from the centre of the fight with his jersey completely ripped off him.

Otautahi got the penalty and Justin carried on the game as if nothing had happened.

That just shows you what Justin's like. No matter what game he plays in, he gives it everything.

At halftime Sumner's regular halfback asked Justin if he'd move to centre so that he could have a chance to play alongside an All Black legend. So Justin played centre in the second half.

Sumner won the game. It was the semifinal. And the Otautahi boys and their supporters loved it. At the after-match they were all coming up to Justin and saying, 'Cher, bro, too much.' They were buying him beers and giving him a hongi. The atmosphere was amazing at that game. And I'm sure it was a great experience for Justin too.

2003 — a good vintage

John Mitchell: I remember Mike Anthony, the trainer, telling me once that Mehrts and Justin had the same fitness levels when he started working with them in 1995. The difference was that while Mehrts progressed normally and his body showed the normal wear and tear of the ageing process, Justin made huge shifts in terms of his physical ability. He defied the ageing process because as he got older he kept getting fitter and stronger. That shows the amount of work he puts in to improve his fitness.

Mike Anthony: I worked with him in the All Blacks going into the 2003 World Cup. He worked harder than any other player I've had. He was outstanding. I keep a record of training sessions completed. I've got all the Crusaders guys from that period. And he completed the most out of the lot of them. That's probably why he's been able to stay at the level he has for so long. He works as hard if not harder than anyone else does.

And because he's so competitive he pushes himself to the limit on that stuff. He competes against himself and his previous bests. From a physical perspective he's actually got better as he's got older. Going into the World Cup he was hitting personal bests on all his fitness levels. He's so driven he wanted to beat himself from previous years.

John Mitchell: An example of what I liked about him is that he challenged a selection of mine during Tri-Nations 2003. We didn't give him the start against South Africa in Pretoria.

He'd just come back from a huge hamstring injury against England. It was a spectacular injury because he was through for a try. He just had to pass the ball inside to set the last man away. And at the crucial moment, snap, his hamstring went and he died with the ball. That was the match we lost 15–13 in Wellington.

So Justin was coming back from that. We already knew quite a lot about Justin. But we needed to find out a lot more about our second and third halfbacks going into World Cup year. I wanted to select Steve Devine. But Justin didn't want to give anyone else a chance.

He disagreed with our decision, which he was entitled to. But I told him that at the end of the day I'd decide who was in or out of the team. He never liked those situations. But it was bloody good because, once again, it showed how much it meant to him.

His philosophy was 'never give a sucker an even break'. You could see it in his eyes. And it builds up in him emotionally too. But that's what you've got to love about the bloke. He really wears his heart out on his chest sometimes.

And I don't have a problem with that. I actually love guys being quite deep and deeply affected by their rugby because you feel confident they're the ones who are going to give you everything out on the pitch. And that's how it is with Justin. We beat South Africa 52–16 and he got the last 20 minutes. So it worked out all right.

After being dropped for the semifinal in 1999, the World Cup in Australia in 2003 was huge for Justin Marshall. It's doubtful whether he would give his left arm to have won it. But he would've thought seriously about a small toe or finger.

Once again the All Blacks went in as favourites.

They'd lost to England in Wellington in the first test of the year. John Mitchell and Robbie Deans assured the country it was just a glitch. And the country tried to believe them . . . even though it felt like swallowing a fur ball. That annoying hiccup was stuffed down into a dark corner of New Zealand's consciousness by the All Blacks' next two results: 50-point thrashings of South Africa and Australia away from home. New Zealand felt relieved. We hadn't understood a word John Mitchell had told us about what he was trying to achieve. His dialogue with the media was deeper and more mysterious than the dialogue in the *Matrix* movies. But we didn't care. He was thrashing the old enemies. New Zealand celebrated. But maybe we should have celebrated a little bit more, because those two matches were when the All Blacks played their best under John Mitchell and Robbie Deans. The All Blacks peaked at the wrong time.

They ground out a 19–11 win over the Springboks in Dunedin. They fought to a 21–17 win over the Wallabies in Auckland. New Zealand interpreted that as meaning this team knew how to hold on and close out the tight ones too. There was sensibility and grunt along with all that talent, flair and genius.

The World Cup started and the All Blacks annihilated Italy 70–7. They trounced Tonga 91–7. They almost lost to Wales. They what? Okay, that may be overstating it. They allowed Wales to fight back from a hefty deficit to take the lead. But the All Blacks came home strongly, to win the match 53–37.

They beat South Africa 29–9 in the quarters. And lost to the Wallabies 22–10 in the semifinal.

If we're being brutally honest, that semifinal came down to one pass. And the fact is we don't have to tell anyone in New Zealand or Australia or anywhere in the rugby world for that matter which pass we're talking about. But for the benefit of those readers who've just stumbled out of a cave in Outer Mongolia after years of solitary meditation: Carlos Spencer's ambitious cut-out pass early in the first half.

Overall, I think if Carlos Spencer's pass had hit its target out wide in the backline we would have scored the try and from there the game would have taken a different course. Instead, Stirling Mortlock intercepted and scored down the other end. And Australia won.

Having said that, I thought we scored before that anyway. Mils Muliaina had a try disallowed in the corner. And I'm certain that was a try. So maybe if that had been allowed, we might have dictated the match instead of them.

Anyway, after Mortlock's try the Wallabies got an incredible amount of self-belief and confidence. We decided to kick deep at the kick-off. We kicked what we call a four, which is deep into the 22. The intent was that they'd either kick the ball back to us or kick it out and we'd attack from there. But they put about 12 phases together from that kick-off. And for some reason they were able to play like that for the rest of the game and we just couldn't get the ball back.

We started better than them, they got that lucky break — although Mortlock will never call it lucky — and that turned the game. I don't know if you've ever taken an intercept in rugby but I've only taken about two in my entire career. You have to be in the right place at the right time. Reading the play's only part of it. You do need an element of luck. It's not the same as taking an intercept in rugby league, where the play's a lot easier to read.

I got an intercept once against the Queensland Reds. Elton Flatley always does that inside pass to Chris Latham in the blind spot. I noticed that and it was just good luck that he threw the pass, because Flatley did slightly hesitate but then threw it anyway and I intercepted it.

It's not even a fifty-fifty thing. So, regardless of whether or not the Aussies knew we were going to do that move, Mortlock needed to have a touch of luck and be very accurate, which he was. And for the rest of the game they were just so clinical.

Taken out

Aussie flanker George Smith hit me late in a tackle off a short lineout about 25 minutes into the first half. Lying breathless and unable to talk on the ground, I knew he'd done a good job on me. I remember getting up fuming, not only because he'd hit me late but more importantly because I knew he'd done some major damage. I started walking towards the lineout from the penalty we received and I was pointing at him, shouting all the nasty words I'd learnt from my mates in Mataura.

Taine Randell: I think everyone knows what a big job Justin does as a senior player. And that was best seen in the World Cup semifinal in 2003, when George Smith whacked him in the ribs. When I saw that I thought, 'Oh no, the game's definitely over now.'

Justin: The tackle from George was so hard that I struggled for the rest of the first half. I was furious. As far as I was concerned it was a cynical professional foul. The referee agreed. George was penalised, so it was definitely illegal. But I had a feeling he'd punished me much better than the ref had punished him.

The worst thing for me was that I knew there was something wrong with my rib. I couldn't breathe and it was really sore and I didn't want to take any impact on it. They did a blindside scrum move about five minutes from halftime and I had to run right across to the other side of the scrum with Mortlock running straight at me. I went low on him and he got away from me because I just couldn't grip on to him properly. We ended up giving up a penalty in that move and they took the three points. I felt terrible. It was about then I began to have doubts whether I could do my job properly out there.

I made it through to halftime. And though I tried to get involved in the team talk at halftime, I was too busy dealing with the doc to get a real feel for what the boys and the coaches were talking about.

'You've got to jab it,' I said to the doc. 'Put something in there so I can't feel it.'

'You're not allowed to,' he said. 'And even if you were allowed to and we did, you've definitely either broken or cracked your rib and if you get hit there again you could puncture your lung and you wouldn't know. So I can't do that for you.'

That was disappointing because I knew I was in trouble. And when he said that, I thought, 'Well, I don't really want to puncture a lung. I understand what you're saying.'

So he taped it right up and it actually wasn't too bad when I went out for the second half. The worst thing was that there were opportunities to run and I didn't. I just didn't want to get tackled. I could feel myself shielding the injury as I ran with the ball because it was actually hurting. At times I felt there were opportunities where I felt I could have made a break. We were actually starting to string some passes together and go all right.

There was one chance when I went through a gap, but Mortlock came from my blind side — Mortlock again — and smashed me. It actually really hurt me and that's when I knew I was gone. I walked off to the sideline 10 minutes into the second half.

Reuben Thorne: I was gutted when I saw Justin holding his ribs. I could see the hurt in his eyes and I could tell he didn't want to go off. He was a vital part of our team, and the organisation of our team. And no disrespect to anyone else, but when we lose Justin off the field, we really lose something. He's a real competitor, he's real tough, he's got experience and he directs the forwards better than any other halfback I've ever played with. And when you lose someone like him in a game that big, it's a big blow to the team.

Justin: Afterwards, George Gregan said to me, 'I don't know what happened out there, mate. We haven't been playing very well up until this game.'

And he was right. They were absolutely bloody awful against Scotland in the quarterfinal. They only scraped in.

'Look, mate,' he said, 'I can't explain the way we played today. But everything just happened for us.'

Us and them

I know it was a big deal for a lot of people that John Mitchell often struggled to express himself clearly when he was talking to the media. But to me, that was irrelevant. As long as he was able to express himself clearly to the players and we were then able to express his vision successfully with the ball in hand, what did it matter what he said at the press conference?

To be honest, I didn't take a lot of notice of what Mitch was saying to the media. I don't watch a lot of the TV news and I only flick through the odd thing in the newspaper. I'd heard about it: that he was uncomfortable and he wasn't himself in front of the media and so on and so forth. But I didn't think twice about it.

For us players, he was brilliant because he, to a certain extent, did what he felt was best for the team. For that reason he flagged the odd sponsorship thing we were supposed to do. He'd just say, 'No, I'm not getting the players to go to this dinner. It doesn't suit.' And what he was actually doing was really looking after us, but getting himself more and more offside with the people at the New Zealand Rugby Football Union. And he was making it more and more crucial that he won that

World Cup because they were just waiting for an excuse to jump on him. And that's all it took.

The minute he didn't win that game, he was never going to have the backing of the Rugby Union. He'd put the players' needs over the union's needs far too often. The result was that we loved him, but they hated him. In a nutshell, he'd pissed off too many important people.

In the end they were never going to back him. And I got that feeling straight away. The thing I will always vividly remember, and that to this day bemuses me, was that it actually happened when chief executive Chris Moller and chairman Jock Hobbs came into the changing rooms after the semifinal loss. Nothing wrong with that in itself, but it's what they said.

We were all down. And if you can think of the real low points in your own life when you feel just awful and drained, well, that's what we felt like. We were devastated.

But then Chris Moller and Jock Hobbs told us there was going to be a full review of the entire World Cup campaign. There was going to be a decision made on the future of the All Black coaches within the next week or so. All this was going to be happening from that moment on.

So, how appropriate was the timing of that? I was absolutely disgusted.

They pulled Mitch and Robbie out first and had a word to them and then they came back in with them and told us about the review. So how are Mitch and Robbie supposed to feel? They're suffering anyway from the loss, and yet the first thing they get told is, 'There's going to be a full review of your positions.' It's just absolutely poor business practice for a start off, and I think it's disgraceful to treat people that way.

And regardless of what process the union had to go through from there to satisfy themselves and the media and the public, I still say it was inappropriate to announce the review in the changing room after such a big loss.

I really felt for Mitch and Robbie. And the NZRU, in handling the situation that way, lost a lot of respect from the players, particularly the players in that room. And it's something that we have been trying to rectify ever since.

The players' trust of the union was almost irreparably damaged. They felt isolated from the union and insulted by it. That scene in the dressing room created a big gap between the union bosses and the players.

And there were other wedges that had pushed us apart. The World Cup bonus wrangle was one of the main ones. Before the tournament, we were at loggerheads with the NZRU over how much we should be paid for each game we played at the World Cup. We were being offered significantly less than some of the other countries. And we wondered if we were being taken for a ride.

In 2004 I was part of a group of senior players who met regularly with Chris Moller, Steve Tew and Jock Hobbs to try to build some bridges. The idea was to ensure that the All Blacks and the union were working together instead of against each other.

Since then, we've made a lot of progress, significant progress. Prior to these meetings, we'd both lost a lot of ground. And we weren't the only party with complaints. They also had issues about the way the All Blacks did things or would like to do things. So it's an ongoing process.

Scapegoats

After that semifinal loss, I went on record that the coaches and the captain would be made the scapegoats and that it was wrong. I've been around long enough to know how things work. Well, Mitch, Robbie and Reuben Thorne were made the scapegoats. And I still believe they were unfairly blamed. I also thought it was such a typical New Zealand response for everyone to blame the coaches.

Their record was brilliant and it certainly wasn't their fault we lost that game.

I've travelled around Australia, South Africa and England since that loss and people overseas keep saying to me: 'What happened with John Mitchell? He had a phenomenal record in charge.'

And they're right. His sacking following the World Cup defies belief.

While Mitchell was coach the All Blacks played 28, won 23, lost four and drew one. He presided over an unbeaten Northern Hemisphere tour, two back-to-back Tri-Nations championships and a Bledisloe Cup victory. His winning percentage with the All Blacks was 86 percent.

But I knew his would be the first neck to feel the axe. It's just indicative of how ridiculously ruthless rugby has become in New Zealand.

Mitch and Robbie were absolutely crucified after losing that World Cup semifinal, yet they were given only two years to prepare for it. That's not long enough to build a team for a World Cup. It takes longer than that to decide on the players and then get them to a point at which they can execute flawlessly the game plan the coaches are trying to achieve.

I know Mitch promised New Zealand he would bring back the World Cup and said openly that his head was for the chopping block if he didn't. But once you get the job, you'll say anything. You say what you believe needs to be said. Of course you're going to tell New Zealand the All Blacks are going to win the World Cup.

You have no choice when it comes to that. In New Zealand more than any other country, your job description isn't so much national rugby coach, but World Cup winner. Anything less is considered dereliction of duty.

We got to the semifinal. We were playing good rugby. But in Sydney on 15 November 2003 we were outplayed by a better Australian side. That's all there is to it.

Accountability

The All Blacks always get the blame when a World Cup is lost. But I think the New Zealand Rugby Union has a lot to answer for. They keep on changing the coaching staff every two years. And none of them get a really fair go. Surely, the first two years in charge of the All Blacks — or in any job — is where you're going to make most of your mistakes and learn most of your biggest and most valuable lessons.

But in my time the All Blacks have never had the benefit of those lessons because, straight after learning them, the coaches are pushed out. In comes a new coach. And it's back to square one for all involved.

Imagine if John Mitchell had suffered that semifinal loss, learnt from it and was allowed to coach at the next World Cup. Now do you think he'd have any more chance of winning it? I believe he would. I believe that, given the chance, he would have been a good bet to coach the All Blacks to World Cup victory in 2007.

John Mitchell had us playing exciting rugby in 2003. The big issue that year and throughout the World Cup was that we had no real goal-kicker. A lot of experts damned Mitchell for not having a specialist kicker. But as a squad we were okay with that.

During the late 1980s and early '90s the New Zealand rugby public became silent partners with the All Black selectors in a contract that included the very important Fox clause. That clause stated that if the All Blacks couldn't beat a team with forward grunt and backline wizardry, they were allowed to call on Grant Fox.

Foxy was the ideal clean-up man when things got messy. His weapons of choice were perfectly weighted kicks for field position and pinpoint penalties and conversions.

When Foxy Mark I retired from the international game, the prototype for Foxy Mark II, Andrew Mehrtens, arrived with a few extra features: an eye for the gap, a deceptive burst of acceleration and a wide range of passing options.

But in 2003, the All Black selectors opted not to pick Mehrtens. Many couldn't believe this because Mehrts was such a reliable kicker. And Foxy Mark III, Dan Carter, hadn't been perfected yet. He was still at least a year away.

But the selectors were dying to try out this flashy new experimental model, known as Carlos Spencer.

When it came to first fives, Foxy, Mehrts and Carter were like Rolex watches. They could run for about 10 years without missing a second. In contrast, Spencer was one of those made by Q for James Bond. You could fire missiles with it, cut through steel with its laser beam or use it to become invisible. It was just a bit unreliable when it came to telling the time.

But, hey, who could blame Mitchell and Deans for picking Carlos? In rugby terms, Carlos was the ultimate boys' toy. He had bells, whistles and flashing lights everywhere. The temptation was too much. And, anyway, at that time Carlos Spencer was the best first five in the country. Even Foxy, Mehrts and Dan Carter would agree with that.

But convince the average punter? They're often harder to convert than the experts. The New Zealand rugby public was used to having a Foxy-type first five as insurance when things got iffy.

But Carlos was the guy who was firing up the coaches' imaginations. He was the excitement machine. And he epitomised the style of rugby Mitchell and Deans were aiming for, a blend of structured percentage forward play and free-spirited creative backline moves.

With guys like Carlos, Mils Muliaina, Doug Howlett, Joe Rokocoko and Tana Umaga ranging out wide, Mitchell and Deans backed the team's ability to score tries.

Okay, so they'd gone down to England in the first test of 2003. But when Aaron Mauger slotted in at second five for the thrashings of South Africa and Australia everything seemed to click. And the All Blacks went on to win the Tri-Nations and the Bledisloe Cup.

Having glimpsed the possibilities, Mitchell and Deans felt they were on to something big. They were loath to compromise their vision by tampering with or decreasing the attacking firepower the All Blacks had with ball in hand. If that meant no specialist kicker, then so be it. They took a gamble and the players were just as excited as the coaches were.

And let's face it, we didn't lose the World Cup semifinal because we didn't have a specialist kicker.

Reuben played bass

Another aspect of Mitchell and Deans' leadership that polarised New Zealand rugby enthusiasts in 2003 was their loyalty to Reuben Thorne and their faith in his captaincy.

The detractors said Thorne wasn't doing enough to hold his place in the team let alone lead it. The media dubbed him Captain Invisible. Fans started playing 'Watch Reuben' during tests to help make up their own minds. And even former All Blacks questioned his contribution as blindside flanker and his leadership.

It was a fairly one-sided debate. The modest Thorne never hit back with a list of his good points or even defended his selection. John Mitchell explained Thorne's low-key presence by describing him as the man who did the 'shit jobs'.

Big, calm, silent types like Thorne and Mitchell can absorb a lot of criticism and abuse and keep functioning. But, while they might not want to get dragged into a dogfight with their critics, maybe what they needed was a smaller, angrier, louder type to state their case.

Everyone has their strengths. The strengths of Jerry Collins, one of the other guys people wanted to play blindside flanker, are his tackling and his ball running. Those are things that people take notice of because they're quite spectacular. But he doesn't get turnovers and he doesn't make 20 to 25 tackles in a game; he makes 10 effective ones.

Reuben's strengths are different. They're things like his work in the lineout and how he operates within the scrum and how he works with the other forwards. Probably his biggest asset within the team is his work in the clean out, the so-called 'shit jobs'. He's an excellent body mover.

You know the only reason we get good ball is because we have guys like Reuben getting rid of the opposition players at ruck and maul time so that I can get at the ball. Now not everybody lines up to do that, because it's pretty unrewarding. It's work you do *for* the team that goes unnoticed by everyone *except* the team.

Now, if the All Blacks were into music the first five — particularly if it was Carlos Spencer — would be the front man, the star, the singer, the self-appointed leader of the band. He'd co-write the songs with the halfback. The duelling lead guitarists with all their flashy fretwork and soaring notes would be on each wing. Second five and centre would strum out the rhythm and strike a few poses, while the fullback would shore up everything with those long-held chords on the keyboards. The front row would set the tempo with the regular driving beat of the bass drum while the locks would fill out the rest of the percussion. Openside flanker and No. 8 could be the horn section, driving in every now and then to add momentum and fill out the sound. And Reuben Thorne at No. 6 would play bass.

Now if I was a forward I'd rather be looping around the ruck with the ball in my hand, not cleaning out people so someone else can have a run. But if someone doesn't do the clean-out work then we don't recycle the ball and we can't set the backs away.

Now, when you think about it, which person in New Zealand rugby is best positioned to comment on the effectiveness of Reuben Thorne's clean-out work? The answer's obvious: me.

I've played halfback behind Reuben for years with Canterbury, the Crusaders and with the All Blacks. If Reuben was really Captain Invisible, I, more than anyone else, would want him out, because if he doesn't do his job — removing players who are stopping me from getting to the ball — I can't do mine. And I wouldn't put up with that. Anyone who knows me knows that.

Having said that, if you're going to pick Reuben Thorne, you can't pick Jono Gibbes, because they're actually quite similar players. If you've got those two guys, then you've got no one to carry the ball. So you have to balance it out.

It's the same with the props. Kees Meeuws will often carry it up while the other guy does the tight, less glamorous work. That's why Kees has scored all those tries for the All Blacks, because the other prop and the hooker free him up.

Reuben Thorne also suffers from the same problem I've had with my passing: no matter what he does the same old complaint is trotted out. It's laziness on the part of the critics really. Reuben could carry the ball up 10 times and be quite noticeable in the action, yet have an average game in the tight and drop a couple of lineout balls. But instead of criticising the aspect of his game that genuinely deserves criticism, they'll say, 'Where was he? We didn't see him.'

How many times have you watched a rock band and noticed the bass player standing there, calm, unmoving, inscrutable, hidden behind dark glasses while all hell breaks loose around him. The bass player is like the eye of the hurricane.

Take that old band The Who. Roger Daltrey would leap in the air and smash his microphone down onto the stage. Pete Townshend would swing his guitar like an axe into the amplifiers until it was reduced to a humming, wailing mess of splinters and twisted metal. Keith Moon would blow up his drums, kicking over anything left standing. While a bored-looking John Entwistle carried on playing his bass, enabling the creative free-for-all to become just another element of the music, part of a logical progression.

Another thing you might have noticed is that during the whole period that he was getting criticised, not one single player who had actually played alongside Reuben Thorne bagged him. The critics were all former players who were just watching it all on TV.

And the game has changed since they were playing. That's not just a stock defence either. It *has* changed.

When we first started playing we used to just go from scrum to lineout. The whole forward pack would rumble around the field following the ball like bees around a honey pot. The halfback would nip in behind them and the backs would organise themselves on either side of the swarm.

Nowadays the All Blacks work in what we call two pods, which is two groups of forwards. So the forwards get split in two. Each pod has guys to charge in and do the tight stuff, guys to do the clean out and guys to carry the ball up. The pods can work on their own, depending on who's closest to the ball, or complement each other. For instance, say Daniel Carter sets the ball up in the middle of the field: one pod will go there and do the clean-out body-moving work and the other pod will wait for the next person to carry the ball up. They work like that, in tandem.

So Reuben would often be in a pod with the likes of Greg Somerville, Chris Jack and Keven Mealamu. Now as much as Reuben and Greg would love to be the guys to run the ball, the coach is probably going to appoint Keven because of his explosiveness and Chris because his sheer size makes him a menace for tacklers.

Now Reuben Thorne has very good ball skills. Often he shows more skills than anyone else at training. And earlier in his career he played a much more flamboyant style of rugby. But he isn't given much opportunity to use his skills these days. He's busy doing another more disciplined and specialised job, the type of job that requires a unique sort of person. And maybe sometimes he looks back and wishes he could have been given more scope to show off his skills. But I must admit I've never wished that for him. Because the way he's played has served me, Canterbury, the Crusaders, the All Blacks and, whether they realise it or not, the fans perfectly.

That brings to mind a David Bowie concert at Western Springs. And a regular exercise: listening to the music and trying to pick the bass line. It was like tapping a Gib wall, trying to find the studs. Then, suddenly, there was *no* bass. Maybe an amp had blown or a cord pulled loose. And all that was left was this tinny, empty sound, the sound of all the other instruments.

Poor old Bowie! Seeing him up there with no bass lines was like seeing the emperor with no clothes. Without that simple bass line, the music caved in, just like a house without a frame. You don't always see the frame or pick out the bass line . . . but without them you're in Shit Street.

Child's play

Having kids puts a whole new twist on things. They show you that you aren't as important as you think you are.

They're so unknowing when they're that young. Nicolle had Lachlan with her in Australia for a little part of the 2003 World Cup. He was only 14 months. And during that time he learnt to walk. I thought I'd miss that. But I got to see him walk for the first time.

Coming home from the World Cup in 2003 was worse than in '99. I was dreading coming back to New Zealand and facing the repercussions of that loss. We were already getting put through the mixer and we knew it was going to get worse. I just wanted to get away from it all.

But I completely forgot about all that stuff when I got to Christchurch airport.

I picked up my bags and walked around and there was Nicolle. I spotted her. But there was Lachlan beside her. And when he saw me, his face broke out into a huge smile and he ran for the first time. That, for me, just blew me away. I couldn't talk to anybody after that. I had bloody tears in my eyes. I just had to get away. It was really emotional because it put it all in perspective. He didn't care. He didn't know anything about rugby. To him, it was just Dad coming home. Dad didn't lose the World Cup. Dad just came home.

Things didn't go well and things didn't work out. And I wanted to win that World Cup because I knew it was going to be my last. But that moment made me realise that there were still a lot of things for which I could be very thankful.

I know people say that marrying Nicolle and having kids have changed me as a person and they have, definitely.

Errol Collins: Apart from the culture shock he got when he first arrived in Christchurch as a little ratbag, there have been two big changes in Justin's life. The first was when he met and later married Nicolle. She had an incredibly settling influence on Justin. There were still quite a few rough edges before she came along. And she smoothed most of them off. The second big change came when his first son, Lachlan, was born. Justin took the responsibility of having a child very seriously and accepted everything that came with it.

Nicolle: I think marriage and children have given Justin another focus. Rugby's been the biggest influence in his life. His family lives and breathes rugby. They are a real New Zealand rugby family, whereas I don't come from that.

I'm from Palmerston North. We're a city family. Dad's a hardware manufacturer. He and Mum had three children — a boy and two girls — and Mum stayed at home and looked after us while we were growing up.

My family would watch the All Blacks on TV and my brother played rugby. But we had a holiday home in Taupo and we'd be out trout fishing and boating and snow-skiing. All our neighbours used to drive to Wellington to watch All Black tests or go on tours to South Africa to follow them. But we never did that. Mum's English. She was probably more a football fan than anything. Now she's a fanatical rugby convert.

Justin: The day Lachlan was born was the strangest day of my life. I wouldn't say I'm a deeply emotional person. But I cried my eyes out when he was born, just being in there and seeing him be born and then waiting for that first cry and then hearing him cry. You can't explain that experience. I wouldn't even try to describe it. You don't know what it's like unless you've been in there and seen it happen.

It's difficult to be the husband because you feel so helpless. The strangest part was being with him and Nicolle all day — he was born really early in the morning — and then about 6 pm visiting hours are over and you go home on your own to an empty house.

I just wandered around in a daze not knowing what to do. Then I woke up the next day, went in to see Nicolle and Lachlan and I saw that my life had changed. There was something else to think about all of a sudden.

And it was just the same when Fletcher was born. I was just as emotional. I didn't think I would be, but I was.

We were worried how Lachlan would be about having a little brother. We shouldn't have bothered. He was fine.

Nicolle: I'm at the rugby and people are right next to me yelling out things like, 'Marshall, you prima donna. You're hopeless. Send the stroppy bastard off.'

They see him on the field and they think they know him. But there's a lot more to Justin. On the field he wears his heart on his sleeve for all to see. But off the field he can take a while to get to know.

I often hear people say they think he appears arrogant and aloof. I guess they don't expect him to be reserved when he's so open about his emotions during a game.

He has varied interests, which help him relax away from rugby. He is a fantastic cook, with his own vegetable garden, and he's as fanatical about his golf game as he is about making the perfect cup of coffee. Off the field he's a very well-balanced man.

But I find his on-field persona quite attractive too. He gives it everything and he'll never take a backward step. And that's why he gets picked.

Excuse me for expressing myself

I scored a try against the Stormers in the semifinal in 2004. It was late in the game and we needed the crowd behind us. So I started jumping and skipping around behind the goal line and motioning to the fans like a hyperactive conductor.

The crowd took up the challenge and got behind us. The most bizarre looks were from my team-mates, who are unused to seeing me express that type of emotion.

A lot of people told me later it was great to see somebody showing their feelings on the field and that it really got them going in the stands because it was a bit quiet before that. But I also received two or three hate letters.

The punters send them to the Canterbury Rugby Union and they just get stuck in my mailbox. We had the final that following week and we lost to the Brumbies. And that's when I received these letters. They were saying things like, 'We don't see you strutting around showing off now, do we, Marshall. You're not so smart any more. When things don't go your way it's a bit different, isn't it?'

It just goes to show, in New Zealand, you express yourself at your own peril.

The nude video

I get more questions about two incidents in my career than about any others. One is my super-quick recovery from the Achilles tendon injury in 1998; the other is the nude video on *Lion Red SportsCafé* during the 2004 Super 12.

What happened was that we'd seen the nude video segment on *SportsCafé* quite a bit so we knew what sort of things made it on to the programme. A few of the guys like Scotty Waldron and Ross Filipo decided between themselves, 'Maybe we could go up to Marshy's pool and do a bit of a streak and send in the video.'

They asked me if that was okay and I said, 'Yeah, I've got no problems with it and, if you like, I'll get involved.' Of course, management didn't know anything about it at that stage.

Anyway, we've got this pantomime-style horse's head at Canterbury that's absolutely brilliant. The guys carry out dares in the horse's head. And it pops up everywhere around Christchurch. We'll do silly things like spot a guy in Cathedral Square sitting on a bench eating fish and chips; the next minute the horse will come cruising right across the square to the guy, pick up some of his chips and start eating them. Then the horse will just shake the guy's hand and run off. We often video what the horse is doing. It's a bit like *Candid Camera* or *Beadle's About*. Actually, I suppose the closest thing on TV is the 'Can a Mascot?' segment on *Pulp Sport*, where they just film the fox mascot doing stupid things.

So when we decided to video one of the players streaking in my pool for *SportsCafé*, we figured the horse's head would be useful, so no one would know who the streaker was.

So what they did was they filmed the horse coming up to my place in Sumner. You can hear the boys going, 'Go, go . . . go on, do it,' in the car. I'd told them to go through a paddock around to the side fence of my property so you see them doing that (plus I didn't want any nutters to see the front of my house on TV).

We'd decided that after the player wearing the horse's head jumped into the water he was going to pretend to lay a cable in the pool and a Picnic bar would float to the top.

So he jumps in the pool and he's gritting his teeth with a concentrated look on his face and the guy with the camera's saying, 'Hurry up, hurry up. I think he's coming.' Eventually, the old Picnic bar floats to the top.

While they're still down at the pool I'm up in the top room yelling, 'Hey, what are you doing? What are you doing on my property? What's that in my pool?' I'm getting really angry. I grab one of my golf clubs and shake it in the window.

They're saying, 'Let's get out of here, let's get out of here.'

As the guy's getting out of the pool, I'm coming flying down the hallway with my golf club.

They make it out the door but I'm right behind them, yelling my head off. And as they're driving off, I'm yelling, 'Get off my property! I'm gonna get you! You just wait!' The final shot is me standing in my driveway waving my golf club.

It only took us about an hour to film the sequence. We had it all set up and we planned all the shots. The funniest thing was the first time he jumped in he didn't take the Picnic bar. And the one thing I said to them was, 'I'm fine with you guys jumping in the pool but it's the middle of winter and the water's only about 14 degrees. It's freezing.'

So by the time the guy was ready to jump in the second time there was a fair bit of shrinkage.

Once it was filmed and cut the next hurdle was getting *SportsCafé* to show it on TV. So I rang Ric Salizzo, who's one of the presenters, and who used to be the media liaison manager for the All Blacks. And I said, 'Look, Ric, a couple of guys from one of the local clubs have made a nude video where they come up to my house and streak in my pool. I'm just letting you know that I'm okay with it.'

Ric said, 'I dunno, Marshy. We don't really want to encourage that sort of stuff. We're quite aware that people can hassle elite athletes. And we don't want to be associated with that.'

I said, 'Thanks, mate. I know what you're saying. But I've seen this video. The guys involved showed it to me. And I actually think it's a bit of a laugh.'

So Ric had no idea that the other guys in the video, including the streaker, were all Canterbury guys. Nobody knew, apart from the other guys in the Canterbury team.

So the video went to air on *SportsCafé* but it was edited slightly. They cut out the bit with the Picnic bar. Even the *SportsCafé* team thought that was a bit over the top. And they shortened it down a bit. But it was still pretty funny. And it went down a treat because my acting surprised even me.

After that everybody thought that some guys from the public had gone up to my place and one of them had jumped into my pool naked. And that they'd filmed the whole thing.

Since then there've been hundreds of people, wherever I go around the country, coming up to me and going. 'How'd you feel about those guys coming up to your house and running around in the nude?'

I always admit that I knew about it and they're always genuinely shocked and say, 'But you looked really pissed off.'

I know it sounds a bit wanky, but I was getting a bit of coverage on the TV at that time. It was coming up to the Super 12 semifinals. And I think that may have helped the video stick in people's memories.

The weekend before I'd scored a try against the Stormers and carried on behind the posts like an idiot, leaping and jumping and waving my arms about trying to get the crowd behind us. And I'd polarised a fair few people with that performance.

The Crusaders' management didn't know anything about the video until it appeared on TV. But because the horse's head disguised the streaker and I looked like a genuinely aggrieved property owner, we were sweet. They just let it slide.

Hooray Henry

Graham Henry took over from John Mitchell for the 2004 season with Marshall's old Crusaders coaches Wayne Smith and Steve Hansen filling out the selection panel. Henry and Hansen had worked together with Wales and Hansen had coached them to that mighty effort against the All Blacks in the World Cup.

But before the new panel had even coached their first All Black test together, they had a problem on their hands.

I actually asked the New Zealand Rugby Union to release me from my contract about half a dozen games into the Super 12 that year.

I got an amazing offer from Welsh club the Newport Dragons. It was what's commonly described as an offer I couldn't refuse.

So I phoned the NZRU and said, 'I'd like to have a meeting with Steve Lancaster (who works on the player contracts for the union), Steve Tew and Graham Henry.'

I wanted a release from my contract at the end of that Super 12. I said to Nicolle, 'This is a huge risk. I'll be effectively telling the new All Black coach that I'd rather go overseas than play in his team. If they say no, he might decide, "We don't want him because there's no future in him and he's not interested."'

So I went up to Wellington and what I was asking wasn't what they wanted to hear.

I said, 'Look, I've given a lot to New Zealand rugby. I've given 10 years. Now I've got a genuine opportunity to take my family overseas to do something we're really excited about. So I hope this request will be approached in the right way.'

So they said no.

Graham Henry said, 'We can't afford to lose you.' That was nice to hear actually. 'We see you as the No. 1 halfback and a player who could possibly last right through to the World Cup.'

I was contracted through to the end of 2005. So in the end they compromised.

They said, 'Look, we'll give you a release after the Lions tour.' And that's what we agreed to.

The international season couldn't have started better with 36–3 and 36–12 wins over world champions England. But many felt the second test was ruined when England lock Danny Grewcock was controversially sent off in the first half.

We don't pat ourselves on the back anywhere near as much as we should, especially when we win test matches. When we won that test match against England at Eden Park in 2004 people said, 'It was a good performance but it wasn't good enough.' Well, why not? It was a test match. We won the bloody thing. 'Well, they only had 14 men.' Well, they deserved to have only 14 men and we still put 20-odd points on them and they were a good side. My personal opinion on the sending off of Danny Grewcock? He got what he deserved. He kneed our guy in the head, end of story.

The All Blacks followed up their thrashing of England with a 41–26 win over the Pacific Islands at Albany.

But there was a genuine feeling that the Aussies and the South Africans would provide much stiffer opposition in the Tri-Nations. And that feeling was spot on.

My cheap shot?

I'm not a huge fan of the Wallabies' coach Eddie Jones. And I almost had a fight with him after our 23–18 loss in Sydney in 2004. It was our second of two matches against Australia that year and to tell this story properly I really need to go back to the first match, the All Blacks' 16–7 win in Wellington. Actually, I need to go back to the day before that first match.

I met George Gregan for a coffee. As I've said, we always catch up before a big game. Anyway, this time he had Wallaby lock Justin Harrison with him.

I was telling them about this *Player* magazine that had come out. One of the main articles was about George, and Justin was teasing him about being a media star.

They hadn't seen the article so Justin and I went down to Whitcoulls and bought it. He took it back to the hotel and showed it to the Aussie boys, who poked a bit of fun at George over it. So Justin Harrison and I got on okay in the build-up. But it was a different story during the match.

It didn't just rain that night in Wellington, it bucketed down. It was freezing out on the field and at times the rain was so heavy you could hardly see the players out wide. But it was a satisfying night for us. We ground out our win sensibly, keeping the soapy ball in nice and close to the ruck for most of the match and waiting until the final moments to push it out wide for Dougie Howlett to score.

But that wasn't the most memorable image of the match. That dubious honour belonged to Brendan Cannon, the Aussie hooker, who whacked our poor No. 2 Keven Mealamu smack in the face during a maul. It was a beautiful punch, but a pretty cheap shot as Keven was trapped with nowhere to go.

As a rule the All Blacks refuse to be bullied, and those times we have let it happen, we've been doubly dealt to by the merciless New Zealand rugby public. So first of all Keven had a go at Cannon. Then Carlos Spencer and I instinctively went after him too. As far as we were concerned he'd crossed the line. And we just laid into him. I didn't know Carlos was in there at the time. But when you see it on TV you can see we both arrived almost simultaneously and started pounding him.

Eventually it broke up and there was a lot of pushing and shoving. And a few of the Aussies were really angry, particularly Justin Harrison. 'What are you doing?' he said. 'That's just a cheap shot.'

I said, 'What about him?' pointing at Cannon. 'Hitting someone with their arms pinned. That's not a cheap shot?'

'Go away, mate. You know what you guys did was just a cheap shot. You're better than that, aren't you? What are you doing?'

'Fuck off. If you bastards wanna start it, well, that's what happens.'

The Aussies were just shaking their heads. I honestly don't think I've ever seen them that angry before or since.

Anyway, I learned later that the Aussies were holding a grudge against me. I talked to George and he thought it was terrible what Carlos and I had done. And he said all the Aussies were furious.

I thought they had a bloody cheek after what Brendan Cannon had done to Keven. Did they expect us to just stand by and let our team-mate get a hiding?

Anyway, I didn't think much more about it. I just thought, 'Oh well, if they're going to feel that way when they start a fight, well let them be like that. And if they want to hold it against me, well I've got no time for them.'

George Gregan: He might have thought I was disappointed but those sorts of things that happen in a game aren't going to put a strain on our friendship. I might have a couple of chips at him that he's getting cranky in his old age. But that's about it.

That's certainly not something I've been thinking about. I moved on from that a long time ago.

What about your cheap shot?

As the preparation for the test against South Africa the next weekend intensified, I stopped thinking about the problems I'd had with Australia. We snuck home against South Africa 23–21 in Christchurch and our attentions turned once again to the Aussies and our return game in Sydney.

About seven minutes into the first half of that game I became reacquainted with Justin Harrison.

I was carrying the ball and went to ground. I felt somebody come from behind, right over the top of me, and then an excruciating pain in my eye. If you see me in the footage, I'm on the ground, almost in the foetal position, holding my eye. I thought that I'd been punched and that my eye had closed right over, because I couldn't see a thing, nothing. I was blinded, my eye was really sore and it was weeping. I just lay on the ground and stayed there for a while. I was trying to get up by the time the doc and physio came on. I was holding my eye. And they said, 'What's wrong?'

I said, 'I've been punched. My eye's closed over, isn't it?'

'No. Your pupil's really dilated. But your eye's not closed over at all.'

'Oh. I can't see. I can't see anything. I'm sure my eye must be closed over.'

'No, it's not. But it's really, really, really wide. Your whole eye's gone red. And it's scratched. You've been poked in the eye.'

I couldn't see. But I battled my way through to halftime. It was still weeping really badly and it hurt like hell. There were photos taken after the game. It looked terrible.

Anyway, I went out and played the second half. My vision had improved slightly but it was still blurred.

After the game we grabbed the doctor and decided to have a look at the incident on the video. So we had a look and the only person near me was Justin Harrison. And I thought, 'Mmm. That's interesting.'

Did he do it deliberately? In my opinion, yes, well and truly. On the video you can't see him actually doing it, and he did come out later and say he's not a dirty player. But, well, there's nobody else who could have done it.

And the thing that really annoys me was that he was the big macho man and so staunch the week before. He was the one preaching to me about dirty shots.

Maybe it was an accident. But I would have preferred it if he'd accidentally waited until I got up from the tackle and accidentally smashed me when I was looking at him. And then we could have sorted it out from there.

Fast Eddie

Anyway, we lose the match 23–18. So my bad mood has just got worse. After viewing the video of the incident, I head upstairs with All Black manager Darren Shand and our legal counsel Steve Cottrell to get the judicial process moving.

I look around and notice someone else following us up the stairs — Eddie Jones.

I said to Darren, 'What's he coming for? It's got nothing to do with him. He's not supposed to come because none of the coaches are allowed to sit in on this.'

Darren said, 'Look, I don't know. As far as I know, he shouldn't be there.'

I'm just shaking my head in disbelief. So we get up into the room and I'm really annoyed. (You've got to remember this wasn't that long after I'd been taken out by George Smith in the 2003 World Cup semifinal against Australia.) So I'm not in the greatest of moods. And to cap it all off Eddie Jones is actually up there, when, as far as I know, he isn't supposed to be.

Now I've been an outspoken critic of the judicial system in rugby for years. And this was a prime example of what a cock-up it can be. We're all up in this tiny little room, about three by three metres, and there's an Australian official in there studying the footage of the game. And then he explains, 'I'm not actually the Citing Commissioner. He's a South African watching the game on TV in South Africa. But I will report the information to him and he'll report back about it.'

I couldn't believe it. And to describe the set-up as ridiculous is too kind. The information was obviously going to be all over the place.

Anyway, we explained to this official that we were reporting Justin Harrison for an alleged eye gouge.

The official told Eddie Jones he could stay and listen just so he was aware of what was happening, but he wasn't to say anything that might influence the process. So that was fine.

We watched the footage and I explained what I saw and what I felt. I said, 'I went to ground. Somebody came over the top. I felt an excruciating pain in my eye. But I could not see who did it to me. However, seeing the incident on the videotape it's clear that the player was Justin Harrison. And that's all I can say.'

The official said, 'Well, we can see your eye and it's a real mess so obviously *something's* happened.'

Then Eddie Jones says, 'Well, how do we know this is when the incident actually happened? How do we know it happened at this time?'

And I said, 'It's pretty fuckin' blatantly obvious, isn't it?'

And he said, 'Excuse me, you better watch your mouth, Champ.'

I instinctively moved towards him and stuck my face right in front of his. 'I'm sorry,' I said. 'I thought you were in here just as an observer.' It was really uncomfortable by now. But I was furious at him calling me Champ, especially after they'd just beaten us. 'You weren't supposed to even say anything.'

'You better watch what you're saying, Champ.'

'For fuck's sake, this is ridiculous!'

Darren Shand tried to move between us. 'Settle down, Marshy,' he said. 'Settle down.'

'Hang on,' said the citing official. 'Hang on, hang on.' He was getting all flustered.

By this stage, Eddie Jones and I are standing face to face.

The citing officer's saying, 'There's no need for this.'

Eddie and I are still glaring at each other.

'We've seen the evidence,' the official says, 'and now I've got to pass it on to the Commissioner in South Africa.'

By this stage I think Darren Shand can see the look in my eye. He can see that if Eddie keeps arguing and calling me Champ I'm going to whack him one. And Eddie looks pretty fired up too. So Shandy's quite keen to get me out of there.

But it was really starting to get too uncomfortable anyway. We were still standing right beside each other, and in the end I just said, 'I've had enough of this,' and I just left.

We got outside and I said to Darren, 'What is it with that guy? He wasn't supposed to say anything and then he basically accuses me of lying. I mean, what a cheek.'

Darren just said, 'I know, Marshy. I know.'

'Well, I bet you nothing comes of it.'

It would've been 45 minutes later on my way out to the after-match I met Steve Cottrell and he said, 'Oh, we've just heard back from the Citing Commissioner in South Africa. He says there's no case to answer.'

I said, 'That doesn't surprise me. It's ridiculous, the way the whole thing's run.'

'I know how you feel, mate. But there's nothing we can do about it.'

And that was that.

Well, not quite. The next morning I was photographed at the airport. And the picture of me with my injured eye appeared in all the papers. It looked really bad. My eye was scratched in two places and it was red as hell. Everyone started talking about Justin Harrison and me on the talk-back radio. The TV news and the sports shows got into it too.

I heard about it but I couldn't follow it that closely because we went on to South Africa for the last game of the Tri-Nations.

I've spoken to a couple of the Australian guys since that test and they said, 'Jees, Marshy, you obviously did something to fire up old Eddie. That must have been a real blue you guys had. He was pretty angry when he came back down to the dressing room.' They all thought it was quite amusing.

In the rough

Believe it or not, Justin Marshall genuinely dislikes trouble, hates it with a passion and avoids it whenever possible. But it tends to creep up and swamp him before he's even noticed it's nearby.

A few brushes with trouble can put you on your guard. You start to sense it lurking around every corner. So what do you do? You stay away from the corner. Because two steps behind trouble comes guilt. And that's worse than trouble.

I'm a pretty enthusiastic golfer. I have two sets of golf clubs, which I have absolutely no need for. I've always been into it, right from when I was working seasons at the freezing works down home. In the off-season I had basically five or six months when the works weren't doing anything to try and fill in time. And golf was one of those things that we used to do. So I got passionate about it at the age of 16 and have played ever since.

But this particular day, I had a very average round of golf. And when I have an average round it frustrates me. I don't mind so much if I don't score very well. But if I'm not striking the ball properly it really irritates me. I'd rather have good ball-striking and not have a great score than score okay but just hit the ball along the ground and fluff it so many times. So on this particular day my ball striking was crap.

I was cleaning my car outside my home later on and my golf clubs were lying in the back boot, staring at me. I got them out to move them into the garage and I started thinking, 'What was happening to my swing today?' Then I started thinking, 'I wonder if I was doing this. Yeah, that'll be it.' So I grabbed my five iron out.

I live on a hill section. So I went out on to the back lawn and in front of me was just open space down into Sumner. So being up on the hill I was just hitting out into the paddock heading down into the township. I had a couple of practice swings and I thought, 'Yeah, that's it. That's what I was doing.' And I decided to hit the golf ball.

So I lined it up and I hit it and I hit it really well, much better than I'd been hitting it that day. I was watching the ball flight and I was thinking, 'I've actually caught that quite well with that tail wind behind me.'

It was heading towards these pine trees that are right down by the edge of the road that leads on to a footpath that then leads down into houses.

The ball flight was good. It carried down towards the trees and I thought it was going to hit the pines. But it actually flew over the top of them and I lost sight of it.

Well, I swear it would have been about five seconds later that I heard someone yelling, like a kid, down in the area where I'd hit the golf ball.

Well, I just panicked. I jumped behind the wall, as if somebody could see me, which they probably couldn't. It was just instinct. And then . . . nothing. So it was just somebody yelling, like a kid, and then no sound.

So I sneaked my head back around the wall of the house, and had a look in the direction that I'd hit the ball and started thinking all of the worst things. 'Oh no, I've hit somebody with the golf ball. What if I have? If the golf ball hit somebody it could kill them, particularly coming from this height.'

So I was absolutely petrified. I ran with my golf club back to my car. I hopped in and drove down into Sumner to the area where I suspected my ball had landed. I had my window down. It was quite a quiet evening. And I was listening for noises. And I was driving around and around this little area, trying to see whether, first of all, there was anyone lying unconscious or, secondly, I could pick up any signs that something had happened where my golf ball had landed.

I wasn't feeling that great to be honest. And the thing that was going through my head was: 'What happens if it's gone into someone's yard? What happens if there's been a kid running around in his back yard or riding around on his bike and the golf ball's hit him or her and that's it, they're dead in their backyard? And nobody's going to know. Or it could be somebody who lives alone. And it's hit them. And they yelled out. And they're just lying there, dying potentially.'

So after I'd snooped around for a while I drove back home and went inside and just sat around feeling really uneasy for about 10 minutes. Then I said, 'Nicolle, look . . . ' And I told her the story.

Nicolle: I was inside the house and I looked outside and I saw Justin. And he was holding a golf club in his hand and he was kind of slunk against the side of the house. He looked quite concerned and I wondered what on earth he was doing. After a while he came inside. I didn't realise he'd already been down the hill in his car to have a look around.

But he came inside and sat down at the computer and started to do a few things. He sat there for about 10 minutes and then he said, 'Nicolle, look, I feel really bad.'

I said, 'Why? What's happened?'

'I was practising my golf swing and I hit a golf ball into the field and I think I might have hit something down in Sumner.'

'What do you mean, you think you might have hit something?'

'Well, not long after I teed the ball off and the ball cleared the trees, somebody started shouting.'

'What do you mean they started shouting? Like screaming?'

'No, sort of shouting. I actually went down the hill in my car to have a look.'

'Seriously?'

'Yeah.'

I said, 'Oh no.' And anyway, I started to laugh and I thought, 'That's ridiculous.' And he said, 'I think we should call the police.'

'What?'

'I feel terrible. Somebody might be dead or injured down in Sumner. I think I should ring the police. I can just tell them I've hit a golf ball down towards Sumner. I'm not sure if anything's happened. But . . . '

'You can't just ring the police. What are you going to say? "Hi, it's Justin Marshall here. I've hit a golf ball off my hillside home. I don't know whether I've actually done anything. But just in case I have, I thought I'd better ring you and tell you." I said, 'Really, you'll be the laughing stock. They'll dine out on that for weeks.'

Justin: But I just had this really guilty conscience about it. She said, 'Oh, you can't do that. Don't be silly.' She said she'd go down and have a look around, down in Sumner. She was going to the supermarket actually and she said she'd do a sweep-by, see if anything had come of it.

I said, 'Thanks, that'd be great. I still think I should ring the police.' She advised me against it. Then about 10 seconds after having that conversation, the local fire brigade sirens went off and they started roaring and then I heard the fire engines cranking up. Now, where they practise, they actually head down past the area where I hit my golf ball and go down to the rugby field, which I look down on from my house. So I could hear all the sirens and see all the fire engines heading in that direction. So by that stage I was just freaking out.

Nicolle: I looked out the window and said, 'Oh no.'

Justin said, 'What?'

'You know that man you hit? Well, he was probably standing in the kitchen frying chips and now his house is on fire.'

Anyway, I had to go out to the supermarket so he asked me, 'Do you think you can do another drive by past the houses and just check that there's nothing amiss down there?'

I said, 'Yeah, of course. I'll check it out when I get down the hill.' But, look, an hour and a half had passed by then.

Justin: Nicolle, of course, thought it was hilarious and I was feeling really guilty. And that's how it ended. To this day, I don't know, someone still could be lying in their backyard.

The world is flat

When Graham Henry, Wayne Smith and Steve Hansen took over the All Blacks they had a really clear idea of where they wanted to go. Their big thing was to flatten the All Blacks' play across the park.

The media fed this concept to the public as the 'flat backline'. But there was a bit more to it than that.

They were trying to keep the forwards flatter and closer to the advantage line as well. It makes sense, I suppose. It would defeat the purpose to have a straight backline that's trying to hold on to every inch of ground behind a forward pack that's straggling around like Brown's cows. If the forwards are nice and flat then the backs are already significantly flatter.

But it was easiest to watch the theory in action in the backs. Fans could spot the difference straight away. They were used to seeing Tana Umaga steaming on to passes like a runaway train. Mils Muliaina gliding on to the ball from a deep position and with a jink here and a feint there tying the opposition in knots before he even came into tackling range. Marshall himself charging out from behind a ruck like a wounded rhino ready to set the backs away but also questioning the defence, threatening to burst through a hole inside the first five. Carlos Spencer being Carlos Spencer, shuffling up the body language, conjuring up little illusions, 'Now you see it, now you don't.' The backs had been given a freer reign under John Mitchell. With a deeper backline they had more room and time to express themselves and were encouraged to use them and be creative.

The theory behind flattening your attack is that you cut down the time your opponents have to adjust on defence. That means they can't slide off the ball carrier to the man outside him because the ball's moving too fast. The aim is to get the ball out wide through the hands as quickly as possible so you can out-flank the defence.

The All Blacks don't have that long together each year. So the flattening of our play was pretty much all we worked on in 2004.

During the Tri-Nations the whole country started questioning the All Blacks' strategy of using a flat backline.

It was more Wayne Smith's pet project than Graham Henry's. Smith was convinced the flat backline was the way of the future. But as the Tri-Nations progressed, one problem emerged. New Zealand's backs weren't scoring many tries.

Grant Fox, widely regarded as one of the shrewdest tactical brains in New Zealand rugby, defended the coaches' tactics on 3 News. Other former All Blacks openly criticised them.

But you had to wonder if all this open discussion was working against the All Blacks. As a kid you're told, 'Don't telegraph your passes,' meaning, 'Don't make your intentions obvious.' But the All Blacks were telegraphing their whole attacking philosophy to their opposition. The management seemed to take an entrenched position: We Will Defend the Flat Backline Till the End. When that happens the roles get reversed. You're no longer using an idea to help you achieve your aims. You're enslaved by it. And that makes you predictable and easy to read.

Wallaby coach Eddie Jones put the whole debate in perspective with a couple of throwaway lines in a radio interview. When asked about it he said: 'Yeah, we've used the flat backline here and there. It's a high-risk, high-return scenario.'

Using the flat backline is like driving a Rolls-Royce with a time bomb strapped underneath. The only way to diffuse the bomb is by cutting two particular wires at precisely the right time. If you're up to the task, you're left with a Rolls-Royce to drive around. And that's pretty much the definition of high risk-high return.

The way I see it, there are two main risks involved in using the flat backline and each can be nullified by asking the right question at the right time and having total faith in your answer. The first risk arises before you take the flat backline on the field. And you must ask yourself: Can this team translate this theory into practice flawlessly? If the answer's yes, then go for your life. But if it's no, don't take it on the field. The only way the flat backline can work for anything more than a short 10- or 20-minute burst is if the team can execute the plan exactly as the coaches envision it. That means no mistakes. And that takes incredible accuracy. And to demand that much accuracy in the pressure of a test match, you must be sure the players are ready for it.

If you were directing a play that depended on rapid-fire dialogue delivered so naturally it appeared to be made up on the spot you'd make sure the actors had learnt their lines thoroughly. It's the same with the flat backline. You have to be well-rehearsed.

The other risk arises on the field. And it poses a question that every player in the backline must ask himself when he has the ball in his hand. Shall I pass it or do I need to hold on to it?

Everyone asks this question anyway. But when you're using the flat backline the question is much more urgent and the consequences of your answer much more black and white. The defenders are always pushing the offside law as far as they can. That means the attacking line and the defensive line are in each other's faces. When you get the ball a defender is usually about to smash you. And when you look at the man you intend to pass to, he usually has a defender waiting nearby like a hungry shark waiting for you to toss a hunk of red meat.

The ball for a player in a flat backline is like the cape for a matador in a bullfight. The

Early days with Nicolle. She had a dream job with Allied Liquor. Mehrts and I thought it was, anyway. Here we are helping her out at a vodka promotion.

A special moment for one of my oldest rugby mates, Taine Randell, on his wedding day, with Tony Brown, myself, Nicolle and Tabai Matson.

Happy days (December 10, 1999). Nicolle and me and my groomsmen, Hamish McKay, Daryl Gibson, Mark Morton, Tabs Matson and Mehrts. And they all got on like long-lost mates.

The Marshall clan. Darren, Warren, Justin, new member Nicolle, Lois and Paul.

Being a husband to Nicolle and a parent to two boys has made me a more mature and mellow person . . . and a better rugby player.

View from the top. Lachlan's loving airport greeting after the 2003 World Cup semifinal loss helped me put life into perspective.

Rebirth. I didn't think becoming a father for a second time would be as incredible as the first. But it was.

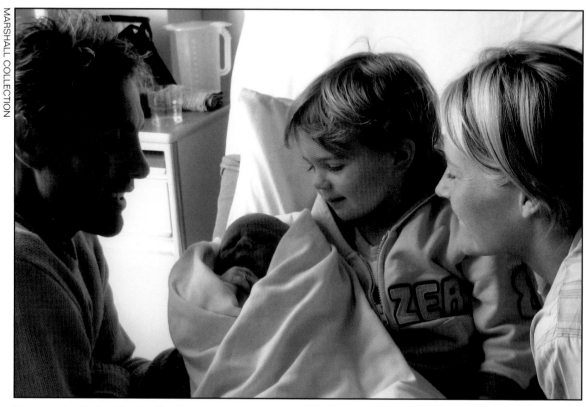

Meet the family. Lachlan finally gets to meet his little brother Fletcher.

Boating and water sports were a big part of family life for Nicolle and me when we were growing up. . . and water-skiing is something we both still enjoy.

Men from the Deep South. Diving in the Marlborough Sounds with my cousin Daryl Gibson and lifetime Mataura friend Mark Morton.

Mister Competitive. I take all sports seriously. I can't help it. And I play to win, not just to have fun. Here I am reading a difficult, breaking putt early in my golfing career.

'Nice outfit, Razor.' Scott Robertson gets caught out by The Prankster and is forced to wear his Speedos over his shorts.

Hairy contest. The Crusaders hold a moustache-growing competition while in South Africa. Slade McFarland, kneeling in the second row, second from right, won the prestigious event . . . and the bottle of wine.

My greatest fans. Nicolle has brought Lachlan to his first game, the Crusaders' 59–24 win over the Reds at Nelson in 2005.

only difference is the matador will always try to get out of the way of the charging bull, whereas the rugby player sometimes has to take the hit . . . and hope like hell that help arrives soon. There's no room for error.

During the 2004 season the All Blacks regularly out-flanked teams. But our accuracy let us down at crucial times. We'd get outside the opposition, but something would go wrong between there and the try-line. The last pass out wide might be dropped. The pass inside might be dropped. A little kick would bounce out of play. We had lapses in both skill and confidence and they let us down.

The other thing was the opposition knew what we were trying to do. That was the problem in our 40–26 loss to South Africa in Johannesburg in the last match of the Tri-Nations. We had plenty of room out on the flanks and it looked on to spread the ball out there. But they were really effective in shutting us down in midfield.

And in hindsight the Springboks weren't silly. They played the All Blacks the way a fly fisherman plays a trout. They showed them all that inviting space out wide as if they were setting and casting a fly. And every time the All Blacks took a bite, they invariably ended up caught in a net with a hook in their mouth.

Leading man

That whole period was an interesting time for me. The week before we'd lost to Australia and I'd been eye gouged. It did affect my game but afterwards the coaching staff and the players voted me as their man of the match. You can't get a higher endorsement than that. Yet Nicolle reported to me over the phone that I was still being heavily criticised in the media and on talk-back radio. No prizes for guessing whose opinions I valued most.

Then Graham Henry came to see me in the lead-up to the match against South Africa at Ellis Park. I'd been making a fair few calls in the other games and showing a lot of leadership. That's what he asked from senior players when he took over the job. And I'd responded as strongly as I could.

But he told me to take a step back in the next game and let some of the other people take some responsibility. I don't mind saying his request irritated the hell out of me. I wasn't trying to take over. But I'll always do whatever's necessary to help us get the right result.

Anyway, Graham said, 'A lot of the guys are turning to you but we want to get some leadership in other areas for this game.'

He felt there were other players in crucial positions who were too quiet. I had to back off so that these guys could come out of their shells. And it made it hard for the management to develop other leaders. It felt to me as if I was being penalised because I'd developed leadership qualities and these other guys hadn't.

My other concern was that maybe we were doing too much analysis too close to the game.

The night before that Tri-Nations test in Johannesburg Smithy had the backs down looking at clips and called an impromptu meeting to look at a few different things.

Well, I don't think the night before a test match is the appropriate time to be cramming your head full of technical information. I don't like doing it anyway. It's not how I like to prepare. As far as I'm concerned, that work's got to be done earlier in the week. Doing it that late in the week just creates confusion and indecision on the field. It's too fresh in the mind.

Now this brings me to another aspect of the flat backline debate that Eddie Jones touched on. He said it's high risk, high return, suggesting it should be used in situations when that sort of game is needed. You might gamble with it to catch the opposition by surprise or use it when you're playing catch-up on the scoreboard and running out of time. And I agree with Eddie on that. You need to have a balance. There are times when the flat backline is a great tactic. And there are times when it's not the right choice. And one of those times was in the test against South Africa that next weekend at Ellis Park. We lost that test and I think the main reason was because we chose the wrong tactics and stuck with them to the bitter end.

I actually recognised very early on that we needed to change the way we were playing. I noticed that while there was plenty of space out wide, their backs were rushing up and stopping the ball from getting there. They were rushing up and chasing our first and second fives. And I believed we should have started attacking inside their first five because there were holes opening up there.

But that wasn't our game plan and I'd been told not to do that. In hindsight, I should have just said, 'Bugger that,' and started attacking the channel anyway. I should have stormed in at halftime and said, 'I can't understand why people are sticking to this game plan when it's obviously not working. We're just running into a brick wall here.' When you're on the field, you have to accept responsibility for what's happening out there. The training and the team talks are all useful. But players need the courage to change things as the game demands. No coach in his right mind will punish you for saving his arse. And nobody congratulates you for successfully following a losing game plan all the way to the final whistle.

I listened to what some of the other players were saying at halftime and they seemed confident attacking wide was still going to work. To follow my instincts I would have had to disagree with them as well as the coaches. So I kept quiet and continued to play my role in executing the original tactics. At the time I decided to hold my tongue. But in hindsight I wish I hadn't.

That's not to say I had a bad game. I missed one crucial tackle. Otherwise I played well. I just think that if I'd taken more control and, basically, disobeyed orders and worried about the consequences later, we could have won instead of lost the test.

Marshall's partner in the halves against South Africa that night was Andrew Mehrtens. It was the forty-third time they'd played together for the All Blacks. It's amazing that nine years after they made their All Black test debuts they were still running the show for the most respected rugby team in the world.

Andrew Mehrtens: I have no doubt that he helped me in terms of consistently making the team. I think our partnership has helped us a lot over the years, certainly me.

And we did complement one another. He's obviously a big, strong, robust sort of a guy who can bustle stuff in close and then I've been the one who just sits back and kicks a wee bit more and tries to do things tactically. At times I can take the pressure off him and at other times he can take the pressure off me by having a crack himself.

There have been so many times when I've been changing direction and switching play and he hasn't heard the call — so he's run one way and I'm going the other — and he still manages to find me. Things like that are priceless and that's the secret of a good combination. It's getting used to one another. After a while we hardly even needed to call. We could just read each other's body language.

We've always liked to have a crack at each other. He gives me heaps about the outside backs not seeing the ball because I keep kicking it.

And I say, 'Yeah, well I might kick it, if I ever see it again. But you keep tucking it under your arm and going for a run yourself.'

We've still got the same jokes we had 12 years ago. For everyone else it's probably like playing alongside a grumpy old married couple.

Justin: If I'm brutally honest, the flat backline wasn't invented with a halfback like me in mind. I like to run with the ball and use the players around me to manipulate the defence. If everybody outside me is at the same depth and standing flat, I have no time to do what I want with the ball.

In a nutshell, my experience of playing with a flat backline is that it puts much more pressure on the team's skills. It also restricts players like Carlos, for example, in asking questions of the defence as he has no time. And, to me, that's not ideal in test match rugby when the pressure's on.

And I actually sent Graham Henry an email after the Tri-Nations. I can't quote it verbatim. But the gist of it was pretty much what I've been saying.

The thing that I've found quite concerning since and had to be concerning for the coaches was that nobody bothered using it in the 2005 Super 12. So if they were going to persist with it against the Lions, the players would almost be starting from scratch again.

Wayne Smith: The term 'flat backline' is someone else's, not mine, so I never use it. We are simply trying to apply logic to our attack and vary our positioning accordingly. It's based on some pretty simple and sound principles and while it's often easier just to follow what everyone else is doing, you then usually get the results that everyone else gets.

Definitely, early on our plans for our backline attack weren't executed as well as we wanted. But I don't think you should mix up bad execution with it being a bad idea. We've proved that if executed well and if the players understand why they're doing it and how its use differs in different situations it can be an effective way to play. But I think Justin's right. It was adhered to in the wrong situations. And it didn't work under pressure in some of the Tri-Nations games.

Some of the ball skills weren't up to it and we found that out. Certainly on the end-of-year tour, we went back to some fairly basic drills to try and overcome that. But he's got a fair point. It needs a certain level of skill to be able to do it. But if any country in the world has the potential to achieve that skill level, it's New Zealand.

It makes you wonder whether the All Black coaches should be trying to reinvent the wheel every time they get a group of players together.

Maybe they should be looking at what the State of Origin league coaches do: get the players together, psyche them up until they want to run through walls and set them loose.

As far as the Maroons go, the biggest play is learning how to shout 'Queenslander!' properly. They don't over-coach. They just fine-tune. And let the quality of the players shine through.

Justin: I was really happy with my form coming out of the Tri-Nations and the coaches were really happy with me too. Graham Henry said, 'Look if we were picking the Lions team right now, you'd be our starting halfback. But we're leaving you behind on the Northern Hemisphere tour because we want to develop some more depth at No. 9. You won't be around forever.'

Sterling idea

Straight after all that, English club Leeds Tykes offered me a two-year contract to play for them in the Zurich Premiership.

I also got an offer to play for the Barbarians against the All Blacks at Twickenham.

So it turned out quite well for me. Because Mehrts, Carlos and I were all rested, not dropped, for the Northern Hemisphere tour, we received full pay from the NZRU. I was allowed to play in the Barbarians match, which was quite lucrative, and also used the trip to England to talk through my contract with Leeds.

Beating the All Blacks with the Barbarians would have topped it all off nicely. (I know it sounds awful because I'm an All Black. But that's just the competitive person I am.)

Another thing that helped me decide to head overseas was the decision by Sanzar to change the Super 12 to the Super 14, and increase the Tri-Nations to six tests. My problem with that structure is that it's only increasing the number of times we're taking on South African and Australian players and teams. It's not providing any variation in our calendar. And I don't think there's the depth to warrant two extra teams in the Super 12.

When the story broke that I'd signed with Leeds, reporters kept asking me whether it was because of the money. I played it right down. I put an emphasis on the challenge of playing in a totally new environment. But it's fair to say the financial rewards had a big part to play in my decision. I've been an All Black for 10 years and the NZRU have rewarded me well for my service. So it needed to be a good offer to get me to leave New Zealand.

My agent actually told me that the contract we negotiated with Leeds was in the top three or four, alongside the likes of Jonny Wilkinson.

Lions fever?

In early 2005 New Zealand sports fans were in a state of breathless anticipation waiting for the arrival of the British Lions for the first time in 12 years.

Strangely, Justin Marshall found himself nonplussed about the whole thing. While he was the form New Zealand halfback in the Super 12 and enjoying his rugby with the Crusaders, he was seriously considering making himself unavailable for the All Black team to play the Lions.

He said that if he was to play, his main motivation would be that he'd never played the Lions before and he wanted the jersey to add to his collection. He felt that wasn't the motivation he needed going into a tough series like that. Basically, he needed to be fired up. And he wasn't.

He'd talked to George Gregan, who'd played a home series for the Wallabies against the Lions. 'Aussie was the same, mate,' said Gregan. 'Everyone went crazy while they were here. But when they jump on the plane and go home, when all's said and done, it's just another series. It doesn't loom any larger in your memory. So just do what you've got to do.'

There were a number of reasons why I thought about making myself unavailable for the All Blacks to play the Lions. The main reason is that if I'm honest with myself my heart's just not in it. I think when I made the decision to leave New Zealand rugby, it signalled a new phase in my life and I'm ready to move on.

That's the way that I'm feeling right now, as we're writing this book. But that's not to say that feeling can't leave as quickly as it came, knowing my impulsive and competitive nature.

Call me oversensitive, but I don't feel the All Black management team have encouraged me to be part of the Lions series. After missing the Northern Hemisphere tour I was feeling vulnerable about my place in the team. I needed some contact and reassurance from the selectors. Hell, I'll admit it. I probably needed my ego stroked a bit. Who doesn't when they feel their job's under threat?

But I hardly heard a peep from the All Black coaches and nothing from the New Zealand Ruby Union.

I had one conversation with Graham Henry. I told him, 'I think by the end of next week I'm going to sign a contract to go to Leeds. I haven't signed it yet.' I said that twice to him. 'I haven't signed anything yet.'

He said, 'I think that sounds like a good sound future for you and your family. It'll be great. Okay . . . okay. That's fine. All right. Yeah . . . Okay.'

The next week I signed the contract and that was that.

I never heard from anybody. I didn't hear from Steve Lancaster. All I got from Steve Tew was an email after I'd already signed, saying thanks for everything and good luck.

Nobody wanted to sit down with me and say, 'Perhaps we can work out something to make you want to stay.'

I had to phone Steve Hansen. And I've known him for years.

I never heard from Wayne Smith either.

Maybe they just wanted me to disappear quietly. Well, that's what it felt like.

For one, they left me out of the Northern Hemisphere tour and they gave me a piss-poor reason for that. Then there was my decision to go to Leeds being met with a wall of indifference, and no contact since. I feel they don't have any interest in me, so why should I accommodate them or even leave myself open to being their afterthought if things aren't going well.

They had meetings with all the All Black guys who went on tour. They had a catch-up with those guys to see how their pre-season's gone. I've had nothing. Not even a chat over a cup of coffee.

That's all making my decision easier. That's pushing me away from making myself available for the Lions. But if they were talking to me, including me in their plans, keeping in contact, I'd probably get my enthusiasm back.

There was one other thing. I asked them to tell the media what they'd told me, that I'd been rested, not dropped, for that tour, and that I was still their No. 1 halfback for the Lions. I didn't want any extra pressure going into that series.

Well, I spoke to Steve Hansen to tell him about Leeds. And one of the only things he said about leading into 2005 was, 'You just need to go out there and play well and be positive and have good form because these guys on the end-of-year tour went really well.'

And I said, 'Thanks for the pressure, mate. Thanks very much.'

He said, 'Come on, mate. You know what I mean. Don't take it the wrong way.'

'Yeah, yeah, whatever.'

He could have said, 'Have a good Super 12. We'll keep in contact and if everything goes to plan, we'll see you for the Lions.'

Instead he's telling me how well all these other guys did.

It's like: 'It's not my fault. You left me behind. How am I going to go well?'

There was going to be no pressure. Then suddenly I'm No. 3 in the pecking order because these guys on tour have gone well. That pretty much sums it up for me.

Steve Hansen, All Black selector (interviewed before the Lions tour): Justin rang me to tell me he was going to Leeds, which was really nice of him. I told him I didn't feel that would get in the way of him making the Lions team. I said he'd make the All Blacks to play the Lions as long as his form was good. That's always been the criteria.

I did mention the fact that the others had played well, which obviously makes it a bit harder for him, now he's got some genuine competition.

I certainly didn't say that he'd dropped to No. 3 or No. 4. I wasn't implying that. If he read that into the conversation, then that's disappointing.

He knows better than anybody what I think about him. I coached him at High School Old Boys in senior rugby, provincial rugby, Super 12 rugby and All Black rugby. I should think that he understands that I'm not there to try to put pressure on him. I'm there to help him.

The way I understand the conversation was that if you play well, son, you'll be back in. If you don't play well, then you're not going to make it. I think that's the criteria for selection in any team.

As for no one asking him to stay and not sign the contract for Leeds, well we'd had exhaustive conversations about that previously, he and I and the rest of the All Black management. And he'd made it pretty clear that he wanted to go. Initially it was straight away, then it was agreed we'd let him go, myself included, after the Lions tour. Short of getting down on our knees and begging him not to go, there was nothing else we could do.

When they get to the point where we felt Justin was at, I think you've just got to support them, because they've made up their mind what to do.

It's the same with retiring. There's no point in trying to talk someone out of retirement. I've never done that and never will do that. They're big boys and to have made the decision they've obviously thought about it long and hard.

He's been a great All Black. He still is a great All Black. He's a very proud one. And the rest of his Super 12 form will be good because he'll make sure it is. And if that's the case, I would think you'll see him running around against the Lions. Then no doubt he'll move on to the next part of his career and we'll support him in that as well.

If he turns around and decides not to go overseas, we'll be happy with that.

Since writing up this section of the book, Justin Marshall has been contacted by Graham Henry, who wanted to let him know he was still in the frame for All Black selection.

This was four weeks into the Super 12 and it's amazing what a difference a phone call can make. Suddenly, I felt wanted again and the obsession started to take hold immediately. I couldn't get the thought of wearing the All Black jersey again out of my head. So much of top level sports is psychological. And that call, coupled with the fact that I was really enjoying my rugby with the Crusaders, rejuvenated my enthusiasm. As for playing against the Lions, well, yes, it was a real possibility again.

Part Four:
After-match comments

Passing judgement

Andrew Mehrtens: Everyone has got into him at various times about the speed of his delivery. But nobody, because most people don't know enough about it, has gone back and looked and said, 'Look at the crap he was getting served up. Look at the amount of slow ball he was getting served up. Look at the amount of legs and limbs he had to crawl over to get the ball.'

Australia's really gone ahead of us in the last 10 years with their ball presentation. We're starting to get better now. But New Zealand's just been so into individual skills and beating guys and stepping that we lost our emphasis on just doing the basics really well. We had guys who could spin the ball on their finger for hours and hours a day but couldn't do a simple draw and pass.

So people do overlook that for a long time Justin was getting crap ball. And I could see it probably better than anyone at first five, the sort of shit that was getting served up. That goes for the All Blacks, the Crusaders and Canterbury.

Apart from his first couple of years with the All Blacks, the best ball he would have got would have been in the Crusaders from 1999 onwards.

I don't think you heard anyone questioning his pass when he was getting decent ball. And I've certainly never had a problem with it at all. He's got as quick a pass as anyone out there.

Laurie Mains: I do have an opinion on the argument over Justin Marshall's pass. You cannot get a halfback that is strong in every facet of the game, strong in every skill that a halfback has to have. But you'd have to ask, when Justin's team has been getting good-quality ball, when has Andrew Mehrtens been under pressure? You'd find it extremely difficult to pinpoint a time when he has been. If the first five-eight is not under pressure, then that tells me he's getting the ball fast enough.

Sure, Graeme Bachop might have been a faster, crisper passer than Justin. But his passing in my opinion was always more than adequate. It was of a quality that allowed his first five-eight to play the game that he needed to play.

Some first fives that have played outside him have expected far too much and tried to play the game too flat and put themselves under pressure. But one of the great characteristics of Justin's play is that he senses those situations and he takes the responsibility himself to take the pressure off those fly-halves.

The All Blacks possibly don't realise just how damn lucky they've been over all this period of time. And my own view is that it's a tragedy that he's been allowed to leave. He's still at his best.

If there's one player in New Zealand rugby who's 30-plus years old who could go through to the 2007 World Cup it's Justin Marshall because he has proved it time after time that after injury or after a slump he comes back better than ever before. There's some mental and physical capability there that very, very few people have.

I'm of the opinion that we could regret that decision to let him go overseas so soon.

Taine Randell: There are obviously players with better passes and passing's pretty important when you're a halfback. But in terms of his overall game, he's ahead of anyone else. That's why the coaches keep picking him. And when you've played with him, you see what he does and you appreciate it more.

I can tell you that Justin Marshall's held in huge regard overseas and his passing is never mentioned at all.

When teams he's involved with don't perform, invariably, he gets it, instead of critics looking at the real issues. Usually, the real issue has something to do with the crap ball he's been delivered by the forwards. Instead of doing some research about how to rectify that, it's easier for people to blame Justin.

Wayne Smith, former All Black coach, current selector: I think there's been some rubbish spoken about his pass over the years. He's a big man. He generates a lot of power through the air with his pass. Sometimes when he's high, he takes a bit of a skip to get it away. But he generally makes up a lot of ground through the air with the strength of the pass. When he stays down, when he's working with agility and he stays down in the pass, he's pretty effective. But he understands that. He's never had a problem understanding that. Whenever he's come under criticism for his pass, watch the next game or two. He shows a real ability to get his foot in and stay down and generate some real speed with it.

Andrew Mehrtens: We had a practice session for the Crusaders one year at Burnham Army Camp. We were calling different moves and I didn't like where the ball had come off the lineout. It had come off the front of the lineout and we needed it off the back.

He threw this pass. And I decided, 'We're not going to bugger around doing the move if we're not going to do it the way we need it to be done in a game.' So I just kicked the ball down and said, 'No, no, no. Stop. Let's go again. We don't want it off the front. We want it down the back.'

Well, the next one, unfortunately, got thrown down the back so it's quite close to the first five. And all I remember are three sights. There's the ball flying at me at about a million miles an hour straight at my head. And behind it, the two biggest, angriest muppet eyes I have ever seen . . . just underneath those massive big eyebrows. If I hadn't got my hands in front of the ball, it would have taken my brick off.

There have been three or four instances over the years when we've had flashpoints like that or arguments. We stew on it for a little bit and after that we're fine. But I'll tell you what, there was no problem with the speed of his pass that day.

Final whistle

Laurie Mains: I've got to say that I've sat back over the years and watched Justin develop into one of the great All Blacks of all time because of his ability to control games and win matches for the All Blacks. He's gone through some difficult periods with injury and come back even better than he was before. He's one of the truly great players.

Tabai Matson: I give Justin Marshall heaps whenever I get the chance. But I'll tell you, he is one of the greatest All Blacks of all time. There aren't that many people who've played for the All Blacks for a decade. How do you measure the greats? You look at longevity. Anyone who can keep getting picked year after year, coach after coach, has to have greatness. Sean Fitzpatrick had longevity. But he didn't have the rivalry for his place that Justin's had. Fitzy was by far the best hooker around, with Norm Hewitt a distant second. But ever since Justin's been in the All Blacks there have been plenty of good halfbacks. And he's fought them all off and come back from the brink of the international scrapheap so many times it's incredible.

Is he the best halfback in New Zealand?

Robbie Deans: Look, this is only one man's opinion obviously but there's not a contest. Justin's unique. He's the most capped halfback. He's a personality in his own right. And he's a player who has a lot of respect within any group and that's powerful. That takes some doing.

They're going to have to fill the breach obviously when he goes to Europe for the next stage of his career. But who knows, he might be back for the 2007 World Cup.

What makes Justin Marshall a great All Black instead of just another All Black?

George Gregan: All I think of are some of the big test matches. There was the 1999 World Cup semifinal where they put him on the bench and they lost.

Then when he went off against us in the 2003 World Cup semifinal, which I know he was understandably disappointed about, it was just noticeable what a big hole it left.

I think he was a big loss for New Zealand in those two big games because he's got a good head under pressure and he thrives on the big games.

There are a lot of players who are the complete opposite to that. You know they're the complete opposite to that. And you play on it.

He's one of the main leaders in the team. He's got presence out there. And no other New Zealand halfback has ever had that same influence while I've been playing against them. And that's just a fact.

Reuben Thorne: Justin was an invaluable back-up guy for me when I was captain of the All Blacks. I relied on him quite a bit. He was a natural leader and a real team player. I think he's awesome. I've got a huge amount of respect for him. I think we're bloody lucky to have him here in New Zealand. But I think he's one of those people we won't fully appreciate until he has gone. I can't believe the amount of bagging that he gets outside of Canterbury. But we're happy to have had him as long as we have.

Taine Randell: We used to give him shit. I'd say I went to Otago University. So-and-so went to Canterbury University. And Marshall went to the big white university in Mataura . . . that was the freezing works.

He may not be scholastically inclined, but he's a great example of a natural winner. It just shows that you don't have to be the best reader in the world or the brightest chemist to succeed. I don't think he's bucked the system. I think that is the system. If you're talented and you're determined, you can succeed in life.

Daryl Gibson: The main strength Justin Marshall has is that he's very competitive. We play squash quite regularly against each other. But in any sport we play he is more competitive. He won't give up. He'll just keep going and going and going. And he's quite emotional. There have been plenty of times in training where someone's done something to him and he gets all fired up.

I think it all stems from his roots in Mataura. He's a bit of a scrapper. I admire that side of him, the fact that he'll fight through anyone. And it comes out now and then when he's pushed. He just cracks. He probably doesn't like that side of himself that much. Unfortunately, in some areas he's probably not as polished as he'd like to be. But if you were looking for the one thing that gives him the edge over other people that would probably be it.

Nicolle: I remember picking up the newspaper once, looking at the headlines and saying to Robbie Deans, 'I don't know, Robbie, what's he said this time?'

He said, 'Nicolle, Justin's black and white, and you wouldn't have it any other way.'

And he's probably right. That's one thing I like about Justin. He makes a statement. He stands for something. He's an exclamation mark, not a comma.